The Illustrated Guide to the Anglo-Zulu War

A Zulu amulet necklace, or isiqu, *which was worn to ward off the evil effects of having killed a man in battle and thus, by association, represented a deed of valour, shown encircling the South Africa Medal with date bar specifying that it was awarded to a British soldier for serving in the Zululand campaign of 1879.*

The Illustrated Guide to the Anglo-Zulu War

by

John Laband and Paul Thompson

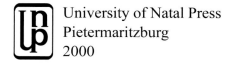 University of Natal Press
Pietermaritzburg
2000

ISBN   0 86980 972 5   (Paperback)
       0 86980 973 3   (Hardback)

Design and layout: The Blue Box

Cartography: M Design

Cover design: Brett Armstrong

Acknowledgments for cover illustrations:
Detail from an oil painting (315 x 340 mm) by M.E. Newman on an engraving from the *Illustrated London News*, 24 May 1879: 'The Final Repulse of the Zulus at Ginghilovo'.   (Local History Museum, Durban)

A Zulu *isiqu*.   (Natal Museum, Pietermaritzburg)

The South Africa Medal, 1879.   (Private collection of Philip Muller)

Typeset by the University of Natal Press, Pietermaritzburg, South Africa
Printed in Great Britain by Unwin Brothers Ltd
The Gresham Press, Old Woking, Surrey

Contents

List of Maps

Preface

Historians are seldom so fortunate as to be afforded the opportunity to revisit entirely a work they wrote twenty years before. Paul Thompson and I first published our *Field Guide to the War in Zululand* in 1979, and since then it has been reprinted three times with corrections and revisions. However, the relatively minor revisions we made then (the last time was in 1987) do not adequately reflect the enormous strides that have been taken in Anglo-Zulu War studies over the past two decades by the many scholars now working in the field. Today we know so much more about the war than we did in 1979, especially about the Zulu side. We are consequently extremely grateful to Mr Glenn Cowley, the Publisher at the University of Natal Press, for inviting us to bring out the new *Illustrated Guide to the Anglo-Zulu War*. That commission has allowed me to rewrite and expand upon the entire text of the last edition of the *Field Guide* (now out of print), to incorporate new illustrative material and, in consultation with Paul Thompson, to generate new maps that reflect our changed understanding of battles and operations.

Forty-nine of the diagrams of fortifications from the original book have been retained. Six have been eliminated since the remains they portrayed have (upon further reflection) proved too doubtful. Human intervention is not being kind to the remaining vestiges of the fortifications, and they are suffering a dynamic process of damage and outright destruction. Therefore, we thought that in this new book – in the interests of preserving a record – we should present diagrams of all those forts we positively identified and charted twenty years ago, even though they might imminently no longer be in existence, or already have been obliterated.

Battlefields, too, are constantly changing as they are encroached upon by human habitations and roads, and as they receive the benefits of interpretation centres and other laudable attempts to explain and preserve them. These interventions mean that the environs of no battlefield will remain static, so we have chosen in this new book to present the terrain only at the time of the war and not – as we did previously – to show current features. To the eight battles previously portrayed we have added four minor engagements since we believe they illustrate other important aspects of the conflict.

The use of full colour is intended to make troop movements on the maps easier to follow. However, the reader should be reminded that nothing is more provisional (when not conjectural) than the portrayal of a battle on a map, for the evidence upon which it is based is unavoidably incomplete, confused and partisan – if not self-exculpatory. Consequently, the battle maps reflect only my present interpretation of the sources. Currently, there is heated debate among Anglo-Zulu War experts centred on the battle of Hlobane, and the protagonists will recognise whose interpretation I have essentially adopted. The battle of Isandlwana remains even more problematical. Paul Thompson and I have reconsidered the sources, walked the battlefield once more and consulted widely with other specialists. In the end, we have adopted my understanding of Zulu movements and the British rout;

while British dispositions reflect more closely Paul Thompson's conclusions, which have been shaped by his pioneering research into the Natal Native Contingent. Some readers will consequently note that our depictions of Isandlwana deviate in some measure from the consensus that has been solidifying in recent years. Naturally, our views will be tested in debate with other historians, and the outcome will, we trust, be reflected in future articles and books on the subject.

In spelling Zulu names, the stem has been distinguished from the prefix through capitalisation. This practice has been adhered to in the index, where Zulu names are entered under the first letter of the stem. Following convention, geographical features have been spelled without the prefix (for example, Zungwini Mountain), as have the names of groups of people (for example, the Ntuli). However, *imizi* and *amakhanda* have retained the prefix (for example, eZulaneni or kwaNodwengu), as have those *amabutho* or people connected with an *ikhanda* (for example, the uThulwana or abaQulusi). We thank Professor John Wright for his guidance in this matter.

Our deepest debt of gratitude is to our cartographers, Di Matheson and Marise Bauer. Paul Thompson drew the bases to the maps, and I imposed the military features and troop movements. With infinite patience, good humour and care Di and Marise transformed my cluttered drafts into lucid and elegant maps that executed my intentions better than I had imagined possible. The stylish page design was devised and executed by Paul de Villiers with *insouciant* flair. We are also indebted to Philip Daniel, Sally Hines, and, most particularly, the meticulous Trish Comrie, all of whom have had a vital role in editing and improving the text. All the above worked long and extraordinary hours to ensure the high quality of this production. Thanks are also due to John Morrison, the Director of the Natal Society Library, for making the illustrative material in the NSL's holdings so freely available to us, and to Professor Clive Graham for his help with Anglo-Zulu War medals and decorations.

We are also properly grateful to the Deputy Vice-Chancellor (Research & Development) and the Research Office of the University of Natal for making available the generous funding which defrayed the cartographic costs and travel expenses incurred during the course of completing this book for publication.

Finally, it is most heartening to have enjoyed the ungrudging and constructive support of other historians active in the same field. Those who have generously shared their expertise and source materials with us are Ian Knight, David Rattray of Fugitives' Drift Lodge, Huw Jones, Ron Lock, Maj Peter Quantrill, Mike Taylor and Steve Watt. David Rattray also read this book in manuscript with close attention, and we are grateful for his valuable comments. Consultation with these experts notwithstanding, the ultimate responsibility for the interpretations and conclusions expressed in this book is ours alone.

John Laband
University of Natal, Pietermaritzburg

Key to Symbols

IN MAPS OF FIELD OPERATIONS AND MILITARY ENGAGEMENTS

Colour identification of military units and works

British	▬ red
Naval Brigade	▬ blue with red border
colonial and imperial (raised locally)	▬ orange
Zulu	▬ blue

Classification of military units

British and Colonial

headquarters	⬛
cavalry	◪
artillery	⊡
engineers	⊞
infantry	⊠
pioneers	⊡
Border Police	⊕
River Guard	△
pockets of resistance	⬭

Zulu

commanders	☆
military concentrations	⬭
marksmen	⇒
scouts and skirmishers	○

Size of military units

squad	⊏⊐
section	⊏⊐
infantry platoon, or division of artillery battery	⊏⊐
infantry company, cavalry troop or artillery battery	⊏⊐
infantry battalion or cavalry squadron	⊏⊐
regiment	⊏⊐
brigade	⊏⊐
division	⊏⊐

Weapons

gun
rocket
Gatling gun

Wagons

wagon train
parked or laagered wagons

Military works

fort
laager or camp
ikhanda (Zulu military homestead)
destroyed *ikhanda*

Engagements

minor engagement
battle

Captured livestock

cattle
goats

Features

umuzi (Zulu homestead)
destroyed *umuzi*

town

Anglican mission station
Hermannsburg mission station
Norwegian mission station
Swedish mission station

farmhouse

track
railway
drift
pont

international boundary

PART I

The Anglo-Zulu War

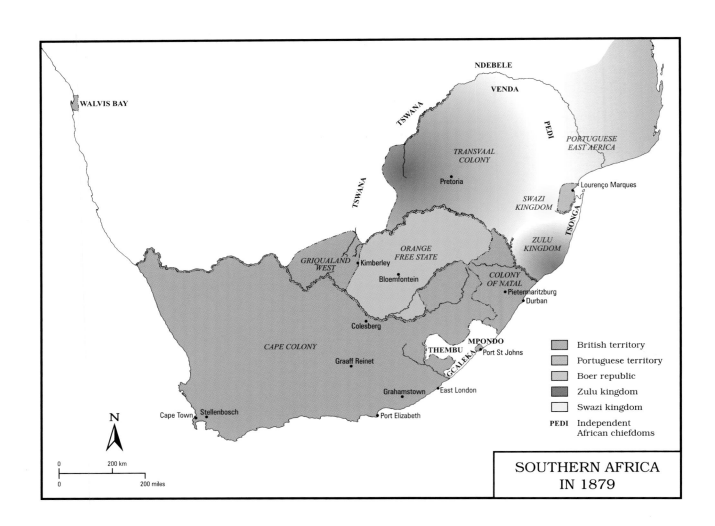

WALVIS BAY

NDEBELE

VENDA

TSWANA

PEDI

PORTUGUESE
EAST AFRICA

TRANSVAAL
COLONY

Pretoria

Lourenço Marques

TSWANA

SWAZI
KINGDOM

TSONGA

ZULU
KINGDOM

GRIQUALAND
WEST

Kimberley

ORANGE
FREE STATE

Bloemfontein

COLONY
OF NATAL

Pietermaritzburg
Durban

Colesberg

CAPE COLONY

THEMBU

MPONDO

Port St Johns

GCALEKA

Graaff Reinet

Grahamstown

East London

N

Cape Town

Stellenbosch

Port Elizabeth

	British territory
	Portuguese territory
	Boer republic
	Zulu kingdom
	Swazi kingdom
PEDI	Independent African chiefdoms

0   200 km

0   200 miles

SOUTHERN AFRICA IN 1879

The Causes of the Anglo-Zulu War

By the 1870s the tide in southern Africa was running against the independent, pre-industrial Zulu kingdom. In general terms, the sub-continent's economy was at the threshold of being transformed by the burgeoning mineral revolution set off by the recent discovery of diamonds. Mining, finance, commercial agriculture and trade were being stimulated, and closer links with the capitalist economies of Europe were being forged. Associated with these developments were increasing demands for productive land and a dependable supply of cheap wage-labourers. Even though the young men of Zululand were obliged to serve their king through the *ibutho* (age-regiment) system, and were not permitted to sell their labour beyond its borders, the kingdom could not resist indefinitely the pressures exerted by neighbours like the British Colony of Natal to unlock its labour, open up markets and carve out plantations.

For imperial planners seeking in the 1870s to consolidate, rather than expand, the British Empire, however, the significance of southern Africa's growing economic potential was viewed in wider terms. It was India – not the African sub-continent – that was central to British commercial interests and her status as an imperial power. And India's security depended on the Royal Navy's control of the sea routes to India through the Suez Canal and around the Cape, which entailed possession of suf-

ficient ports and coaling-stations along the way for steam-driven ships. Southern Africa's prime importance, therefore, lay in her strategic position and it was essential for Britain to remain the paramount power there, as well as in Egypt.

Yet the difficulty in maintaining Britain's dominance in southern Africa lay not so much with the ambitions of rival colonial powers (as was the case with Egypt), as with the political and economic fragmentation of the region. Besides the British colonies of the Cape, Natal and various other lesser possessions, there were the Boer republic of the Orange Free State and the South African Republic, as well as several surviving independent black kingdoms, of which the Zulu was the most powerful. The boundaries between these settler and African states were ill-defined in many cases and hotly contested, and conflict was consequently endemic and debilitating. Nevertheless, the developing economic viability of southern Africa suggested how – with suitable guidance – a comprehensive political structure might be erected that would enable the sub-continent to fulfil its imperial strategic role.

The Earl of Carnarvon, who in February 1874 joined Benjamin Disraeli's Conservative administration as Colonial Secretary, believed that he had found the

Sir Bartle Frere, GCB, GCSI, KCB, who had been a senior administrator in India, arrived in South Africa in 1877 as Governor of the Cape, High Commissioner, and Commander-in-Chief of the British forces. He initiated war against Zululand to effect the confederation of the southern African states under Britain, but the disastrous campaign led to General Sir Garnet Wolseley superseding him in May 1879 in the Zululand theatre.

Sekhukhune woaSekwati, the Pedi chief, who between 1876 and 1878 successfully resisted both the Transvaal Boers and the British. In colonial opinion, this was only possible because of the Zulu king's moral and material support, and gave substance to their suspicion that Cetshwayo was heading a 'black conspiracy' dedicated to overthrowing white rule in southern Africa.

ideal means in the confederation of all the white-ruled states of southern Africa. Because a settled environment would be created for greater economic integration and progress, such a confederation would be able to bear the costs of its own centralised and streamlined administration. And since internal conflict would be all but eliminated, the confederation would need to maintain only its own small, affordable armed forces, and not have to rely as previously on a large and expensive imperial garrison for its security. Moreover, besides fulfilling its prime purpose as an unassailable link in the British route to India, Carnarvon hoped that the strength and self-reliance of the proposed confederation would position it as the base for future British economic and political expansion into the interior of Africa.

There was, however, a major obstacle in the path towards Carnarvon's idealised confederation; namely, the security risk posed by the continued existence of the independent black kingdoms neighbouring the settler states that would make up the new structure. Not only might they threaten settlers with raids, but their very existence would unsettle Africans already living under white rule and foment resistance. For confederation to succeed, therefore, it was also necessary to assume some form of British supremacy over all

the indigenous peoples of southern Africa. What made the fulfilment of this requirement all the more urgent was the reluctance of the Cape Colony (the largest and richest piece in the proposed structure) to commit itself until it was entirely assured that confederation would not entail fresh and costly wars with neighbouring Africans.

With such difficulties standing in the way of confederation, Carnarvon had to select a very special proconsul for its successful implementation. His choice for appointment as Governor of the Cape Colony, High Commissioner for South Africa and Commander-in-Chief of the British forces in southern Africa fell on Sir Bartle Frere. Frere had enjoyed a distinguished and successful career as one of the senior administrators of India. As such, he was used to shouldering great responsibilities and taking vigorous executive action. His scope to act on his own initiative in southern Africa was increased when Carnarvon resigned in February 1878. Sir Michael Hicks Beach, his replacement as Colonial Secretary, was beset by many international difficulties and was only too happy to leave the consummation of South African confederation in Frere's practised hands.

Frere arrived in South Africa in March 1877. He instantly approved the process which would culminate in the anarchic and bankrupt Boer South African Republic being annexed to the Crown on 12 April 1877 as the Transvaal Colony. With that territory's increasingly obvious potential as a source of considerable mineral wealth, and standing as it did across the road to the interior with its untapped riches, its annexation was essential to secure the northern component of confederation. The incorporation of the Transvaal was also necessary to placate the Cape. Between May 1876 and February 1877 the South African Republic had been involved in precisely the sort of mismanaged and unresolved conflict with the Pedi under Sekhukhune which the Cape so strongly wished to see concluded before consenting to confederation. With annexation, the understanding was that British troops would swiftly succeed against the Pedi where Boer commandos had failed. Frere also executed a series of strategic annexations aimed at stabilising the Cape eastern frontier and securing the remaining potential ports along the southern African coast.

Yet, for all these successes, in Frere's estimation one major hurdle still stood in the way of confederation. This was the powerful Zulu kingdom, popularly believed in settler and official circles alike to be the inspiration behind a growing conspiracy among Africans to rise up and overthrow white supremacy in southern Africa. Frere consequently used every argument and incident (no matter how trivial) to persuade the Colonial Office that Zululand, as a savage and barbaric state ruled by a blood-thirsty tyrant, where civilizing missionary endeavours were thwarted, and whose military system threatened the stability of the rest of the sub-continent, had to be eliminated.

In any case, intervention against Zululand was made imperative by developments in the Transvaal where many of the Boers were becoming increasingly unreconciled to British annexation. The Administrator, Sir Theophilus Shepstone, believed that to convince them of the advantages of British rule, the unresolved 'native question' would have to be settled in their favour. This required, firstly, the subjugation of the Pedi, whom Shepstone believed were encouraged in their resistance by the Zulu example; and, secondly, the settlement of the long-standing boundary dispute between the Zulu kingdom and the Transvaal over what was known as the Disputed Territory.

Previously, because the British had wished to block the landlocked South African Republic's attempts to drive through Zululand to secure a seaport, the Zulu had relied upon British support to maintain their control over the Disputed Territory. Now, to the bewilderment of Cetshwayo kaMpande, the Zulu king, the British performed a complete turnabout and championed the Boer claims. A meeting at Conference Hill on 18 Octo-

ber 1877 failed to resolve the dispute, intransigent words were exchanged and Frere thought the way was clear for a military solution to the Zulu question.

At that crucial moment, the Lieutenant-Governor of Natal, Sir Henry Bulwer, who feared the effects on Natal of a full-scale conflict, offered to mediate. Cetshwayo accepted with relief his proposal for a Boundary Commission and, though Frere was disappointed, he could not refuse. The Commission duly began its sittings at Rorke's Drift on 17 March 1878, and Frere received its scrupulous report on 15 July. The High Commissioner realised with dismay that he could not make its finding public since, in upholding in large measure the Zulu claims, the Commission's award threatened to cause an explosion in the Transvaal where the situation was already seriously deteriorating.

In April 1878 Shepstone had commenced military operations against

> 'Mpande did you no wrong, and I have done you no wrong, therefore you must have some other object in view in invading my land.'
> (King Cetshwayo kaMpande, 29 March 1881)

King Cetshwayo kaMpande photographed in August 1882 wearing European dress during his visit to London. He was pressing the British government to allow him to return to Zululand from the Cape where he had been exiled since his defeat in the Anglo-Zulu War.

Sekhukhune, but the campaign was proving a disaster, and by October the British would have withdrawn from Pedi territory. Frere believed that the unfavourable boundary award, coming on top of this debacle, would prove to the Boers that the British could not guarantee their security against their African neighbours. Such knowledge, he feared, would spark a Boer rebellion in the reluctant Transvaal Colony which would likely draw in Boers elsewhere in South Africa, and encourage the Zulu and other Africans to fall upon the whites as they fought among themselves. To extinguish the fuse to this general explosion, it was more urgent than ever to neutralise the Zulu. Minor border incidents between July and October 1878 along the Mzinyathi (Buffalo) and Thukela rivers, and in the Disputed Territory, provided the grateful Frere with the opportune excuse and the justification (vital for his superiors in the Colonial Office) for punitive action.

By September 1878 Frere's military and naval commanders were preparing, on a contingency basis, for war against Zululand. During September and November they moved troops in a steady trickle to the Zululand border to be in position should war break out. Considering that Frere and all his advisers were agreed that confederation remained contingent on the permanent removal of the Zulu threat, the alternative of taming Zulu power through diplomatic means was never seriously explored. Frere doubted whether any verbal undertaking could be binding on the Zulu, especially if the dreaded military system remained intact, and it was impracticable to maintain a large British force on the Zulu border to ensure compliance.

Consequently, the ultimatum to King Cetshwayo, which Frere drafted with the advice of Shepstone and Bulwer, required, among other stipulations, that the Zulu military system be abolished and the king submit himself to the authority of a British Resident. Since such requirements would have subverted the social, economic and political structure of the Zulu kingdom, it was never supposed that Cetshwayo was left with any option but to fight in defence of his sovereignty and his people's independence.

As Frere hurried events to a military conclusion, the Colonial Office became increasingly uneasy. A war was brewing in Afghanistan, relations with Russia were strained, and Hicks Beach had absolutely no wish for a campaign in Zululand as well. But Frere was entrusted with considerable discretionary powers, and he coolly exploited the conveniently slow communications with London to keep his superiors in the dark while he executed plans that he knew would not have received their prior sanction. Yet he took the risk because he was confident of his policies, and he had been assured by the military that a swift, cheap and decisive

A view drawn in February 1879 by Brevet Lt-Col John North Crealock, Lord Chelmsford's Military Secretary, of the lower drift across the Thukela River.
It shows the pont in operation, Smith's Hotel, and the tree at the water's edge under which the British ultimatum was delivered to King Cetshwayo's emissaries on 11 December 1878.

campaign was all that was required to effect them. Any censure he might have earned would be wiped away by his triumphant clearing of the way for the creation of the new South African Dominion, of which he expected to be the first governor-general.

In this steady build-up to invasion, in which the Zulu kingdom was to be sacrificed on the altar of British paramountcy in southern Africa, the Zulu themselves were the bewildered victims. King Cetshwayo's own policy towards his neighbours had undergone no radical change which might have explained Britain's sudden enmity. The border incidents upon which the whites unaccountably placed such store were clearly no real justification for war, while the partial and short-lived Zulu mobilisation in the final months of 1878 was only in response to the growing British military presence. King Cetshwayo made frequent attempt to negotiate to avert what he knew would be a disastrous war, but his increasingly desperate overtures had no chance of success since Frere was determined on a military solution.

On 11 December 1878 Cetshwayo's representatives were summoned to the Natal side of the Thukela River at Lower Drift to hear the long-delayed boundary award. Their satisfaction rapidly turned to dismay when the welcome details were followed by the impossible terms of the ultimatum. Though given 30 days in which to comply with them, Cetshwayo had no real alternative but armed resistance if he were to avoid abject and complete surrender. He therefore mobilised his army for the coming campaign, and allowed the ultimatum to expire unanswered. On 11 January 1879 British forces invaded Zululand.

Yet, as events were to prove, Frere's military experts had gravely miscalculated. It required eight months of hard fighting to break Zulu resistance. The costs, whether in terms of casualties sustained, the damage to Britain's military reputation or the financial outlay, were considerably higher than the British government was willing to countenance for a colonial campaign. Frere was disgraced as a consequence, and plans for South African confederation were put on hold for another 20 years. Yet if Frere's invasion of Zululand failed spectacularly in its primary objective of securing a grand political solution through military means, it nevertheless facilitated the eventual integration of the ravaged and fragmented kingdom into a colonial and capitalist southern Africa.

> 'After the boundary award had been made know, a sense of relief was manifest on the countenances of the Zulu deputies . . . An hour's adjournment then took place, and on resuming the conference, the ultimatum was interpreted to them. A change then passed over the Zulu faces – those faces got longer and longer.'
>
> (*Natal Mercury*, 11 and 12 January 1879)

Prominent members of the Zulu deputation of fourteen izinduna *who heard the British ultimatum on 11 December 1878. Gebula, an* induna *of the kwaGqikazi* ikhanda, *sits on the extreme left, and Vumandaba kaNtati, the* induna *of the uMcijo* ibutho, *is third from the left in front of the wagon wheel. They were photographed by James Lloyd of Durban, and their faces express some of the disquietude they experienced when he levelled his strange, three-legged instrument with its polished tube at them.*

Two photographs, both apparently taken at King Cetshwayo's coronation in 1873,
contrasting the traditional and new-style Zulu fighting-man.

Above: *A member of a young* ibutho *(note his appropriately dark-coloured war-shield) poses proudly in full festival panoply, his body covered in a profusion of cow-tails. His spectacular headdress is of leopard skin and of ostrich, crane and lourie feathers.*

Below: *Prince Dabulumanzi kaMpande stands centre with a number of his adherents, dressed as they would be on campaign, and carrying firearms rather than spears. The men at either end hold old-fashioned Tower muskets. The seated man wearing a jacket and the man on Dabulamanzi's left have smaller, muzzle-loading sporting rifles. Dabuluamanzi and the man on his right with a leopard skin carry breech-loading shotguns.*

The Zulu Military System

The Zulu army was never a separate, professional institution like the British army, but was integrated into the whole fabric of the nation's life and formed the basis of the king's power and authority.

The *ibutho* system

The military system was built on the institution of age-set units called *amabutho* (singular – *ibutho*), which seems to have developed from the ancient practice among the Nguni-speaking people of banding together youths of similar age in circumcision sets. By the early nineteenth century, among the chiefdoms in the area later to be dominated by the Zulu kingdom, the practice of forming *amabutho* was changing its function from that of assembling youths simply for initiation purposes into that of grouping them together for various forms of service, economic and military, that would facilitate the more effective management of resources in Zulu society. In the 1820s King Shaka kaSenzangakhona, the founder of the Zulu kingdom, brought this evolving *ibutho* system to its fully developed form as an instrument for integrating the members of conquered chiefdoms into the new state and weaning them from their loyalty to their original chiefs. During King Cetshwayo ka-Mpande's reign, which began in 1872, the *ibutho* system persisted (with modifications) as the central pillar of the Zulu state.

When Cetshwayo was king, Zulu boys age between 14 and 18 would gather at military homesteads or *amakhanda* (singular – *ikhanda*), which, as the focuses of royal authority in the far-flung districts of the kingdom, were presided over by representatives of the king in the form of members of the royal family, or trusted royal officers or *izinduna* (singular – *induna*). There youths might serve for two to three years as cadets, herding cattle, work-

A view taken in September 1847 across the great parade ground at the kwaNodwengu ikhanda towards the isigodlo with King Mpande, King Cetshwayo's father, reviewing two of his amabutho. Although this lithograph by George Angas was made 30 years before the Anglo-Zulu War, a review at Cetshwayo's oNdini ikhanda would have presented a very similar aspect.

An engraving in the Graphic *of 22 February 1879 of the oNdini ikhanda, King Cetshwayo's chief residence. The name was derived from the Zulu word for a rim, as of a bowl, and was an alternative for the Drakensberg Mountains. The archaeological evidence confirms the relative accuracy of the artist's impression, which gives a good idea of the scale of the* ikhanda *which consisted of as many as 1 400 huts.*

ing the fields (otherwise essentially a woman's task in Zulu society) and practising military skills. Once enough boys of an age-group were congregated at the district *amakhanda*, they would all be brought before the king. They usually reported to him at his kwaNodwengu *ikhanda* in the Mahlabathini plain where the annual first-fruits ceremony (*umKhosi*) was being celebrated at the time the moon was at the full and about to wane in late December or early January. The king then formed them into an *ibutho* with orders to build a new *ikhanda*, often bearing the name he had given the *ibutho*. Sometimes, as with the uVe in 1875, the new *ibutho* was incorporated into an old *ibutho* – in that case the iNgobamakhosi – whose strength the king had decided to maintain, and quartered with it in the mature *ibutho*'s existing *ikhanda*.

Not all the *amabutho* were made up of cadets from every district of the kingdom. The abaQulusi in north-western Zululand, for example, or the emaNgweni along the coast, had each developed out of an *ikhanda* founded to establish royal authority in that locality, and they each formed a separate *ibutho* composed only of men living in the vicinity that they had come to dominate.

Women were part of the military system in that they formed the major agricultural labour force in Zulu society and produced food to feed their male relatives when they were away from home serving the king. Girls in Zululand were also formed into *amabutho* primarily for the purpose of regulating marriage. At intervals the king gave members of a female *ibutho* leave to be married, but only to middle-aged suitors from male *amabutho* who had received royal permission to put on the head-ring or *isicoco*. This was a circlet of tendons or fibres sewn into the hair, coated with beeswax or gum and then greased and polished. It seems that the custom of the head-ring was a substitute for the defunct circumcision ceremony, which had marked the attainment of manhood and full incorporation into communal life. By withholding the *isicoco* from the men of his *amabutho* until the age of 35 or 40, the king was prolonging the period in which they would be regarded as youths, or *izinsizwa* (singular – *insizwa*) in Zulu society. This meant they could not marry, set up their own independent households and rear children, but would remain under the authority of their elders and, by extension, of the king. When eventually granted the privilege of assuming the *isicoco*, each man paid *ilobolo* (bride wealth) of up to three cattle to his bride's family to formalise the marriage transaction, and set up as an *umnumzane* (plural – *abanumzane*), or married head of his own household.

By Cetshwayo's reign there was apparently a considerable degree of flexibility in the *ibutho* system. Enrolment in an *ibutho* was no longer compulsory, and the possibility existed (as was the custom in the neighbouring Colony of Natal) of putting on the *isicoco* and establishing a homestead, or *umuzi* (plural – *imizi*) without having first served the king. The penalty, however, was exposure to the scorn of the vast majority of men in Zululand who continued to conform to the system.

When serving their king, the *amabutho* were stationed in the *amakhanda*, of which there were 27 in Zululand in 1879. Thirteen of them – including oNdini, Cetshwayo's 'great place' – were concentrated in the Mahlabathini plain and in the emaKhosini valley to its south-west over the White Mfolozi River. With its estimated 1 000 to 1 500 bee-hived huts of wood and thatch with floors of clay and dung, oNdini was larger than most, though typical in its construction and layout. At the upper end was the *isigodlo* (plural – *izigodlo*), or royal enclosure, where the king lived with his wives and the women of his household. In other *amakhanda* the king's representative would occupy the royal enclosure. From either side of the *isigodlo* swept two wings of huts, or *izinhlangothi* (singular – *uhlangothi*) housing the warriors, which surrounded the large elliptical parade ground. Here the king inspected his *amabutho* who danced for him, sang his praises and practised deployment into various military formations like circles and columns. At the upper end of the parade ground, in front of the *isigodlo*, was a cattle enclosure, or *isibaya* (plural – *izibaya*) sacred to the king where his councillors would consult, and where the king would perform the required national rituals and ceremonies. Behind the *isigodlo*, and outside the main complex, stood two smaller *imizi*, one where the royal women bore their children, and the other where the king's grain and milch cows were kept.

The 13 central *amakhanda* were occupied by unmarried *amabutho* for seven to eight months immediately after their initial formation, and thereafter for only a few months a year when they gathered to serve the king. Otherwise, they were used by all *amabutho* when they congregated during the annual *umKhosi* ceremonies when the king and the army were ritually purified of evil influences and strengthened, the ancestral spirits, or *amadlozi* (singular – *idlozi*) praised and the allegiance of the people renewed. The remaining 14 *amakhanda* were widely dispersed as regional centres of royal influence and mobilisation points for local elements of the *amabutho*. Young men (as we have seen) gathered there as cadets before being formed into *amabutho*, and married men assembled there for short periods of two to five months, often with their wives. While serving at an *ikhanda* the members of an *ibutho* kept it in repair, herded and milked the royal cattle attached to it, and cultivated the king's land. Although supposed to be maintained through the king's bounty, the men were actually dependent on food supplied from home by their women. Daily intricate dancing and praise-singing effectively doubled as military exercises.

Yet it must be emphasised that the king did not only mobilise his *amabutho* for the national ceremonies and for going

The emaNgweni ikhanda, the centre of royal influence in the coastal plain north of the Mhlathuze River, sketched just before it was burned by the British on 4 July 1879. Note the western-style house in the isigodlo, *similar to the one built for Cetshwayo at oNdini.*

Zulu imizi, *shown in this photograph of the 1890s typically scattered over the rolling countryside, were each the self-sufficient home of a married man and his family. A thousand or more of them were burned by the British in 1879 in an attempt to break Zulu resistance.*

to war. Sometimes he would call up a limited number of *amabutho* (perhaps only one or two) for special tasks: building him a new *ikhanda* in a region where he wished to assert his authority (such as the one constructed in November 1877 near the little German missionary settlement of Luneburg); repairing an old one damaged by fire, as often occurred, especially during the dry winter season; participating in great hunts (especially at the game-rich confluence of the White and Black Mfolozi rivers); supplying him with exotic foodstuffs, like bananas from the coast, and with rare feathers and skins for apparel; or collecting tribute from outlying subordinated people, such as the

Sigcwelegcwele kaMhlekehleke, a minor chief of the Ngadini people, was a successful courtier whom King Cetshwayo appointed induna *of his favourite* ibutho, *the iNgobamakhosi. Sigcwelegcwele fought at both Isandlwana and Gingindlovu.*

Tsonga. The *amabutho* also served as a police force, collecting cattle fines from offenders against the king, or 'eating them up' by destroying their *imizi* and executing them and their dependents. The cattle and commodities which the *amabutho* accumulated for the king on their forays (most spectacularly on full-scale campaigns against an enemy), or as a result of their labour at the *amakhanda*, provided a vital source of royal power. By redistributing a portion as rewards to the *amabutho*, or to the great men of the kingdom, the king was able constantly to consolidate his position and to ensure the loyalty of his subjects.

The *ibutho* system, in other words, was an instrument of both internal control and external defence. It enabled the king to exercise real social and economic control over all his subjects, and to divert their productive and military potential away from their own households, localities and chiefs to the service of the state. But besides operating as a system of taxation, where labour was substituted for money or goods, the *ibutho* system also served to integrate the men and women of the various chiefdoms subsumed by Shaka and his heirs into the Zulu kingdom, and to ensure that they recognised the Zulu king as their sole ruler.

Structure of the *ibutho*

Each *ibutho* was divided up into a number of sections, or *amaviyo* (singular – *iviyo*). Each *iviyo* consisted of men of the same age-group, drawn from a particular locality, who had been formed into the section during their days as cadets at one of the district *amakhanda*. Each *ibutho* was commanded by an *induna* (who might even be a member of the royal house) appointed by the king. His was a position of great power and prestige. Under him were a second-in-command and two experienced wing officers, all of an older generation than the men they led. There were also a number of junior officers, at least two to each *iviyo*, who had been chosen by their contemporaries in their days as cadets.

It is not possible to put a firm figure to the strength of an *iviyo* as this depended, as did the number of them comprising any particular *ibutho*, on the degree of royal favour involved. The iNgobamakhosi, for example, was Cetshwayo's favourite *ibutho* and consequently the largest in the army. Thus an *iviyo* at the time of the Anglo-Zulu War could vary on average between 40 and 60 men (though it could go up to 100 or more), and an *ibutho* could consequently muster between several hundred and a few thousand. These discrepancies, and the fact that elements of the same *ibutho* could well be engaged simultaneously in different theatres during the same campaign, make it difficult to compute with any ac-curacy the number of Zulu taking part in any of the battles of 1879.

Dress

The ceremonial attire of the *amabutho* that distinguished them one from another was lavish and intricate, and contained many rare and fragile skin and feather items supplied through the king's favour. Members of an *ibutho* were expected to keep their dress neat and clean in conformity with regulations. If improperly dressed, a member of an *ibutho* would be thrashed with light sticks by his companions and sent home. Developments in ceremonial costume were related to the continuing availability of materials. By Cetshwayo's reign, when hunting had seriously depleted supplies, attire was simpler than it had been 40 years before. White ox and cow tails were fastened around the neck to hang down the back as far as the knees, and down to the waist in the front. Others were tied below the knees and above the elbows. Flaps of the skins of rare animals such as leopard were worn as part of the headdress (held together by a thick, padded skin headband), either to hang down either side of the face or down the back of the neck. Various forms of skin tassels could also form

Men of what is reputedly the uNokhenke ibutho, *photographed in c. 1879. They are arrayed as for the hunt or war. Note the typical lack of uniformity in their apparel. They carry small shields of the pattern introduced by Cetshwayo during the civil war of 1856, and which were often preferred on account of their manoeuverability over the more unwieldly standard-sized shield, especially among men carrying firearms.*

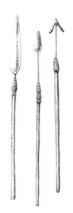

part of the headdress, as invariably did combinations of valuable feathers. These could be arranged in bunches, or in single plumes worn upright or pointing backwards. The loin cover had evolved by the 1870s to become a bunch of tails in the front and an oblong of cowskin behind, sometimes supplemented with further tails. The king and important men wore the same style of festival dress as did ordinary *amabutho*, but differences in status were marked by the costliness or profusion of the materials used.

An abbreviated form of this precious and constricting costume was worn to war, and it seems that it was a matter of rank and some personal taste as to which items were retained. During the Anglo-Zulu War, men of status sported more of the festival regalia than did ordinary warriors as an indication of their rank; while the more conservative men of the older *amabutho* preferred to keep to the usage of their youth and wear more decorative pieces than did the younger men, who laid aside all items except the loin cover, possibly some abbreviated form of headdress, and their weapons.

Weapons
In 1879 Zulu fighting-men carried traditional and modern weapons in varied combinations. The basic traditional weapon was the spear (today still popularly called the 'assegai', after the Arab term for the weapon), of which there were some 10 varieties. The deadliest was the short-handled, long-bladed stabbing spear, or *iklwa* (plural – *amaklwa*), reputedly introduced by Shaka, though probably a refinement on a weapon already used by other people of the region. It was wielded only at close quarters, when an underarm stab – normally aimed at the abdomen – was followed by withdrawing with a rip. This methodical operation required considerable skill and practice. In addition the warrior carried two or three throwing-spears with long shafts, or *izijula* (singular – *isijula*). Used also for hunting, they were well-balanced in flight, and could find their target at up to 33 yards (30 m). Some warriors might also carry a wooden knobkerrie, or *iwisa* (plural –

amawisa), for close fighting, or perhaps a few might have a battle-axe with a crescent blade (*isizenze*), of Swazi or Pedi origin. The making of spears was a specialised task that was concentrated among blacksmiths in the regions of the Nkandla forest and Black Mfolozi River. The spears, as a national asset, were handed over to the king, who distributed them to his *amabutho*.

The war-shield of cattle-hide, or *isihlangu* (plural – *izihlangu*), which took great care and patience to manufacture and was a most valuable item since a hide produces only two shields, was also supplied by the king (whose property it remained) and was kept in a special hut in the *ikhanda* because of its ritual properties. By the 1860s the shield had generally shrunk to two-thirds of the man-height originally stipulated by Shaka, though in 1879 full-sized ones continued to be carried by chiefs as a sign of distinction, and by some veterans of the older *amabutho*. The uniformity of shield colours and patterns, which distinguished the different *amabutho* in Shaka's time, was no longer observed since sufficient cattle with the required markings were no longer available. By 1879 many *amabutho* carried shields of no particular hue, although the convention (which dated from Shaka's time) seems generally to have been observed that younger *amabutho* should carry predominantly black or reddish shields, and married *amabutho* white ones.

Firearms had been entering Zululand through Delagoa Bay and Natal in significant numbers since the 1860s. By 1878 it was estimated that there were 20 000 firearms in Zululand, of which 500 were breech-loading rifles, and a further 7 500 percussion rifles. The balance were inferior, obsolete weapons like muskets, no longer required by European armies and dumped by unscrupulous dealers on the African market. Acknowledging the power and prestige conferred by firearms, Cetshwayo tried (not entirely successfully) to keep possession of them a royal monopoly, and issued them to his *amabutho* in exchange for a cow apiece.

However, the Zulu seldom made full

use of firearms or developed new tactics that would have exploited their potential. They preferred to rely on the traditional weapons on which their tactics had been based since the time of Shaka, and tended to employ firearms only as secondary weapons in place of throwing-spears, to be cast aside when the hand-to-hand fighting began. Yet more than military conservatism was responsible for the Zulu reluctance to exploit the new technology fully. Muskets were labourious to load, and wet weather could put an end to any firing. Old, condemned muskets and poorly maintained firearms generally could be positively dangerous to their users as well as inaccurate. The Zulu use of eccentric bullets like stones and metal pot legs exacerbated poor marksmanship by men lacking adequate training in firearms, and particularly in the correct use of sights. The poor quality of gunpowder available adversely affected range and penetration. As a consequence, warriors blazed away while out of range, and almost invariably fired high. The Zulu army probably contained a few hundred men familiar with modern firearms through involvement with white hunters and gun traders. Such men were best used as snipers, and were most effective against small British scouting or foraging parties. These specialists made good use of the hundreds of Martini-Henry rifles captured from the British during the course of the war, but modern breech-loaders were wasted in the hands of most Zulu who used them. Equally, the British 7-pounder guns and rocket-troughs that fell into Zulu hands were never exploited for lack of the necessary expertise.

Mobilisation and ritual preparation for war

The king sent orders by runner or signal to the commanders of the various *amakhanda* to collect their *amabutho* and proceed to the king's 'great place' in the Mahlabathini plain. In 1879 Cetshwayo's order to muster for the impending war coincided with the *umKhosi* festival scheduled for 8 January. The *amabutho* would routinely have attended the *umKhosi*, but on this occasion they were ordered to leave their ceremonial dress at home and come prepared for active service. As it turned out, the *umKhosi* festival did not take place because of the impending hostilities, but the *amabutho* concentrated in oNdini and the nearby *amakhanda* were 'doctored' for war in rituals that were an abbreviated form of the *umKhosi* ceremonies.

The Zulu believed in a mystical force, *umnyama*, which was darkness or evil influence. It reduced resistance to disease and created misfortune. A person polluted by *umnyama* could only be purified by symbolic medicines and rituals. In its worst form it could be contagious, people being treated withdrew from society and all pleasurable experiences, as if they were in mourning. Warriors about to go to war were in particular danger of pollution since taking a human life caused an especially virulent form of *umnyama*. They needed to be purified of evil influences and strengthened against them through black medicines that symbolically represented death.

On the first day of the essential rituals, the *amabutho* collected great heaps of firewood and green mimosa. A black bull, which represented all the evil influences in the land, was caught on the second day and killed bare-handed by an *ibutho*. War-doctors, or *izinyanga* (singular – *inyanga*), cut strips of meat from the bull, treated them with the black medicines and then roasted them on a fire of the wood collected the previous day. The *izinyanga* then threw the strips of meat into the air and the *amabutho*, who were drawn up in a great circle, caught and sucked them. Meanwhile, the *izinyanga* burnt further medicines and the soldiers breathed in the smoke and were sprinkled with cinders from the fire. Then, finally, to expel all dangerous influences, each warrior drank a mouthful from a pot of medicine, and a few at a time vomited the contents into a specially dug hole. This ritual vomiting took all day to complete and was intended to bind all the men together in loyalty to their king. Some of the vomit was later added to the great *inkatha* of the Zulu nation, the sacred grass coil which was the symbol of the

> 'A gun is a coward's weapon and a man has to be a man to fight with assegais, if a man is a man he will fight at close quarters'.
>
> (Mangwanana Mchunu of the uVe *ibutho, c.* 1936)

> 'The men catching the doctored strips of meat would immediately bite off a lump which is chewed and then spat out on the ground whilst the juice is swallowed. Because many of the troops are extremely hungry or even emaciated, they sometimes swallowed the piece bitten off, although it is quite contrary to custom.'
>
> (Mpatshana kaSodondo of the iNgobamakhosi *ibutho*, 24 May 1912)

nation's unity and strength, and which was kept in the esiKlebheni *ikhanda*. On the third day the warriors went down to any running stream to wash, but not to rub off the medicines. Once these rituals had been completed, the men, who had undergone a symbolic death and were in an intensified and contagious state of *umnyama,* had to behave like bereaved persons (*ukuzila*) and observe ritual abstinence. They could no longer sleep at home or on their sleeping-mats, nor have anything to do with women.

While these rituals were going on, the king called into the royal cattle enclosure a few favoured pairs of *amabutho* who were of similar age and strength, and who regularly accompanied each other into battle. Members of the rival *amabutho* would hurl ritual challenges and praises at each other and *ukugiya* (perform war-dances) until sunset, promising to outdo each other in the coming war. During battle *izinduna* would spur on their men by reminding them of these challenges. In 1879 Cetshwayo first called the uMcijo and iNgobamakhosi (his favourite *ibutho*) to challenge each other, and then the uMbonambi and uNokhenke.

The Zulu believed that good fortune depended on the favour of the *amadlozi.* The most important spirits in the hierarchy of the other world were those of the king's ancestors who were concerned with the welfare of the whole nation. The Zulu communicated with the *amadlozi* through their cattle, who formed a direct link between the ancestors and their living descendants. To ensure that the royal *amadlozi* approved of the decision to go to war in 1879, the *amabutho* sacrificed cattle at the graves of the Zulu kings in the emaKhosini (valley of the kings) and requested the spirits to accompany the army when it set out. The *amadlozi,* so the Zulu felt assured, responded positively through the bellowing of oxen late at night.

On the march

The king decided which *ibutho* would have the honour of leading the army against the enemy, or of 'drinking the dew'. The others followed according to their status. Until it reached enemy territory, the army marched in one great column. Five months after the army had marched to Isandlwana, its track was still plain, the long grass all trodden down in one direction as if a huge roller had passed over it. Every man carried his shield rolled up on his back. Boys of over fourteen years of age accompanied the army as carriers, or *izindibi* (singular – *udibi*), moving in the rear or some kilometres off on its flanks. These *izindibi* were attached to the chiefs and principal officers, and carried their mats, headrests, tobacco and the like, as well as driving the cattle required for the army's consumption. Some of the men of importance were accompanied by girls carrying beer, corn and milk. After a day or two, when these supplies had been exhausted, the girls returned to their homes, as did those *izindibi* who could not keep up with the army's advance. When this happened, even the *izinduna* would have to carry their own belongings. Every man had with him iron rations in a skin sack, but these also soon gave out.

The increasingly hungry *amabutho* tried to spare their own civilian population as much as possible, slaughtering the cattle they brought with them, and camping whenever they could at *amakhanda* where there were stores of food. In enemy territory an army could forage mercilessly, but even when on its own soil – as in 1879 – it was often forced to raid the grain-pits and cattle of its own civilians who, in turn, did their best to remove their precious supplies. Sometimes the army advanced in skirmishing order, driving wild game to the centre to kill for consumption. However, by 1879 there was little game left to kill. Lack of water and wood fuel for cooking and warmth added to the army's privations.

A Zulu army might continue its march after darkness fell, but it did not undertake night marches as such. Despite legends about the extraordinary speed of its advance, in 1879 it averaged only about 12 miles (19 km) a day, normally by fairly easy stages with often quite extens-

'Men selected for scouting were men of courage, who on coming across detached sections of the enemy perhaps driving cattle, would attack and seize the stock. There are also spies sent in twos and threes to locate the enemy for purposes of their being surprised and ambushed.'
(Mpatshana, 28 May 1912)

ive halts during which there would be the opportunity to forage.

Once an army neared the enemy, the column split normally into two divisions which would advance parallel to and in sight of each other. Bodies of scouts about 500 strong, especially selected for their courage, preceded each division in extended order by about 10 miles (16 km). Their numbers were supposed to trick the enemy into thinking they were the main body, and so if attacked to draw the enemy onto the rest of the army which had been alerted by runner. Besides these advance-guards, which moved provocatively in the open as decoys, sometimes driving cattle to tempt the enemy, the Zulu also sent out spies in twos and threes to locate the enemy and give the army the advantage of surprise.

Once the enemy had been located, it was up to the Zulu commander, who had been appointed by the king, to consult thoroughly with his subordinate officers on whether or not to engage. Once the decision had been taken, the army was drawn up in an *umkhumbi*, or circle. *Izinyanga*, who had accompanied the army, sprinkled it with further medicines. The commander then gave his instructions, and took up position with his staff on suitable high ground at some distance from the coming engagement. From this

eminence he was able to direct operations by runner, to despatch an *induna* to rally his men, or even to retire unscathed should the battle go against the Zulu.

Battle tactics

The Zulu tactical intention was to outflank and enclose the enemy in a flexible manoeuvre, evidently developed from the hunt, that could be readily adapted to either a set-piece battle or to a surprise attack. Not for the Zulu the harassing tactics employed by other black warriors, such as the Xhosa and Pedi, against whom the British had fought in southern Africa. Indeed, modern commentators have been perplexed by the Zulu failure to develop new tactics better suited to confronting the devastating fire-power of the invading British. One rejoinder is that it had been 41 years since the Zulu had last encountered a white army, and all battles in the intervening years had been fought employing the conventional tactics dating back to Shaka against African foes. Another response is that the Zulu believed they could win against whites carrying firearms if the invaders could be forced to give battle in the open field outside prepared defences. Experience in the campaign of 1838 against the Voortrekkers had proved this, for although the Zulu had been repeatedly repulsed at the

> 'When actually in battle, the *izinduna* recall what a rival regiment said at the time when they were challenging one another in the presence of the king; e.g. as Sikizane kaNomageje of the iNgobamakhosi did at Isandlwana: 'Why are you lying down? What was it you said to the uMcijo? There are the uMcijo going into the tents.'
> (Mpatshana, 25 May 1912)

Charles Fripp, a special artist for the Graphic *in Zululand, much admired the bravery shown by the Zulu. He worked in the field and his drawings were very accurate. His depiction of charging Zulu catches them in typical open order with an assortment of weapons (including firearms) and a minimum of personal adornment.*

Boer wagon laagers, they had twice beaten Boer commandos in the open. Besides which, Zulu tradition as an aggressive and conquering people demanded the manly frontal assault and merciless hand-to-hand combat. Night attacks and ambushes might well be resorted to, but the norm was battle by daylight, in the open, and according to a predictable tactical formula.

For the purpose of executing this standard manoeuvre, the army was divided into four divisions in a formation likened to an ox. The 'chest', or centre (*isifuba*), which consisted of the veteran *amabutho*, advanced slowly, while the flanking 'horns', or wings (*izimpondo*; singular – *upondo*) of younger, more agile *amabutho* were rapidly sent out. One horn made a feint, while the other, concealed as much as possible by the terrain, moved with greater speed to effect a junction with the less advanced horn. The chest then charged the surrounded enemy and destroyed him in close combat with the stabbing-spear. The 'loins' or reserve (*umuva*), traditionally kept seated with their backs to the enemy so as not to become unmanageably excited, had the task of supporting an engaged *ibutho* in difficulties, or pursuing the defeated enemy. Similarly, a reserve of youths, or a very young *ibutho*, was sometimes held back from joining in an attack, but was later sent in for support, in pursuit, or to round up captured cattle. Auxiliaries and irregulars, not incorporated into the *ibutho* system, usually supported the army operating in their locality, and sometimes also took full part in the battle.

Contrary to the now generally accepted impression, the Zulu did not attack shoulder-to-shoulder in a solid body. Instead, they advanced rapidly in lines of skirmishers in open order several ranks deep (at Isandlwana 10 to 12 ranks was the mean), coming on in short rushes and making good use of natural cover. They only concentrated when upon the enemy and about to engage in hand-to-hand fighting, and this they prefaced with a shower of throwing-spears or gun-fire to distract the foe as they rushed in at close quarters. When battle was actually joined, and especially when the spear was being thrust into the enemy, the national war-cry was shouted which, during Cetshwayo's reign, was 'uSuthu!'. Imbued with their military ethic, each man vied to be first among the enemy, and rival *amabutho*, spurred on by the ritual challenges they had exchanged before the king, contended to gain the honours. No quarter was even given in battle, and not even women were generally allowed to escape, on the grounds that they bore fighting-men. The enemies' cattle, on the other hand, usually fared better than they did themselves, for they were the prized booty of war.

Caring for the wounded and disposing of the dead

Wounds inflicted by spear and British sword-bayonet, as well as superficial bullet grazes, could be healed with the simple remedies the Zulu possessed. For flesh wounds the Zulu had a poultice made from the leaves of the ubuHlungwana herb (*Wadelia natalensis*), or the powdered bulb of the uGodide (*Jatropha hirsuta*), which prevented inflammation. Open wounds could be tied up with grass. But most bullet wounds, especially those inflicted by the heavy lead slug fired by the Martini-Henry rifle, smashed bones and caused considerable internal injury, requiring more sophisticated care than the Zulu had available. Fractures were set with splints, and certain herbs – particularly the powdered root of the uMathunga (*Cyrtanthus obliquus*) – were rubbed into incisions made at the point of breakage. Some Zulu had the limbs smashed by bullets amputated – and lived, and some *izinyanga* had the ability to open broken skulls and remove harmful blood clots. But most of the Zulu wounded in 1879 (whom British-style medical attention could have saved) never survived the long march home.

The bodies of the Zulu fallen were disposed of in dongas, antbear holes and grain-pits by friends or relatives, for they had the obligation to see to their decent burial. Otherwise, the dead might be allowed to lie where they had fallen, simply covered with a shield. Slain enemies, by

'Those of our impi were here and there covered with their shields – It is put over by a relative or friend. Many were not covered because their friends etc. did not look about sufficiently and find the corpses'.
(Mpatshana, 25 May 1912)

contrast, were left to the wild animals and the elements.

Dispersal and ritual purification

After a victory, it was customary for a Zulu army to return in triumph to the king in order to report and to share out the spoils. If beaten, the warriors would scatter to their homes, leaving it to the unfortunate commanders to inform the king of the army's misfortune and to take the responsibility and possible punishment. Whether victorious or not, a Zulu army could not stay long in the field after combat. There were the wounded to bring home, and lack of supplies forced a rapid return or dispersal. Besides which, as a militia, the *amabutho* had their interrupted domestic functions to consider. But overriding all these considerations which made it difficult to wage an extended campaign, was the ritual one.

When a Zulu killed in battle, or ritually stabbed a brave fallen enemy in fulfilment of a custom related to the hunt in which a fierce and courageous animal was thus honoured, it was necessary afterwards to perform certain rites to remove the contagious ritual pollution of *umnyama*. It was essential to disembowel a slain enemy lest *umnyama* should follow and the killer swell up like the dead. Equally part of the rites was the stripping of the dead man's apparel and the wearing of an item by the slayer in place of his own (which had been polluted by the harmful influences of his victim's blood) until he had been ritually cleansed.

Because they were ritually polluted, warriors returning from battle could not immediately present themselves before the king, rejoin their companions, or resume normal domestic life before the required ceremonies had been performed. Accordingly, for four days the ritually contaminated were separated from their companions, who were barracked in the *amakhanda*, and were placed in special *imizi* where they were fed with cattle captured from the enemy. Daily, they went out to wash ritually in the run-ning water of a stream, and then returned to *ncinda*, or suck medicine from the fingertips and squirt it in the direction of their foes. In this way they hoped to ward off *umnyama*, and to obtain occult ascendancy over the spirits of their vengeful victims, whose spilt blood formed a dangerous bridge between the dead and the living. Because many of the warriors carried the necessary medicines with them on campaign, an *inyanga* was not required, except to sprinkle medicines on the final day. They were also correctly ornamented with *iziqu*, or amulet necklaces or bracelets of small pieces of willow-wood, which possessed the ritual properties of warding off the evil effects of homicide. Since by association these *iziqu* represented actions of valour in battle, they were borne with considerable pride, despite being inconvenient to wear.

Once they were ritually clean, the *amabutho* presented themselves with their weapons before the king in the cattle enclosure. The king seated himself in their midst, well fortified against *umnyama* by medicines smeared over his face and body. The *amabutho* then exchanged accounts of the fighting and renewed the challenged they had made before setting out for war. The king would already have held extensive discussions to discover which individuals had distinguished themselves on campaign, and which *ibutho* had earned the great honour of having been first among the enemy. He also had ascertained who had revealed themselves as cowards by holding back in the fighting or running away. These he publicly humiliated by ordering to eat cooked meat soaked in cold water, while their more courageous comrades, seated in a semi-circle, enjoyed their meat crisp and warm. Meanwhile, the king rewarded those identified as particularly brave with gifts of cattle. The ceremonies completed, the *amabutho* dispersed to their homes or *amakhanda* to await the king's summons to serve him once again in peace or war.

> 'If he has killed two or more he will take articles from each and put them on. He will not put on his own things until the doctor has treated him and given him medicine to suck from the fingertips.'
> (Mpatshana, 24 May 1912)

The review at Windsor of troops returned from the Second Ashanti War, as portrayed by the Illustrated London News *of 11 April 1874. The 42nd Highlanders march past Queen Victoria, seated in her open landau. Next to her carriage on a black horse is her cousin, Field Marshal the Duke of Cambridge, for 39 years the Commander-in-Chief of the British Army. On his right is Maj-Gen Sir Garnet Wolseley, KCMG, CB, who commanded in the Ashanti War. The extremely pushy but professional Wolseley and his 'ring' of like-minded officers alienated the conservative Duke and those officers who deplored army reform and advanced military ideas.*

The British and Colonial Military Systems

British regular troops, being professional soldiers armed with the latest weaponry, tended to look down on the imperial and colonial units raised locally, especially the African levies. But the mounted volunteers, both black and white, often proved more effective in the field than the regulars who were hampered by logistical difficulties and by tactics ill-attuned to local circumstances.

British regulars

Between 1815 and 1914 the British Army waged more overseas campaigns than any other colonial power except France. Colonial campaigns, fought not against regular troops trained in the European fashion, but against irregulars inferior in armaments, organisation and discipline – and employing varied and unpredictable military styles – were a specialised form of combat requiring strategic and tactical adaptability. The emphasis remained on individual flair among officers and disciplined solidarity among the men, rather than on the technical knowledge and complex managerial skills necessary to cope with the problems of mass organisation and movement that characterised warfare between the great industrialised powers of Europe and North America.

Without the familiarising effects of conscription, the general public in Britain continued to view the small and professional British Army with considerable disparagement and suspicion. Certainly, the army was a self-contained and authoritarian institution in which the forces of conservatism were deeply entrenched. Nevertheless, it played an essential role in imperial defence, and the British government, rather than downgrading the army, made various attempts to improve its effectiveness. Reforms carried out under Edward Cardwell, Secretary of State for War (1868–1874), had a direct bearing on the war in Zululand since they affected the army's ability to wage colonial campaigns.

For the sake of economy and efficiency, Cardwell reduced Britain's military presence overseas by completing the withdrawal of troops from colonies of settlement, and by scaling down garrisons elsewhere, except in India. The introduction of short service in 1870, whereby recruits spent six years in the regular army and six in the reserve, was designed to create a large reservoir of trained reservists, reduce unhealthy service abroad and save money. Cardwell created 69 brigade districts in Britain (usually conforming to an existing county) with two linked battalions to be attached to each depot. The battalions would alternate in recruiting at home and serving abroad, so ensuring (it was intended) that the Empire would be guarded only by seasoned troops. In 1871 the purchase of commissions was abolished and promotion opened to merit to encourage the development of a professional officer corps. Nor had the abolition of purchase changed the nature of the officer corps, for the necessity of a large private income in all except the technical arms (like the Royal Engineers) ensured that the officer corps remained a conservative social elite.

This system did not work in practice, however. Since the reserve was not to be called out except in the event of a national emergency, minor colonial campaigns could only be provided for by calling upon regular and reserve units for volunteers, and by draining standing garrisons. Moreover, as colonial commitments increased, a growing number of home-based and imperfectly trained battalions found themselves serving overseas. Thus, in 1879, 82 battalions were

'There is much work which native levies alone can properly perform – They are excellent scouts, indefatigable & quick witted; perform all fatigue duties most cheerfully; and can be employed with mounted men when necessary, in consequence of their wonderful marching powers – Many of the men are employed as spies; and all cheerfully & willingly perform any duty they may be detailed for such as bringing in wood, repairing roads, searching difficult country, building entrenched posts, &c, &c – '

(Lord Chelmsford, 8 June 1879)

The stone-built Fort Bengough was erected during the fortnight after Isandlwana and garrisoned by the 2nd Battalion, Natal Native Contingent under Maj H.M. Bengough. In the photograph the NNC are drawn up in front of the fort, which was only fully occupied at night. During the day, officers and men sheltered in the huts built on the slope to the right.

abroad, and only 59 at home depots. To maintain establishments and meet the larger turnover of men caused by short-term enlistment, the army had to lower physical standards. Furthermore, as experienced soldiers now left the ranks earlier, the proportion of young men rose to such an extent that the efficiency of regiments on active service was undermined. Indeed, many of the regular troops sent to Zululand in 1879 as reinforcements were young, inexperienced and militarily unsatisfactory. Recruits, if no longer entirely drawn from the least respectable elements of the working class, still came largely from its poorest and least educated elements.

These British regulars formed the main striking-force of Lord Chelmsford's army in Zululand. Regularly paid, trained in the complex manipulation of modern weapons, strongly cohesive in battle and sustained by a comparatively reliable administrative and logistical infrastructure, they were a formidable fighting force. Each battalion of infantry comprised eight companies, nominally made up of 30 officers and 866 men, though the establishment in the field was often considerably lower. The men received a shilling a day and staple rations of bread and meat. Discipline was rigid and punishment by flogging, though abolished in time of peace, was permitted on campaign. The infantry in Zululand were supported by units of the Royal Engineers and by the Royal Artillery. There were six guns to a battery of artillery, divided into three divisions of two guns, each worked by two officers and 45 men. In the Zululand campaign these RA units were supported by the infantry and artillery of the Royal Marines and a Naval Brigade drawn from the crews of warships off the coast of Natal.

Mounted troops retained an importance in colonial warfare long after it had been lost in Europe. They were essential for reconnaissance and raiding purposes, and vital in pursuit of a broken enemy. However, regular cavalry (a regiment on war footing consisted of eight troops – or four squadrons – made up of 27 officers and 607 men), was not available to Chelmsford until the latter stages of the campaign. He had to turn, therefore, to mounted infantry (a squadron consisted of three officers and 110 men drawn from volunteers from infantry regiments), and to units of colonial mounted volunteers of greatly varying strengths.

Imperial and colonial units

British regulars serving in Zululand were too valuable and scarce to be dispersed on garrison and convoy duty and had to be augmented by black levies. In Natal the lieutenant-governor, in his capacity as 'supreme chief', had the right to exact *isibhalo* – or compulsory labour and military service – from Africans living in the colony. Natal magistrates accordingly raised levies from the chiefs in the Native Reserves, encouraging recruitment with promises of captured cattle. The Natal Native Contingent, as this force was called (except for that raised later from the south of Natal and called the Ixopo Native Contingent), was placed under white colonial officers and non-commissioned officers, commanded by seconded or former British officers. They were formed into three regiments of seven battalions – reduced to five after Isandlwana. Each battalion consisted of 10 companies with a nominal establishment of 33 officers, 62 NCOs and 1 011 men. One man in ten was issued with a firearm, and they were paid 20 shillings a month (which was better than the usual

pay for *isibhalo* labour). The NNC, INC, and the three companies of the Natal Native Pioneer Corps, as well as Wood's Irregulars (who for the most part were labour tenants on white farms pressed into service by the landdrosts of Wakkerstroom and Utrecht in the Transvaal), and levies raised from Zulu collaborators such as Prince Hamu's Ngenetsheni adherents, fell directly under Chelmsford's command and were maintained like other imperial troops. By contrast, the part-time levies and small standing reserves of Africans under white levy-leaders, who were raised to secure the border districts of Natal, remained the responsibility of the colonial government. The NNC was poorly armed and ineffectually trained in unfamiliar British drill and tactics. Despite early hopes, it is not surprising that it proved of doubtful morale and effectiveness. The border levies were allowed to retain their traditional style of warfare, though they had little practice in it. They were of even less military value than the NNC.

A far better fighting force, but underestimated by the British regulars with their inflated professional self-esteem and metropolitan contempt for all things colonial, was the colonial irregular horse. The absence of sufficient horsemen was perhaps the single greatest defect in Chelmsford's army, and these colonial troopers played a significant role out of proportion to their small numbers.

Imperial units of irregular horse were raised from whites living in the Transvaal and Cape colonies. They included many foreign nationals, as well as colonials. Some of the units were still in existence after being engaged in other South African campaigns of the 1870s, and were very well versed in the requirements of mounted warfare. Keen and effective African volunteers from the Natal Native Reserves and from the Christian community at Edendale outside Pietermaritzburg formed the five squadrons of the Natal Native Horse and other units, such as Shepstone's Native Horse. They supplied their own horses, but were armed and maintained by the War Office

and commanded by white colonial officers.

The Natal government also contributed mounted men to the invasion of Zululand. Its most effective force was the Natal Mounted Police, a small standing body of quasi-military police, created in 1874. They approached the discipline and professionalism of regular troops. Only the mounted men of the Natal Volunteer Corps, first raised in 1855, and which consisted of one artillery, three infantry and 11 mounted corps, played an active part in the invasion. Drawn predominantly from the English-speaking colonists, they elected their own officers, provided their own uniforms and horses, if necessary, and were issued with weapons and maintained by the Natal government.

Besides the Volunteers, there were other colonial troops available in Natal. The Mounted Burgher Force, which dated from 1863, was an irregular body of volunteers, bound to respond when called out for service by the local field cornet of each ward. With its similarity in form to the traditional Boer commando that had developed on the Cape eastern frontier, this system was favoured by the Dutch-speaking settlers of the country areas. They supplied all their own equipment and found formal, British-style discipline uncongenial. They were not required to serve more than 20 miles (32 km) from their own county, let alone outside the borders of Natal. In this they differed from the Boers of the Utrecht District of the Transvaal, whose commando under Piet Uys crossed into Zululand with the British. And, finally, there were the settler members of the various Rifle Associations which, since 1862, had been organised in some areas of Natal for the purposes of defence. They attempted to train with some regularity, and were encouraged to purchase rifles and ammunition available from the government at a nominal cost.

Dress

In the late 1870s, the British infantryman wore a single-breasted scarlet tunic with brass buttons and coloured regimental

'The muster of the Natal Hussars appeared to be quite a success. Thirty-two troopers assembled out of a total muster-roll of forty . . . The various evolutions of this large (for Greytown) body of men was watched by many with great interest . . . the skirmishing and blank cartridge firing causing considerable amusement as well, for not a few of the horses did not like the smell of powder a bit at first.'
(*Natal Witness*, 29 June 1878)

Men of the 3/60th Regiment (The King's Royal Rifle Corps) on the march in Zululand. Notice their Valise pattern accoutrements (right) and their fixed sword bayonets (opposite page).

'Look at the troops heavy accoutred, plodding their way, under a boiling African sun, over interminable hills and then when arriving at a halting place . . . to find a bed of the river dried up.'

(*Natal Witness*, 19 November 1879)

facings. Trousers were dark blue with a scarlet welt down the outside seam and were tucked into black leather leggings. A co-ordinated set of accoutrements of the Valise pattern was introduced in 1871. It consisted of a black waterproofed canvas sack (or valise) supported in the small of the back by shoulder straps. The straps were attached to a waist belt to which were attached three ammunition pouches holding 70 rounds. The rolled great-coat and mess-tin were secured above the valise. Officers wore either scarlet tunics or the dark blue patrol jackets introduced in 1866, the latter being preferred in the field. No tropical uniform was issued to the British soldier, with the exception of those stationed in India. The only concession to those serving in Africa was the foreign service helmet, first issued in 1877. Instead of the blue helmet worn in Europe, it was of cork covered in white canvas, normally dyed brown with tea when on campaign. Uniforms on active service were not replaced, and became tattered and stained. Officers in the field tended to adopt a strange assortment of jackets and caps.

The Royal Engineers and Royal Marine Light Infantry wore a uniform sim-

ilar to that of the infantry. The Royal Artillery and Royal Marine Artillery wore dark blue tunics with scarlet collars, and blue trousers with the scarlet welt. Mounted infantry retained their regiment's tunic and replaced their blue trousers with brown cord riding-breeches. A bandolier took the place of ammunition pouches. Sailors of the Naval Brigade wore an assortment of styles of blue uniform, which officers sometimes varied with a white jacket and white canvas leggings or trousers. Headgear was blue (sometimes white and blue), though the broad-brimmed straw sennet hat was often adopted. Cavalry uniform was individual to different regiments, and tended to be in dashing combinations of scarlet, blue and white.

Inconsistent attempts at uniform based on European patterns were made by the mounted men of most Natal Volunteer Corps and Native Horse, though some of the better-established units were properly turned out. The Natal Carbineers, for example, all wore blue uniforms and white helmets, and the professional Natal Mounted Police smart black tunics and breeches, and white helmets. Experienced units of imperial horse also tended to be well turned out in similar fashion. The uniform of the Frontier Light Horse was representative: buff-coloured uniform with black trimmings for troopers, and black uniforms with red facings for officers and NCOs. A wide-awake (soft-brimmed felt hat) with a red puggaree (thin scarf worn around the hat) was standard. The Boers, by contrast, dressed in their everyday clothes. The Natal Native Contingent and the various formations raised by the Natal government for frontier defence also wore civilian dress that consisted of little more than the traditional loin cover. They were distinguished from non-combatants and hostile Zulu by a red rag twisted around the head, or, in the case of the Ixopo Native Contingent, by grey armbands with an orange stripe.

Weapons

Since 1874 British infantry had carried the single-shot Martini-Henry Mark II rifle. It weighed 9lbs (4.08 kg) and fired a .450 calibre hardened lead bullet of 1.1 ounces (31 g) with a muzzle velocity of 375 yards (342 m) per second. A lever behind the trigger guard, when lowered, dropped the breech block, allowing the centre-fire Boxer cartridge to be inserted into the chamber. However, the cartridge, which was covered with paper, was difficult to insert, and the thin rolled brass case often became stuck when the chamber was fouled and heated by the black gunpowder propellant, and it was torn by the ejector. Fouling also lodged easily in the rifled barrel with its seven deep, square-cut grooves. This significantly increased the already severe recoil, made the barrel too hot to touch, and affected accuracy since the bullet would no longer spin properly. Breech-loading rifles made it possible not only to fire more rapidly, but to do so while kneeling or lying down. This, in turn, encouraged open-order skirmishing tactics, and firing while standing was confined to close-order formations in defence.

The Martini-Henry bullet flattened on impact, causing massive tissue damage and splintering of bone lengthways. Martini-Henry fire nevertheless did not cause the number of casualties that might have been anticipated, for it depended for its effect on both range and volume. At 'close range' (100–300 yards or 91–274 m), two minutes' fire at six shots per minute would only be 10 per cent effective against a massed attack; at 'medium range' (300–700 yards or 274–640 m) effectiveness would decrease to 5 per cent for four minutes' fire at six shots per minute; while at 'long range' (700–1 400 yards or 640–1 280 m) the effectiveness of six shots a minute over seven minutes would fall to 2 per cent. However, at 'point-blank range' (below 100 yards or 91 m), the wall of fire could be nigh impenetrable for a charging enemy – but only if the troops were sufficiently concentrated. A company of 100 men in close order, two deep with a frontage of 40 yards (36.5 m), could maintain the necessary volume of 12 shots per yard (0.91 m) a minute. However, even at point-blank range a skirmishing

line, with regulation intervals of at least four paces and as many as ten, could not develop the necessary volume of fire to deter a determined charge. At medium to long range volley firing was still preferred because at that distance the enemy still appeared to be a dense mass, and it was easier to control the rate of fire and prevent wastage of ammunition. At the same time the unceasing volleys carried out by each section in turn up and down the line had a terrible psychological effect on the enemy (volley firing set up a thick pall of smoke, and one of the reasons for firing by section was to prevent the smoke obscuring the enemy). Independent fire was employed from close range when the attackers began to emerge as individual targets.

The Martini-Henry was fitted with a triangular socket bayonet, 22 inch (0.56 m) long, universal issue since 1876. Although the 'lunger', as it was known, gave formidable reach in hand-to-hand combat, it was of poor quality and too often bent or broke in action. The Pattern Sword Bayonet was also carried. Ammunition was stored in wooden boxes reinforced by two copper bands. The sliding lid was secured by a single

A drawing of a Martini-Henry Mark II rifle.

two-inch brass screw. It was not difficult to open, though the introduction of the split-pin fastening in 1881 made for quicker release.

Officers carried privately-owned swords and double-action .45 revolvers (usually the Mark II Adams or the Webley Royal Irish Constabulary model of 1867), which were not accurate at more than 25 yards (23 m). The Martini-Henry carbine had been adopted for use of regular cavalry in 1871, though in Zululand cavalry shock weapons, namely the 1864 pattern sword and the 1868 pattern 9-foot (2.7-m) bamboo lance with triangular steel head, were mainly employed. Irregular and colonial cavalry were generally issued with Swinburn-Henry or Snider carbines, both rifled breach-loaders. Initially, only one in ten of the Natal Native Contingent was entrusted with a firearm, usually an obsolete muzzle-loader. The remainder, and the various border levies, carried traditional spears and shields.

Field batteries were normally equipped with 9-pounder RML (Rifled Muzzle Loader) field guns sighted between 1 690 and 2 780 yards (1 545 and 2 542 m). However, these were not employed until towards the end of the Anglo-Zulu War because 7-pounder RML Mark IV steel mountain guns, fitted with a low-slung colonial carriage and narrow track, and pulled by three mules, were considered more mobile and better suited to local conditions. However, they capsized easily if towed over rough ground. Al-

though they had a maximum range of 3 100 yards (2 821 m) for explosive shells, the low muzzle velocity of 7-pounders rendered shrapnel-shot ineffective. Case-shot, or canister, could only be employed at ranges of less than 280 yards (256 m).

Rockets with explosive heads were used in Zululand primarily for their supposed demoralising effect since in flight they made a hideous shrieking sound, and their passage was marked by a thick trail of white smoke and yellow sparks. Hale's rocket, approved in 1867, came in both 24-pounder and 9-pounder varieties. Instead of a stick for stability, it had three flanges at the vent which caused it to spin in flight. It was fired by a hand-lit fuse from a V-shaped trough on a stand, though the Naval Brigade continued to use the pre-1868 rocket tube, which was more suitable for shipboard service. The effective range was no more than about 1 300 yards (1 189 m) and accuracy was very poor.

The Gatling gun (which came into service in 1871 but which was not fired in action until the battle of Nyezane in 1879), was mounted on a carriage similar to that of a field gun. It could fire 200 Boxer .450 rounds a minute from 10 rifled barrels rotated around a fixed central axis by a manually operated crank. The bullets were fed by gravity from a revolving upright case holding 40 cartridges, which was replaced after every 4 revolutions. Though highly effective up to 1 000 yards (914 m), cutting swathes through enemy lines, the Gatling gun proved unreliable because of its tendency to jam.

Tactics

British Army that in countering highly mobile enemies it was necessary to know how to work in loose skirmishing order, making the most of the terrain and natural cover. In the Ninth Cape Frontier War of 1877–8, the British had used the extended firing-line with great success against theNgqika and Gcaleka Xhosa. At the battle of Nyezane in the Anglo-Zulu War, which was a running fire-fight over broken terrain, identical tactics proved equally effective. However, at Isandlwana the extended skirmishing-line could not put up enough firepower to stop the well-concerted Zulu mass assault over open ground.

The contrasting outcomes of the battles of Nyezane and Isandlwana highlight the chief tactical problem in colonial warfare: against the real advantage of dispersal in skirmishing order was pitted the need to concentrate firepower and present a solid line to a rapidly advancing enemy. After the Isandlwana debacle, the British in Zululand unfailingly adopted the latter option. The most effective way of giving maximum effect to the destructive weight of fire of modern rifles, artillery and Gatling guns was to place troops in close order in prepared all-round defensive positions, such as fieldworks (whether of earth or stone), or wagon laagers. The infantry square, an archaic formation in European warfare, devised originally as a tactic for repelling cavalry, was also still effective in colonial warfare where the enemy was highly mobile and manoeuvred not unlike cavalry. The disadvantage of all these tightly packed formations was vulnerability to gunfire or artillery, though this did not apply in Zululand where the Zulu made inadequate use of their firearms and had no artillery. The main weakness of the rectangular wagon laager or fieldwork, or of the infantry square, lay in the corners where the same weight of fire could not be developed as along the sides. The partial solution was to place artillery and Gatling guns in the corners, but even so the less well defended corners were repeatedly targeted by the attacking Zulu.

Mounted troops were required for long-range reconnaissance and vedette (mounted sentry) duties, for patrolling the lines of communication, and for drawing the enemy into range of prepared infantry positions. They were also the main instrument for unexpected strikes against Zulu concentrations, for the destruction of enemy *imizi* and provisions, and the capture of livestock.

Mounted infantry skirmishing with the Zulu as portrayed by the special artist, Melton Prior, for the Illustrated London News *of 4 October 1879. Skirmishing tactics had been employed successfully by the British in the 9th Frontier War, though – as the battle of Isandlwana proved – they were not suited to Zulu mass attacks. In major engagements thereafter the British kept close order to maximise their firepower, though open order remained customary in minor skirmishes.*

The charge of the 17th Lancers at the battle of Ulundi, illustrated in the Graphic *of 20 September 1879. Though anachronistic in modern warfare, the lance proved very effective against irregular troops scattered in flight, especially when, as with the Zulu, they flung themselves flat or took shelter in crevasses. The only problem for the cavalry was that the lance had a tendency to stick in the shield it had penetrated.*

Regular cavalry was most useful for shock action with sword and lance when they could turn the enemy's orderly withdrawal into a rout. However, irregular cavalry was more effective in Zululand because, operating as mounted infantry, they combined the horseman's speed and range with the infantryman's firepower, and generally fought dismounted except when in pursuit.

The Natal Native Contingent was primarily employed (as were other levies) in providing border patrols, garrisons and cattle guards. It took part regularly in skirmishes, though generally in a support role. Sometimes it found itself in the front line during battles, though in pitched engagements its main task was to sally out of the prepared position once the Zulu were routed, and despatch the enemy wounded.

Logistics

Effective logistics, the basis of any successful campaign, were built on the accumulation of necessary supplies and ammunition, as well as on the organisation of sufficient transport. During the Zululand campaign an establishment was required which eventually numbered 748 horses, 4 635 mules, 27 125 oxen, 641 horse and mule carriages, 1 770 ox wagons, 796 ox carts and 4 080 conductors (drivers of wagons) and *voorloopers*

(leaders on foot of teams of oxen). However, the Commissariat and Transport Department (created in the course of the army reforms of 1875) was inefficient and unable to adapt to South African conditions. Its inexperience in purchasing methods and in animal husbandry drove up the cost of buying transport animals and of hiring wagons from the colonists. Uneasy relations between the military and the Natal government, which took umbrage at the former's high-handed style, prevented the full co-operation necessary for easing the transport problem. Furthermore, if more importance had been attached to the selection of better trained staff officers to augment the over-stretched officers of the Department, many of the organisational problems might have been minimised. As it was, Lord Chelmsford proved incapable of restructuring the Department, and only succeeded with great difficulty in assembling the transport necessary for the invasion of Zululand.

An army's movement is based on the speed of its slowest component, and the progress of the convoys of wagons, once assembled, was very slow. Enormous distances, as much as inclement weather and unsurveyed and rudimentary traders' tracks – cut across by drifts and dongas which collapsed under the volume of traffic – were among the problems facing

A photograph of a convoy of the 1st Division negotiating the churned-up cutting leading down to the drift across the Matigulu River gives a graphic indication of the problems the British encountered in moving up supplies.

convoys. Wagons, drawn by as many as 18 oxen or eight mules (which had to be regularly rested and given time to graze), could hardly travel further than 12 miles (19 km) a day and, over difficult terrain, sometimes as few as 3 miles (5 km). The loads carried were prodigious. Battalion transport consisted of eight company wagons containing each officer's 40 lbs (18 kg) of personal baggage as well as the bulk of each fully accoutred infantry-man's 56 lbs (25.4 kg) load – or 60 lbs (27.2 kg) in the case of a cavalry trooper. In addition, there were sufficient wagons to carry a little over 8.82 imperial tons (9 metric tonnes) of camping equipment, 1.76 tons (about 1.8 metric tonnes) of reserve ammunition, 90 tents weighing 3.5 tons (3.6 tonnes) when dry and 4.9 tons (5 tonnes) wet, and rations consumed at the rate of almost 0.98 tons (1 tonne) a day. Although able to hold up to 3.5 tons (3.6 tonnes) each, these wagons were never loaded with more than 0.98 tons (1 tonne) because of the inferior Zululand tracks. Transport was also required for the artillery and rocket batteries, engineering and signalling equipment, medical stores, camp kitchens, field bakeries and shoeing smithies. Un-

like draft-oxen, neither English-bred cavalry chargers nor draft-mules could support themselves solely by grazing, and their fodder also had to be carried.

Slowing the convoys even further was the need to replenish rapidly exhausted supplies. For example, despite a great convoy of 660 wagons, the 5 000 men of the 2nd Division had sufficient supplies to last only six weeks. They had to halt at

Something of the effort and tumult of moving a convoy along the rudimentary Zululand tracks can be gauged from this engraving in the Illustrated London News *of 25 October 1879 of British troops evacuating Zululand.*

'It has been impossible to obtain any really reliable information regarding the country even from those who ought to know it well – They have never been accustomed to look at any of the roads from any but a trader's point of view, and are therefore quite unable to give the detailed information which is so important when movements of troops are concerned.'

(Lord Chelmsford, 11 April 1879)

THE AWARDS
During the Anglo-Zulu War only two decorations for gallantry and one campaign medal could be awarded. The Victoria Cross, established in 1856 for all ranks of the armed forces, was the supreme award for conspicuous bravery in action; while the Distinguished Conduct Medal was instituted in 1854 for other ranks only. All those troops involved in one or more of the campaigns in South Africa between 25 September 1877 and 2 December 1879 were eligible for the South Africa Medal. The date bar fixed to the medal specified in which operations the recipient had been engaged.

intervals to establish forward depots for reserve supplies, and to allow wagons to move backwards and forwards between them and the rear supply bases until they were filled.

There was a practical limit to the size of a convoy, however. Wagons naturally required all-round protection on the march, particularly on the flanks, and patrols moved parallel or in advance of the column to give early warning of enemy movements. However, a single wagon in full span took up 60 yards (55 m) in column, making a lengthy train of several hundred extremely difficult to guard, and dangerously thinning out the escort. The ambush of No. 1 Column at Nyezane, strung out on the march (a column would stretch up to a further 25 per cent of its original length on the move), demonstrates the hazard. The vulnerability of an already extended column was increased at drifts across rivers or passes up steep hills where wagons had usually to cross in single file, creating bottlenecks. In open country, on the other hand, wagons could proceed more rapidly at about eight abreast, ignoring the rutted tracks, and making them easier to escort.

Colonists, especially the Boers, advised the British to form defensive wagon laagers when halted in Zulu territory. But, until after the battle of Isandlwana, they were reluctant to laager because it was such a time-consuming procedure and reduced time on the march. Once it became standard to laager at every halt (the site of which was determined by the availability of water and firewood), the

procedure greatly improved with practice. The Flying Column, for example, could laager its 300 wagons in well under an hour if they had been moving over a wide front, and neaer to two if they had been in single file.

Intelligence
Lack of accurate maps of Zululand forced British commanders to rely on reconnaissance patrols to provide information about the terrain to be traversed, and to locate military objectives. Yet the professional accumulation and analysis of intelligence was not adequately addressed in the late Victorian army, despite the establishment in 1858 of the Staff College at Camberley. It was not until the very end of the war that appropriately trained staff officers were sent out at the behest of General Sir Garnet Wolseley, who was renowned for his 'advanced' military ideas. Chelmsford, his conservative predecessor in command, was reluctant to establish a staff along modern lines, and was content to depend on regular officers without specialist training, and on Natal civilians with some knowledge of the country and the Zulu language.

Worst of all, although Chelmsford did his best to study in advance the miliary methods of the Zulu, and commissioned booklets for his officers informing them on enemy tactics and on how British troops should best be managed in the field to withstand them, he and his staff made the initial and fatal mistake of underrating Zulu fighting capability.

Victoria Cross   *Distinguished Conduct Medal*   *South Africa Medal*

War Correspondents

By 1879, war 'special correspondents' and 'special artists' were a standard presence with any British army on active service and were considered the glamorous elite among journalists. Some, like Archibald Forbes of the *Illustrated London News*, became celebrities in their own right and lions of the lecture circuit. They identified with the British Army and its ethos, and enjoyed a quasi-officer status on campaign. To an insatiable public they brought the most detailed and graphic eyewitness accounts of Britain's far-flung colonial wars, reinforced the romance of distant clashes of arms, paid condescending tribute to the valour of warrior foes, contributed to a more favourable image of the gallant British Army and inflamed popular imperialism.

Since war news undoubtedly sold newspapers, there was always a hectic and costly race between correspondents to scoop their rivals. To relay news from the Zululand front it was necessary for a spe-

cial correspondent to ride across country to the nearest telegraph station in Natal, whence his lengthy report was telegraphed to Cape Town to await the weekly steamer to Britain. The steamer then took at least 16 days to reach the island of Madeira where the transatlantic telegraph cable from Brazil to Europe touched land. Drawings by special artists – which could not be telegraphed – had to be carried to Durban to await the first ship sailing for Britain, and it was at least a month before they could be printed.

The professional (and expensive) correspondents retained by the major daily and weekly illustrated newspapers were not alone in the field, however. During the Anglo-Zulu War, many of the correspondents – especially for the small colonial newspapers – were British officers, colonial volunteers with the army, colonial officials and ordinary settlers living in districts affected by the war. Their reports came much cheaper than those of the flamboyant metropolitan correspondents, but were often no less vivid and informed.

Ambitious commanders like Sir Garnet Wolseley knew how to cultivate war correspondents to boost their own reputations; for their part, correspondents were happy to give their readers the heroes they craved. Nevertheless, comment on the conduct of campaigns was always trenchant and sometimes highly critical. Anxious as they might be to preserve the honour of the army with which they iden-

> 'It is more than probable with such a large number of newspaper correspondents in camp, that many false impressions may be circulated and sent home regarding our present operations either intentionally or ignorantly.'
>
> (Lord Chelmsford, 10 June 1879)

F.R. MacKenzie of the London Standard *(armed appropriately with carbine and notebook) was one of the flock of special correspondents who accompanied the reinforcements sailing for Natal in late February 1879 at the urgent request of Lord Chelmsford, who was badly shaken by the Isandlwana disaster.*

Charles Fripp, special artist in Zululand for the Graphic, *drew in small sketchbooks with an HB pencil, working up outlines into larger more finished drawings in pencil and wash. He depicted himself sketching a group of Zulu* amabutho *cut down by heavy British volley fire during the battle of Ulundi. After being engraved, his drawing was published by the* Graphic *on 11 October 1879.*

tified, correspondents also felt that it was in the public interest to reveal deficient planning and leadership. The Isandlwana debacle made the Anglo-Zulu War international news and war correspondents flocked to the front. There they asked awkward questions and subjected Lord Chelmsford to stinging criticism. The offended General responded by refusing his co-operation, and the debate over the proper conduct of the war was transferred – to the considerable embarrassment of the military establishment – to the pages of the popular press.

The public required graphic images as well as reportage of wars. Photographic technology in 1879 did not permit action shots, and photographs taken of the Zululand campaign were confined to static and laboriously posed photographs of military groups, forts, camps, parades and the like. Besides, it was not yet possible to reproduce photographs in newspapers. So special artists made action sketches on the spot, often under fire.

Some, like Melton Prior of the *Illustrated London News*, were renowned professionals, but others (like Lt-Col J.N. Crealock, Chelmsford's Military Secretary) were suitably skilled serving officers. Like the special correspondents, they tended to sanitise their work, emphasising the elements of adventure, heroism, glory and humour, but not dwelling on the horrors of the battlefield. Once their drawings (scribbled over with helpful descriptions) reached the London newspapers, they were redrawn and embellished by teams of staff artists. Then they were traced in reverse onto wooden blocks, engraved, a facsimile made in copper and finally printed. Besides coarsening the quality of the original sketches, this process inevitably transformed them to conform to the conventions of war illustration, and often undid the special artist's accurate observations by imparting a subtle European cast to African physiognomies and landscapes.

Lt-Col Crealock's rough eye-witness sketch with scribbled explanations depicts Lt-Col John Russell, commander of No. 1 Squadron, Mounted Infantry, riding up to the post at Rorke's Drift on 23 January 1879, the morning after the battle.

The finished engraving which appeared in the Illustrated London News *of 8 March 1879 once the paper's team of staff artists had redrawn Crealock's sketch.*

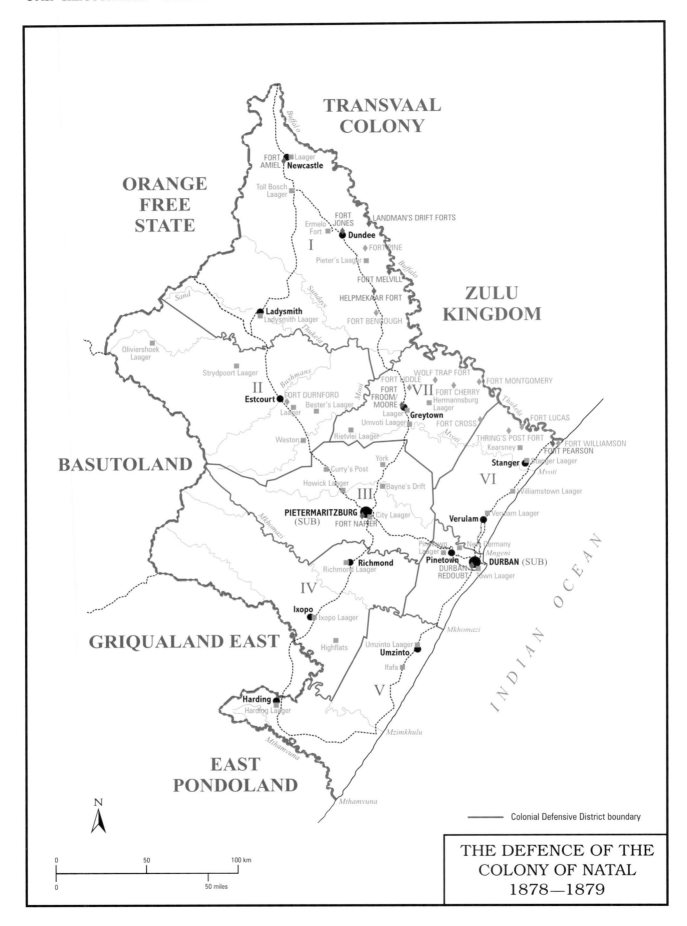

TRANSVAAL
COLONY

ORANGE
FREE
STATE

Buffalo

FORT
AMIEL ● ■ Laager
Newcastle

Toll Bosch ■
Laager

FORT LANDMAN'S DRIFT FORTS
JONES
Ermelo ■
Fort I ● **Dundee**

ZULU
KINGDOM

◆ FORT PINE

Pieter's Laager ■

Buffalo

FORT MELVILL

HELPMEKAAR FORT

Sand

Thukela

Siqadus

● **Ladysmith**
Ladysmith Laager ■

FORT BENGOUGH

Oliviershoek ■
Laager

Bushmans

Strydpoort Laager ■

WOLF TRAP FORT ■

II FORT DIDDLE ◆ FORT MONTGOMERY
FORT DURNFORD FORT VII FORT CHERRY
Estcourt ● FROOM/ Hermannsburg
■ MOORE Laager ■
Bester's Laager ■ Laager ● FORT LUCAS
Laager ■ ● **Greytown**
Umvoti Laager ■ FORT CROSS

Mooi

Weston ■ Rietvlei Laager ■ THRING'S POST FORT ■

BASUTOLAND

Mvoti

Curry's Post ■ York Kearsney ■ FORT WILLIAMSON
FORT PEARSON

Howick Laager ■ III Bayne's Drift ■ Stanger Laager ■
Stanger ●

Mvoti

PIETERMARITZBURG
(SUB) ● VI
City Laager ■
FORT NAPIER Verulam Laager ■

Mkhomazi

Verulam ●

New Germany ■
Pinetown ■ *Mngeni*
Laager
Richmond ● **Pinetown** ● ● **DURBAN** (SUB)
Richmond Laager ■ DURBAN ■ Town Laager ■
REDOUBT

IV

Mkhomazi

Ixopo ●
Ixopo Laager ■

INDIAN OCEAN

GRIQUALAND EAST

Highflats ■ Umzinto Laager ■ V
Umzinto ●

Ifafa ■

Harding ●
Harding Laager ■

Mthamvuna

EAST
PONDOLAND

N

Mthamvuna

———— Colonial Defensive District boundary

0 ⊢——⊢——⊢ 50 ⊢——⊢——⊢ 100 km
0 ⊢——⊢——⊢——⊢——⊢ 50 miles

**THE DEFENCE OF THE
COLONY OF NATAL
1878—1879**

Colonial Defence

Once the British forces invaded Zululand, the frontiers of Natal and the Transvaal would be left vulnerable to Zulu counter-attack. It was therefore necessary to make arrangements for the protection of the colonial population, though these were never adequate to stave off a serious incursion.

Before the war

The search for security against Africans living within the Colony and in the territories surrounding it was a perennial preoccupation for the white settlers of Natal. Internally, the Langalibalele affair of 1873 had seemed to give substance to their anxieties over the possibility of a rising by the Africans of Natal's Native Reserves. Externally, they perceived the independent Zulu kingdom to the north

as the greatest threat to their safety, a belief that events such as the Zulu succession crisis of 1856 and the 'Invasion Scare' of 1861 had done nothing to allay. The situation on Natal's western and southern flanks also gave them cause for apprehension. Basutoland, annexed by the Cape in 1871, remained volatile, while the growing hold of the Cape over the Transkei region could not erase recollection of the very recent Ninth Frontier War and Griqua rebellion. Nevertheless, despite the looming prospect in 1878 of imminent war with Zululand, and the prevailing suspicion among many settlers that recent events (in particular the war against Sekhukhune in the Transvaal) all pointed to the existence of a general black conspiracy to rise up against the white man, the Natal government had taken few special steps to safeguard the colony.

By September 1878 Lord Chelmsford was noting with alarm that the Natal authorities' contingency plans in the event of a Zulu raid consisted of nothing more than advice to the white colonists to take refuge in various government and private laagers already built or under construction. The greatly preponderant and potentially hostile African population was to be left to shift for itself as best it could. On 10 September Chelmsford attended a

'The possibility of resisting a sudden raid into Natal by the present machinery for defence appears to me to be almost hopeless; and I am afraid that this fact must be well known to the Zulus.'

(Lt-Gen Thesiger [Lord Chelmsford], 28 September 1878)

A settler stock farm in the open highlands of Umvoti County in Natal, which bordered on the Zulu country, photographed in the 1890s. Very little of the land was brought under the plough, and the scattered settler families lived a self-contained life looking after their flocks and herds on their large farms.

'The Utrecht town meeting was a failure for want of unanimity on the part of the members: only 16 out of 60 could be got to sign their names to an agreement to stay and defend the Laager, should the Zulus make a raid.'

(*Natal Mercury*, 16 January 1879)

meeting of the Natal Executive Council's Defence Committee and persuaded its members to face up to the dangers of the situation. The chastened Council took note of his suggestions and set about devising appropriate security measures.

For the organisation of its defence Natal was divided on 26 November 1878 into seven Colonial Defensive Districts, with Pietermaritzburg and Durban forming two Sub-Districts. On 3 December the district commanders were named and issued with their instructions. Each was to have command of the colonial forces in his district, as well as all the public laagers and government arms and ammunition. He was to be responsible for the defence of his district until such time as it was placed under direct military command. Yet it remained unclear with what means a district commander was to defend those parts of his district falling outside the walls of the laagers, which would be manned by all the available members of the local Rifle Associations and other similar groups of civilian volunteers. Once the imperial troops were committed to the invasion of Zululand, only small garrisons would remain in Pietermaritzburg and Durban, and along the British lines of communication and supply at Stanger, Greytown, Help-mekaar, Ladysmith and Newcastle. The three corps of Natal Volunteer Infantry,

numbering 272 men, with the 51 men of the Durban Volunteer Artillery, would be available only for the defence of the larger towns. The 11 corps of Natal Mounted Volunteers mustered 430 officers and men but, on 26 November, 10 of the corps, the majority of whose men had volunteered in October for active service in Zululand, were called out. Only the Ixopo Mounted Rifles in District No. IV remained to protect the southern border, along with 32 Natal Mounted Police stationed at Harding. A further 11 Natal Mounted Police were at Estcourt, where a detachment was permanently stationed, but the remaining 130 had been called out for service in Zululand. An uncertain number of Mounted Burghers were liable to turn out for commando duty if called on by their local field cornet, but the limited size of these groupings meant that any patrols they might mount would only be of use in giving warning of Zulu movements, and not in repelling raiding parties. Similarly, the African-manned Special Border Police, placed under especially appointed white border agents along the Thukela and Mzinyathi (Buffalo) rivers, whose strength, augmented for the war, never amounted to more than 190 men, had the primary function of gathering intelligence and monitoring the movements of individuals to and fro from Zululand, rather than actually deterring a

On 26 November 1878 the Natal government called the Natal Mounted Volunteers into active service. The photograph shows the 66-strong Durban Mounted Rifles, in their dark blue uniforms with black facings and scarlet piping, parading in Durban before leaving on 30 November to join No. 1 Column at the lower Thukela.

Zulu incursion. Such considerations made it increasingly obvious to the military that if a passive defence centred on the towns and laagers were to remain the hallmark of the Colony's defensive system, and that if the Zulus were to be dissuaded from raiding the countryside in-between, then a large field-force of levies would have to be raised from Africans living in the border districts.

Despite settler disquiet over the advisability of arming the Natal Africans, during late 1878 Chelmsford recruited seven battalions for the Natal Native Contingent, as well as Pioneer, Hospital and Transport Corps. As imperial forces, they were intended for service in Zululand, and not for defence of the Colony's borders. In December 1878, after prolonged negotiations with the colonial authorities, Chelmsford conceded that additional African levies raised specifically for the defence of Natal should be maintained and commanded by the colonial government. Yet the government could not afford a large standing force, while the economy of the border areas could not afford the absence of yet more of its labour force. Therefore, the government devised a system whereby all the Africans living in the border Defensive Districts (Nos. I, VI, and VII) would constitute the force guarding the border, but not a standing force. According to

the instructions of 20 December 1878, each chief was to furnish a quota of fighting-men, which would assemble at designated rendezvous to take the field under white levy-leaders the moment a Zulu raid threatened. Otherwise, they would remain at home, engaged in their normal occupations and not requiring government upkeep.

Besides these part-time levies, the government provided for small standing reserves of Border Guards stationed at certain strategic points, from which they could promptly move to any threatened stretch of the frontier. By the first week of January 1879 the system was in operation the length of the Zululand border.

During the war
With his columns poised to invade, Chelmsford requested that the whole crucial border region be placed under military control, and on 11 January, the day the British crossed into Zululand, the commanders of Districts I, VI, and VII were subordinated to the British officers commanding imperial bases and lines of supply in their districts.

Defeat at Isandlwana dislocated Chelmsford's strategy, and forced him on to the defensive. To many colonists Natal now seemed thrown open to Zulu invasion. In the general panic they flocked to the government and private

The settlers of Greytown and surrounding districts took shelter in the Greytown Laager on receiving news of Isandlwana. Until their fears of a Zulu incursion subsided with the relief of Eshowe in April, many (especially women and children) stayed cooped up within its walls in increasingly unsanitary conditions. The engraving from the Graphic *of 26 April 1879 is misleading in that it portrays only the male defenders.*

'Nothing is so demoralizing to both Europeans and natives as remaining on the passive defensive – It at once admits an inferiority on our part, and a superiority on the side of the Enemy – I consider, therefore, that the Natal Colonial forces, altho' told off for defence alone, should be made to understand that it may be necessary for them to cross into Zululand if only for a few hours.'

(Lord Chelmsford, 20 February 1879)

laagers, and some even trekked out of Natal to the safety of the Orange Free State. At Pietermaritzburg and Durban there was a hasty improvisation of civil defence, while elsewhere in Natal – even in the southern districts – there were hurried preparations against a possible onslaught. Not until April with the arrival of large British reinforcements did settler alarm finally subside. By then most of the laagers had emptied of their civilian refugees, and the various civilian *ad hoc* corps were being stood down.

The tendency for white settlers to rush to laagers, so leaving the countryside open to Zulu raiders, persuaded both Chelmsford and the Natal government that an effort must be made to raise and organise more black levies. For if the colonists were unable to hold the frontier line, then the burden of Natal's defence would have to fall on the African population. After Isandlwana the 3rd Regiment of the NNC had been disbanded and the 2nd had temporarily dissolved. The 1st Regiment (re-styled the 1st, 2nd and 3rd Battalions, NNC) was stationed at Kranskop and Sandspruit on the middle border. Over the next few months they and the existing Border Guard were accordingly augmented by additional levies which the colonial authorities brought up, chiefly from the defensive districts to the south. By late June the Border Guard in District No. VI had reached a peak of 2 323 men (under 33 white officers), drawn chiefly from District No. V. In District No. VII there were by mid-April 596 Border Guard Reserves under eight levy-leaders, and an estimated potential of 1 500 part-time levies (River Guards) under another eight levy-leaders watching the strategic drifts across the middle Thukela. In addition, the Ixopo Native Contingent, which was raised in March in District No. IV and consisted in May of some 800 foot and 500 horse, was stationed in the same district. During April the Border Guard in District No. I was brought up to a strength of 2 969 men under 11 levy-leaders with the arrival from District No. II of 600 reinforcements, consisting of the Weenen Contingent (the former 3rd Regiment, NNC, now mustered as

'traditional' levies) and African levies from Newcastle and Ladysmith where they were no longer required as part of the laager garrisons.

Strengthening the forces along the border also served Chelmsford's plans for the relief of the beleaguered Eshowe garrison. He intended that while the Relief Column advanced through Zululand the troops on the frontier should create a diversion in its favour by demonstrating along the Thukela and Mzinyathi border line and, if possible, by raiding the Zulu side. Chelmsford argued, too, that if the border forces were to play an effective role in the war they must be prepared to take the offensive against the Zulus, and not merely wait to be attacked: an 'active defence' would eventually force the Zulus to abandon the border zone altogether, disrupting their own plans and thus securing Natal from the threat of invasion. The Natal government, on the other hand, envisaged its forces acting exclusively in defence of the Colony, and resolutely opposed an 'active defence'. It was sympathetic to the growing sentiment among many colonists that white Volunteers in particular, but black levies as well, should not be risked over the border when there were increasing numbers of imperial troops for that purpose. The government questioned also the wisdom of mounting raids into Zululand, which might provoke retaliation, throw the border region into confusion and poison relations between Africans on both sides of the border for a long time to come.

Questions over the employment of colonial troops at the border came down to determining who actually commanded them, Chelmsford or Bulwer. The Lt-Governor clung tenaciously to his claim to do so through his district commanders, even though the three on the border had been under imperial military command since January. Chelmsford could not tolerate a divided command along the vulnerable northern border and tried to circumvent Bulwer to implement his strategy. Thus, without Bulwer's prior concurrence, Chelmsford ordered the imperial commanders along the border to

The Border Guard stationed at White Rock Drift, lower Thukela, in Defensive District No. VI. On 9 May 1879 they saw action when a small body under W.E. Boast (who is probably the white levy leader in the photograph) crossed the river into Zululand and captured 21 head of cattle.

employ all the troops stationed there under them, whether imperial or colonial, in creating a diversion in favour of the Eshowe Relief Column. Accordingly, for a fortnight over late March and early April they demonstrated and raided where they could across the Mzinyathi and Thukela. Bulwer and Chelmsford became involved in violent recriminations over the matter until, in the end, on 19 May, the imperial government decreed that full command of all troops lay with Chelmsford.

In late May Chelmsford ordered the border forces to raid Zululand once more, this time as a diversion for his second invasion. Nearly a month later the Zulus retaliated, as the Natal authorities had always feared they would: they took advantage of the dispersal of the Border Guard in District No. VII for the collection of the hut-tax to ravage with virtual impunity the Thukela valley at Middle

Drift. The raid set off another 'invasion' panic in the district, demoralised the Border Guard, and forced the imperial troops strictly on to the defensive. However, the Zulu army's final defeat at Ulundi and the king's flight discouraged the Zulus along the border from attempting another raid, and they began to submit to the British. In Natal it was realised that the war was definitely over. In July the Natal Mounted Volunteers mustered out, followed in August and September by the African levies and contingents.

On 10 September General Wolseley gave permission for the imperial border posts to be abandoned once the troops in Zululand had passed through for embarkation at Durban. This operation was completed by the end of October, by which date all the colonial troops raised in Natal, including the Border Police, had been disbanded or demobilised.

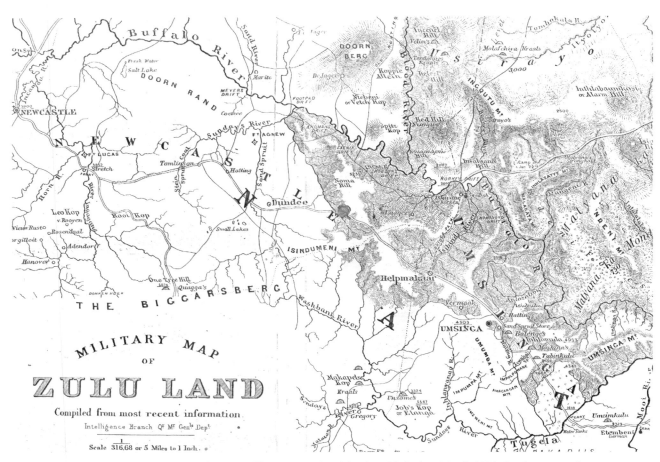

The left-hand corner of Brig-Gen Wood's own Military Map of Zululand, *published in March 1879. Inadequate and inaccurate as it was, it was better than the maps the British had earlier been forced to rely upon when planning their invasion of Zululand.*

Officers of the 2nd Division sketched by Melton Prior for the Illustrated London News *of 26 July 1879 consulting the map of Zululand preparatory to the next day's advance.*

Opposing Strategies

T wo very different military systems opposed each other in Zululand in 1879. Consequently, British and Zulu strategies necessarily differed, especially since the combatants' expectations of the objectives to be gained by going to war were so at variance.

British strategy

For the Zululand campaign, Lt-Gen Lord Chelmsford put together in January 1879 an invading force of 17 929 men. Of these, 5 476 were British regulars drawn from regiments stationed in Natal, the Cape and the Transvaal; 1 508 were irregular colonial horse; and 9 035 were African auxiliaries, raised in Natal. The remaining 1 910 men were colonial conductors, drivers and *voorloopers* necessary to manage the transport and supplies. The strategy Chelmsford and his staff devised for the coming campaign was strongly influenced by their sense of overconfidence fed by their recent successful campaign of 1878 in the eastern Cape against the Ngqika and Gcaleka Xhosa. With misplaced arrogance they underrated the fighting ability of the Zulu and made their plans accordingly.

To achieve the political objective of the war, which was to clear the way for confederation in southern Africa, it was necessary to assert British ascendancy by conclusively defeating the armies of the militarily powerful Zulu state and thereby overthrowing the *ibutho* system that was its mainstay. Naturally, it was preferable to effect this on Zulu, rather than British, soil. Yet an offensive into Zululand would leave British territory vulnerable to Zulu counter-thrusts, especially in the broken terrain of the Natal frontier region where a Zulu raid would be less easily detected and countered than in the open country of the Transvaal. White settlers were in dread of a Zulu raid, not least because they feared it might be the signal for the subjected colonial Africans to rise up in support. The colonial authorities had only enough armed men to hold the fortified posts in certain towns and at various points in the countryside, so to dissuade the Zulu from raiding the farmlands in between, they raised a field-force of over 8 000 African part-time levies and border guards in the border districts. Nevertheless, border defences remained pitifully weak. Rather than rely on the untrained levies to form a barrier against Zulu raids, Chelmsford put his faith in the frontier rivers, which would be unfordable during the rainy season between January and March, except at certain drifts which could be effectively guarded.

Indeed, the seasons determined the timing of the British campaign. Since supplies could not be obtained from the theatre of war, they had to be carried by ox-wagon and mule-cart. Draft-animals subsisted on natural grazing which would be at its most plentiful after the late spring rains – precisely in the same months when the rivers would be in spate. How-

Lt-Gen Lord Chelmsford and his staff, photographed in Pietermaritzburg in late December 1878 while planning the Zululand campaign.
Standing, left to right: Maj M.W.E. Gossett, 54th Regt; Lt A. Berkeley Milne, RN.
Sitting, left to right: Cmdr H.J.F. Campbell, RN; Chelmsford; Lt-Col J.N. Crealock, 95th Regt.

ever, during the dry winter months the rivers would become dangerously fordable, and the grazing would begin to give out and become dry enough to be burnt by the Zulu. January was therefore considered the optimum time for launching an invasion, particularly since it was expected to achieve its objectives within seven weeks and before the unfavourable dry season set in.

Chelmsford initially assembled 10 023 oxen, 398 mules, 977 wagons and 56 carts to transport his supplies, but these had to have all-round protection on the march, turning the army into an escort for its food and requiring the establishment of garrisoned depots along its line of advance. Movement of such convoys was always painfully slow, made worse in January 1879 by the rain-sodden ground and flooded drifts across the rivers. For the British, the war in Zululand consequently became as much a campaign against distance and natural obstacles as it was against the hostile Zulu.

In planning his strategy, therefore, Chelmsford was faced with real constraints. When he advanced into Zululand

he would leave his own frontiers inadequately protected, while his dependence on slow-moving and vulnerable supply-trains would limit both his flexibility and the size of the columns they were to support. His solution was to send in five relatively small columns (later reduced effectively to three) to converge on an appropriate point: oNdini, Cetshwayo's capital. He hoped thereby to move with greater speed and to have more forage at his disposal for each column. The joint advance of a number of supporting columns was also intended to engross more of the enemy's territory, to reduce the chance of being outflanked, and to discourage Zulu counter-thrusts against the Zulu frontiers.

With the possibility of Zulu raids in mind, Chelmsford selected invasion routes in sectors considered vulnerable to Zulu attack. No. 1 Column's advance across the lower Thukela would protect the coastal plain. No. 3 Column, marching into Zululand from Rorke's Drift, would cover central Natal. To strengthen this column, which he decided to accompany, and to improve the defence of the

The interior of Fort Melvill, drawn for the Illustrated London News *of 13 September 1879. The fort was sited to command the drift across the Mzinyathi (Buffalo) River, and a considerable quantity of stores were accumulated there. Note the way in which biscuit boxes have been used to construct the walls of an improvised shelter for off-duty soldiers of the garrison.*

Natal middle border, Chelmsford broke up No. 2 Column which he had originally intended should invade Zululand at Middle Drift. The smaller part reinforced No. 3 Column, and the balance remained on garrison duty above Middle Drift. Chelmsford also kept No. 5 Column in a defensive role, hovering north of the Phongolo to retain a presence against the still undefeated Pedi in the north-eastern Transvaal, and to cover No. 4 Column's northern flank against both the Zulu and the equivocal Swazi. No. 4 Column would advance from the Transvaal through the volatile Disputed Territory where Zulu, Swazi, Boers and German settlers had long contended for supremacy.

By invading at several points, Chelmsford hoped to force Cetshwayo to keep his *amabutho* fully mobilised to face these diverse threats. He knew that the late spring rains of 1878 and the consequently delayed harvest meant that the Zulu armies would be poorly supplied when the campaign opened, and consequently he hoped that their supply problems would be at least as bad as his own and would adversely affect their capacity to stay in the field.

Unreliable maps, inadequate reconnaissance (there were not enough mounted men with the columns for effective patrolling) and the poor processing of intelligence reports meant, however, that Chelmsford had no accurate conception of the terrain over which his columns were to advance, nor any clear idea of the enemy's dispositions and intentions. These deficiencies were to handicap the speed of his advance throughout the campaign (already compromised through logistical problems), and to render the required co-ordination of converging columns impracticable.

Very soon after the invasion began, therefore, Chelmsford abandoned his hopes for a rapid, co-ordinated advance. He decided instead that the columns should halt inside Zululand and send out mobile flying columns to drive the Zulu away from the exposed borders, and to devastate large parts of Zululand. Officially, the British quarrel was only with the Zulu king. After the shock of Isandlwana, however, the British jetti-

Charles Fripp's dramatic depiction for the Graphic *of 7 June 1879 of a patrol of mounted men from the Eshowe Relief Column burning Prince Dabulamanzi kaMpande's eZuluwini umuzi on 4 April 1879. Regular raids by mounted troops asserted British military ascendancy in the area of operations, denied the Zulu shelter and supplies and, in the form of raided livestock, deprived them of their wealth. Inevitably, civilians were the greatest victims of this policy, waged most ruthlessly by Lt-Col Buller's mounted men.*

'Half measures do not answer with natives – They must be thoroughly crushed to make them believe in our superiority . . . I shall strive to be in a position to show them how hopelessly inferior they are to us in fighting power, altho' numerically stronger.'
(Lt-Gen Thesiger [Lord Chelmsford], 21 July 1878)

'The king maintained that from the first he was aware that the English would in the end defeat him, but he said: "I was not a child to let anyone come and take my country, which, as you have seen, is so large and beautiful, without my fighting for it."'
(*Natal Mercury*, 18 September 1879)

soned whatever scruples they might originally have entertained, and Chelmsford sanctioned the complete destruction of the enemy's means of subsistence along the British line of advance. This included the systematic burning of *amakhanda*. As nodes of the king's authority, rallying-points for the *amabutho* and depots for their supplies, their destruction (he believed) would reduce Cetshwayo's capacity to resist and fatally damage his ability to exercise authority. Unfortunately for the Zulu population, the elimination of these 'legitimate' military targets was extended to include civilian *imizi*, and involved the pillaging of grain stores and the capture of livestock. Chelmsford well understood that one of the most effective ways of defeating the Zulu would be 'through the stomach', and a dire threat to their means of livelihood was thereby justified.

One possible means of winning the war, Chelmsford calculated, was to push the increasingly hungry and shelterless Zulu up to the north-eastern corner of Zululand, and provoke Cetshwayo's desperate subjects into deposing him and surrendering. He took serious note of reports of existing dissensions within the kingdom, and hoped to exploit these by encouraging disaffected chiefs through generous terms to defect from the king's cause. He instructed his commanders and Natal border officials to pursue negotiations with Zulu notables, and laid down guidelines for the accommodation of those who surrendered in Natal.

Any possible unravelling of the Zulu kingdom depended, however, on successful military operations in the first instance. One development that Chelmsford wished to avoid at all costs was the degeneration of the Zululand campaign into the protracted, irregular warfare that had favoured the mobile Xhosa fighting on their home ground in the Ninth Frontier War. He knew that the best way to end a typical colonial 'small war' decisively and swiftly was with a pitched battle where all the advantages lay with appropriately trained troops armed with modern weapons. This is why he preferred such a conclusion over the alter-

native strategy of methodically driving the Zulu into a corner and inducing their capitulation. Happily for the British strategists, there was every likelihood that the Zulu, with their strong military traditions, would indeed be prepared to hazard the fate of their kingdom on the desperate throw of a pitched battle.

Chelmsford's operational gambit of dividing his army into several columns must consequently also be seen as a means of enticing the Zulu into attacking one or more of them. Only when they were committed to battle, the British reckoned, would the Zulu discover to their cost that the numerical inferiority of the apparently weak columns was more than compensated for by their superior fire-power from behind prepared positions.

Zulu strategy

In contrast to the invading British, whose poor intelligence-gathering left them in considerable doubt as to Zulu military preparations and strategic intentions, the Zulu were well-informed concerning those of the invaders. In time of war the Zulu always activated spies on a large scale to gain intelligence of the enemy. In January 1879 Zulu spies were out collecting information in Natal, the Transvaal and Delagoa Bay. The advancing British were always aware that they were under observation, for besides the spies who did their best to infiltrate British positions posing as deserters or seeking employment as camp servants, the King's subjects were also expected to keep look-outs and to report the enemy's movements.

It was obviously an advantage to be apprised of the enemy's plans, but Cetshwayo's own strategic options were limited nevertheless. The British might fear that he was attempting to co-ordinate African resistance to their domination over the subcontinent, but this was never feasible. As had so often been the case during the years of colonial expansion in southern Africa, African sectional advantage was placed before wider interests. Thus, as war loomed, Cetshwayo turned in vain to his African neighbours for assistance.

The Swazi kingdom to the north had for too long been a victim of Zulu expansionism to desire anything but the extinction of Zulu military might. Nor was there any possibility of co-operation with the Mabhudu-Tsonga to the north-east, who, since the 1860s, had been in conflict with the Zulu over the lucrative trade to Delagoa Bay. Cetshwayo's emissaries had no success either in raising the Sotho or Mpondo to the south-west and south against the British. Joint operations with the Pedi in the Transvaal seemed the likeliest possibility, but the Pedi had found it hard enough to hold their own against the British in the campaign of April – October 1878, and had no desire to become involved as well in the Zulus' dispute with the imperial power. So when it came to war in January 1879, Zululand had to face the British alone and Cetshwayo had to plan accordingly.

Cetshwayo adopted the defensive as the essence of his strategy. Astutely, he made this strategy conform to his political programme of presenting himself as the victim of an unwarranted attack, forced to fight only in self-defence within the borders of his own kingdom. Accordingly, he insisted that his armies were not to follow up any victory with an invasion of Natal or the Transvaal. He grasped well enough that the British had limitless resources overseas, and that the longer the war lasted the less chance the Zulu had of winning it. Any violation of British territory would only provoke his enemies into persevering until Zululand had been crushed in stark confirmation of British paramountcy in southern Africa.

However, if his victorious armies simply menaced the borders of the British colonies, it was possible that the British might be pressured to enter into urgent negotiations, and a peace favourable to the Zulu concluded before British reinforcements could arrive. To have any chance of success, therefore, the Zulu campaign had to be swift and hard-hitting, but limited.

It must be said that this strategy played into the hands of the British, who also wished to avoid a drawn-out campaign, and sought a swift solution through decisive military encounters. But, as his been explained in the section dealing with the *ibutho* system, for psychological and material reasons the Zulu were not prepared to consider the alternative of a protracted, guerrilla-style defensive strategy. Fundamentally, such

'The final repulse of the Zulus at Ginghilovo', an engraving appearing in the Illustrated London News *of 24 May 1879, based on a sketch supplied by Lt-Col Crealock. The depiction of both British and Zulu accoutrements and weapons is very accurate, and shows the vulnerability of the Zulu to a mounted sortie once their attack on a prepared position had failed.*

hit-and-run fighting (as practised by the Xhosa and Pedi, for example) was foreign to their confirmed methods and traditions of waging war. In any case, had the Zulu avoided pitched battles and withdrawn to their traditional strongholds on mountain-tops and in forests, there is no guarantee that this would have prolonged the campaign beyond British endurance. Conversely, how were the *amabutho* occupying the fastnesses over long periods to have been provisioned? They would have been unable to play their usual part in the agricultural economy, and the women and boys on whom the planting and harvesting of crops and the tending of livestock would have devolved entirely, would have been left unprotected against the systematic ravaging of Zululand by the British. For, as we have seen, there is no doubt that the British would have adopted dire methods against civilians to force the Zulu armies into the open. The consequences of the guerrilla-war option would most likely have been starvation and ruin for the entire community.

In planning for the conventional campaign he intended to wage, Cetshwayo was limited by the number of fighting-men available. The nominal strength of the Zulu army was about 40 000, but some of the senior *amabutho* were too old for active service, and not every member of an *ibutho* could be relied upon to respond to the king's summons. Thus, when the *amabutho* mustered in January 1879, they numbered no more than about 29 000. Their effective deployment would depend on how the British placed their own forces. Cetshwayo knew that the British would invade his kingdom from the south and west at widely separated points. He feared they might also attempt sea-borne landings at St Lucia Bay and Delagoa Bay and, conceivably aided by the Mabhudu-Tsonga, advance from the north-east. The hostile Swazi would doubtless be tempted to take the opportunity to attack over the Phongolo River from the north. Zululand, in other words, faced attack from every quarter.

Since, as we have seen, the King gave priority to defeating the British in the field and threatening her colonies' borders to force a peace, this meant concentrating Zulu efforts against the main British thrust. Because Chelmsford was accompanying No. 3 Column concentrating at Rorke's Drift on the Natal border, and since it was also reported to be the strongest column, Cetshwayo directed his crack *amabutho* mustered at oNdini against it for the decisive battle. A much smaller force was simultaneously sent towards the coast to co-operate with local elements of the *amabutho* in impeding the advance of No. 1 Column. Cetshwayo also sent some reinforcements from oNdini to support the regional abaQulusi *ibutho* and local irregulars who were to face Nos. 4 and 5 Columns operating out of the Transvaal. Local irregulars also collected in the Nkandla forest area to repel any advance across the middle Thukela by No. 2 Column.

By committing the bulk of his forces to the southern and western borders, the King had apparently left the interior of Zululand vulnerable to attack from the north and north-east, and to a possible dash by a mounted British force into the heart of the country. But the British certainly did not have the cavalry available for such a thrust; nor were they any longer contemplating a landing along the coast since their naval reconnaissances had failed to identify a suitable landing-place. Besides which, the people of the Tsonga chiefdoms to the south of the Mabhudu-Tsonga, who were in a strong cultural and tributary relationship with the neighbouring Zulu kingdom, were proving loyal to their overlords. Though not part of the *ibutho* system, they were rallying to the Zulu cause as irregulars. As for the antagonistic Swazi, they were not prepared to risk entering the war as British allies (despite British inducements to intervene to protect their left flank and cut off any possible Zulu retreat northwards) until absolutely certain they would be on the winning side. Cetshwayo was not being unduly rash, therefore, to discount the possibility of immediate attack from any of these quarters. The thousand or so reserves he retained at oNdini were accordingly more a symbolic guard than

'Cetshwayo actually said you are not to go into the hole of a wild beast or else you will get clawed, wait until the soldiers come out of their laager and then fall on them'.
(Mamboola, 29 May 1936)

a serious military deterrent, and consisted mainly of the elderly iNdabakawombe and uDlambedlu *amabutho*, both veterans of the Ncome (Blood) River campaign of 1838.

Cetshwayo sent off his armies in the firm conviction that they could win if the British were forced to give battle in the open. He and his military advisers had learned enough from the disastrous campaign of 1838 to order the Zulu armies in 1879 to avoid storming prepared positions such as laagers, forts or entrenchments. The king therefore instructed his generals to bypass British positions. By threatening both their lines of supply and the territory to their rear, this strategy was intended to force the British to come out of their defensive works to fight. Alternatively, Zulu commanders were advised to surround the entrenched British at a distance and to starve them into submission or a disadvantageous sortie.

Though sound in theory, such a strategy did not recognise sufficiently the difficulties (described in the section on the *ibutho* system) of supplying a Zulu army in the field, nor the lack of patience and restraint likely to be exhibited by headstrong younger *amabutho* vying for glory. Besides, it was the usual Zulu practice to disperse after action for ritual purification and recuperation. These factors made compliance with the king's sensible instructions problematical, and reduced the chance of Zulu success in the field to the unlikely event of catching the British in the open outside their prepared defences. That this is precisely what did occur on a number of occasions was the consequence of Zulu strategic skill combined with British overconfidence and miliary ineptness.

The British caught outside their prepared defences and forced to engage the Zulu in hand-to-hand combat.

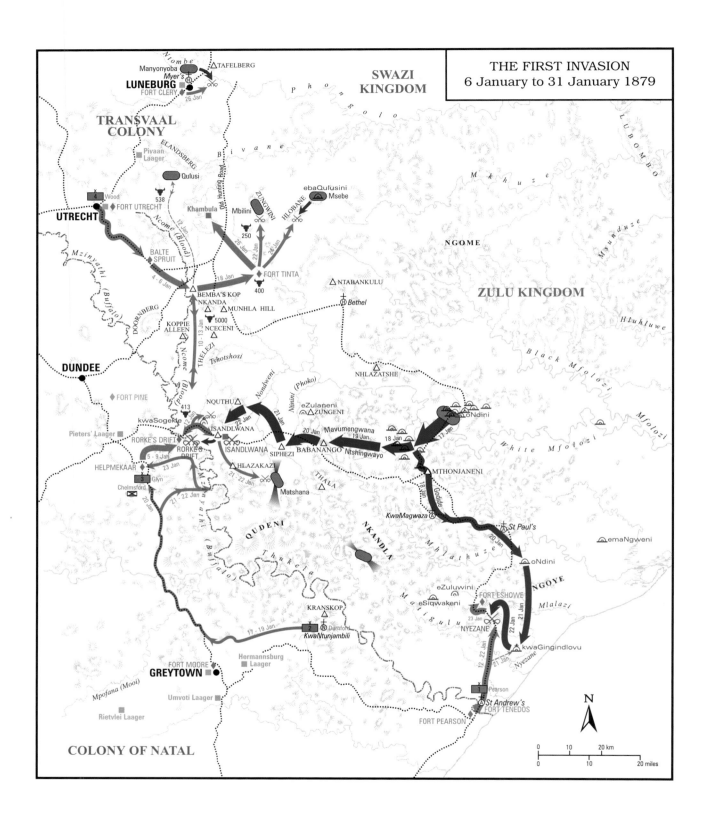

THE FIRST INVASION
6 January to 31 January 1879

Field Operations

The British invasion of Zululand began with the expiry of their ultimatum on 11 January 1879.

The first invasion
6 January – 31 January 1879

The Centre (No. 3) Column of 4 709 men under Col Glyn, accompanied by Lord Chelmsford, had been concentrated at Rorke's Drift on the Mzinyathi (Buffalo) River by 9 January, leaving garrisons along its line of supply through Helpmekaar, Greytown, Ladysmith and Durban. It began its advance across the Mzinyathi on 11 January and the next day won a sharp skirmish in the valley of the Batshe River at kwaSogekle, the stronghold of Sihayo kaXongo, the Qungebe chief. The need to improve the tracks made impassable by the heavy rains delayed the advance on oNdini, and it was only on 20 January that the column halted at Isandlwana Mountain. The camp was not entrenched as it was only intended to be temporary, and patrols continued to be sent out to ascertain the movements of the Zulu and to find a suitable site for the next camp.

No. 2 Column of 3 871 African troops under Col Durnford, positioned above Middle Drift on the Thukela River, was divided by Chelmsford on 15 January. Most of the infantry remained at Kranskop to guard the middle border against local Zulu irregulars concentrated in the Nkandla forest, while Durnford was ordered up to Rorke's Drift to reinforce the Centre Column with the mounted men, rocket battery and balance of the infantry.

The Right (No. 1) Column of 4 750 men under Col Pearson, drawing its supplies through Stanger and Durban, began to cross the Thukela River at the Lower Drift below Fort Pearson on 12 January, and built Fort Tenedos opposite. On 18 January, the column, escorting 130 wagons, began its advance in two mutually supporting sections towards Eshowe, intending to use the abandoned mission station there as a depot for its further advance on oNdini. On 21 January it burned the undefended kwa-Gingindlovu *ikhanda,* and on 22 January continued its advance across the Nyezane River.

Meanwhile, the Zulu army, which had been ritually prepared for war, left the kwaNdowengu *ikhanda* on 17 January and encamped that night in the ema-Khosini valley across the White Mfolozi River. Only a small reserve was left at oNdini to guard King Cetshwayo. The following morning a force of about 4 000 men under Chief Godide kaNdlela detached itself from the main body and set off south-east in the direction of Eshowe to oppose the Right Column advancing up the coast. It bivouacked that night at kwaMagwaza and, because it was suffering from dysentery, only resumed the march on 20 January, when it reached the old oNdini *ikhanda* south of the Mhlathuze River. On 21 January Godide's force, which had swelled to about 6 000 with local reinforcements, reached the burnt-out kwaGingindlovu. Deciding against a night attack on the British camp, it moved back north of the Nyezane to lay an ambush for the Right Column.

After parting company with Godide's force, the main Zulu army of 24 000 men under the joint command of Chief Ntshingwayo kaMahole and Chief Mavumengwana kaNdlela marched as far as the isiPhezi *ikhanda* in the Mphembheni valley. On 19 January the army split into two columns, Ntshingwayo commanding the left and Mavumengwana the right. That night they bivouacked on the tableland near Babanango Mountain. The next night the army camped by Siphezi Hill, and scouts made contact with the British. To avoid detection by British

'We suffered this heavy loss at Isandlwana from a small force; the British army is still there and we are not able to cope with it.'

(Cajana kaMathendeka, 3 February 1879)

mounted patrols, the army moved in small groups on the evening of 21 January and morning of 22 January to the Ngwebeni valley north-east of Isandlwana.

On 21 January Chelmsford sent out a reconnaissance-in-force under Maj Dartnell and Cmdt Lonsdale to scout the broken country south-east of Isandlwana through which it was suspected that the Zulu might attempt a flanking movement. Opposed by a force of Zulu under Matshana kaMondisa massing on the Magogo heights, the two commanders withdrew to the Hlazakazi heights where they bivouacked. A false alarm in the night led to an urgent request to Chelmsford for reinforcements. In the early hours of 22 January Chelmsford moved out of camp with a strong force under Col Glyn, while Lt-Col Pulleine was left in command of the camp with orders to defend it. Durnford was ordered from Rorke's Drift to reinforce him. Chelmsford's forces became involved in a sharp skirmish with the Zulu on the Phindo heights, but the Zulu withdrew north towards Siphezi Mountain, drawing the British after them, away from the camp. During their absence, the main Zulu army attacked the camp at Isandlwana, outflanked and overran the defenders, and cut off most of the fugitives from

retreat across the Mzinyathi. By the time Chelmsford was able to bring his forces back to the camp it was after dark and the victorious Zulu had withdrawn.

The Zulu reserve of between 3 000 and 4 000 under Prince Dabulamanzi kaMpande, who had taken no part in the battle of Isandlwana, went on to invade Natal and ravage the plain between the Mzinyathi and the heights at Helpmekaar. They attacked the hastily fortified post at Rorke's Drift, but were repulsed by its small garrison. In the early hours of 23 January they finally withdrew, avoiding contact with Chelmsford's force, which was marching at first light to the relief of Rorke's Drift. On 24 January the remnants of the Centre Column broke up, leaving strong garrisons at Rorke's Drift and Helpmekaar to bar the way of an anticipated Zulu invasion of Natal.

On the same day as the battle of Isandlwana, the Right Column fought through the Zulu ambush at Nyezane, and reached Eshowe on 23 January. Pearson immediately began to fortify the mission. On 27 January news of Isandlwana reached Eshowe. By the folllowing day Pearson had decided to hold fast to divert Zulu attention from an invasion of Natal. He moved inside the fort on 30 January having sent the mounted men, Natal Native Contingent and oxen back to Natal.

During early January the Left (No. 4) Column of 2 278 men under Col Wood assembled near Balte Spruit, drawing its supplies from Newcastle and Utrecht. On 6 January the column advanced across the Ncome (Blood) River to encamp at Bemba's Kop. Wood led a flying column between 11 and 13 January to within 12 miles (19 km) of Rorke's Drift in support of the Centre Column, capturing large numbers of livestock. From Bemba's Kop patrols were engaged in a number of skirmishes with local irregulars. On 18 January the column resumed its advance and on 20 January halted across the White Mfolozi at Tinta's Kraal. On the same day a mounted patrol under Col Buller was forced to withdraw from Zungwini Mountain by the abaQulusi under Msebe kaMadaka and the adher-

Prince Mbilini waMswati (right), an exiled claimant to the Swazi throne who had tendered his allegiance to the Zulu king, photographed with his induna, *Mbambo. Mbilini was an extremely effective commander of irregular forces and plagued the British forces operating in north-western Zululand until his death in a skirmish in April 1879.*

ents of Mbilini waMswati, a renegade Swazi prince owing allegiance to Cetshwayo. In retaliation, Wood led out the column on 22 January and dispersed the Zulu on Zungwini, capturing much livestock. On 24 January the column broke up another Zulu concentration between Zungwini and Ntendeka Mountain. On both occasions the worsted Zulu retired up Hlobane Mountain. News of Isandlwana reached Wood on 24 January and he withdrew his column via Fort Tinta towards Khambula Hill, where an entrenched camp was formed on 31 January.

No. 5 Column of 1 565 men under Col Rowlands did not join in the march on oNdini as had been intended because of his unsuccessful operations against the Pedi under Sekhukhune woaSekwati. The column remained in garrison on the Phongolo frontier to protect the Left Column's flank from the Pedi and Zulu irregulars, and did not advance beyond its posts at Derby and Luneburg. A mounted patrol from Luneburg defeated Chief Manyonyoba kaMaqondo of the Kubheka on 26 January and captured much livestock, forcing him to take refuge in the caves of the Ntombe valley. From there the Kubheka continued to raid the Luneburg-Derby road and farms in the vicinity.

**Regrouping and skirmishing
1 February – 18 March 1879**
Panic swept Natal and the areas of the Transvaal adjacent to the Zulu kingdom following the battle of Isandlwana. Colonists took refuge in the existing laagers, threw up improvised defences at Pietermaritzburg, Durban and at other posts, or trekked away to safety. Since the Centre Column, besides suffering crippling casualties, had lost all its transport and equipment at Isandlwana, and the Right and Left Columns were bottled up at Eshowe and Khambula respectively, Chelmsford had no option but to stay on the defensive until his forces had regrouped, been reinforced and fresh transport assembled. Isandlwana had also changed the nature of the campaign in that the British now had to prosecute the

war to complete victory if they were to maintain their prestige and hegemony in southern Africa. This meant that a negotiated settlement was no longer conceivable, and Zulu peace-feelers in March were ignored since Cetshwayo was not prepared to accept all the stringent terms of the ultimatum on which the British insisted.

In Britain, the government, reacting to

Col (later Brig-Gen) Henry Evelyn Wood, VC, CB, commander of No. 4 Column, renamed the Flying Column, sketched in early April 1879 by Lt-Col Crealock. The most energetic of the British commanders in 1879, his disaster on Hlobane was masked by his great victory the next day at Khambula.

'The situation of affairs does not appear to me to improve, and I am fairly puzzled when I contemplate our future operations . . . I wish I saw my way with honour out of this beastly country.'
(Lord Chelmsford, 3 February 1879)

Lt-Col Redvers Henry Buller, CB, as seen by Lt-Col Crealock, commanded the mounted troops of No. 4 Column and Wood's Flying Column. He was a ruthless and intrepid leader of irregular horse.

'No fighting has taken place at Eshowe beyond occasional shots between scouts. They [the Zulu] know the camp is very strong, and could not be taken without severe loss.'

(Two Christians from Entumeni, 3 February 1879)

Prince Hamu kaNzibe, King Cetshwayo's elder brother, was induna of the uThulwana ibutho and chief of the Ngenetsheni people in north-western Zululand. He had his eye on the Zulu crown, and was opposed to risking war with Britain. His defection to the British in March 1879 dealt a severe blow to Zulu morale. Lt-Col Crealock sketched him near Utrecht where the British settled him and his many wives until the end of war.

public consternation over Isandlwana, sent out the reinforcements Chelmsford urgently requested. The rapid arrival in Durban during February and March of imperial troops from Britain, St Helena and Ceylon, and of additions to the Naval Brigade, as well as the despatch of imperial and colonial troops from the Cape to Natal, did much to calm the colonists.

The Zulu, despite their victory at Isandlwana, were discouraged by heavy casualties and their repulses at Rorke's Drift and Nyezane. At the same time, the presence of Pearson at Fort Eshowe deep in Zululand was an affront. Cetshwayo had the garrison blockaded and its communications to Natal cut by members of all *amabutho* living in the coastal country, and by local irregulars. Constant watch was kept on the fort by about 500 men in parties of 40 or 50, while the remainder – perhaps as many as 5 000 under the command of Dabulamanzi and Mavumengwana – were quartered in small groups at local *imizi* and *amakhanda,* prepared to re-form to foil a sortie by the garrison, or their relief.

Pearson's lack of initiative and mounted men meant that he only contrived to make one punitive raid from Eshowe. On 1 March a mounted patrol burnt the eSiqwakeni *ikhanda* and three *imizi*, but were harried home by Zulu skirmishers. Otherwise, Pearson contented himself with improving the fortifications and repairing the road along which he hoped a force from Natal would advance to relieve his garrison, which was increasingly short of supplies and suffering from illness.

Wood, by contrast, thanks to his energy and the number of experienced irregular horse at his disposal, retained the ascendancy in north-western Zululand. From his camp at Khambula (which between February and April he twice relocated along the ridge for sanitation and firewood), he sent out repeated successful mounted raids. On 1 February, a patrol under Buller burnt the ebaQulusini *ikhanda*, the centre of resistance in the area, and on 10 February raided Hlobane Mountain, where many Zulu had taken

refuge. On both occasions great numbers of cattle were captured, and the Zulu in the neighbourhood began to submit or retire eastwards out of range of Buller's patrols. But some hit back. The Kubheka of Manyonyoba and Mbilini's adherents, as well as the abaQulusi under Tola kaDilikana, ravaged the Ntombe valley on 10–11 February, striking at farms, missions and Christian Africans (*amakholwa*). In retaliation, Buller raided Manyonyoba's caves on 15 February, and Rowlands, with men of No. 5 Column, advanced from Derby to attack Talaku Mountain held by the abaQulusi. Neither of these raids, nor further minor strikes in late February, were effective in subduing the area entirely, and British lines of supply remained vulnerable to attack. Consequently, on 12 March, when a convoy under Capt Moriarty was proceeding from Derby to Luneburg (No. 5 Column was attached to Wood's command on 26 February when Rowlands returned to Pretoria to deal with the disaffected Transvaal Boers), it was overwhelmed at the drift across the Ntombe River by Mbilini's forces.

Two days before the Ntombe engagement, and overshadowing it in significance, Prince Hamu kaNzibe, one of the major figures in the Zulu kingdom, evaded pursuit by Cetshwayo's forces and took refuge wih Wood at Khambula. There he was joined by many of his Ngenetsheni adherents. On 14 March, a patrol bringing in final stragglers was fired on by Zulu concentrated on Hlobane. Hamu's defection was a clear indication that some among the Zulu leadership had decided that the Zulu cause was lost, and were pepared to make peace with the eventual conquerors.

The turning point
19 March – 5 April 1879

Confronted with Hamu's defection and the prospect of more to follow, and sensing that his peace negotiations were fruitless, Cetshwayo decided in mid-March to reactivate the campaign. By 22 March the veterans of Isandlwana had reassembled at oNdini for ritual war preparations. Since Wood's activities were presenting

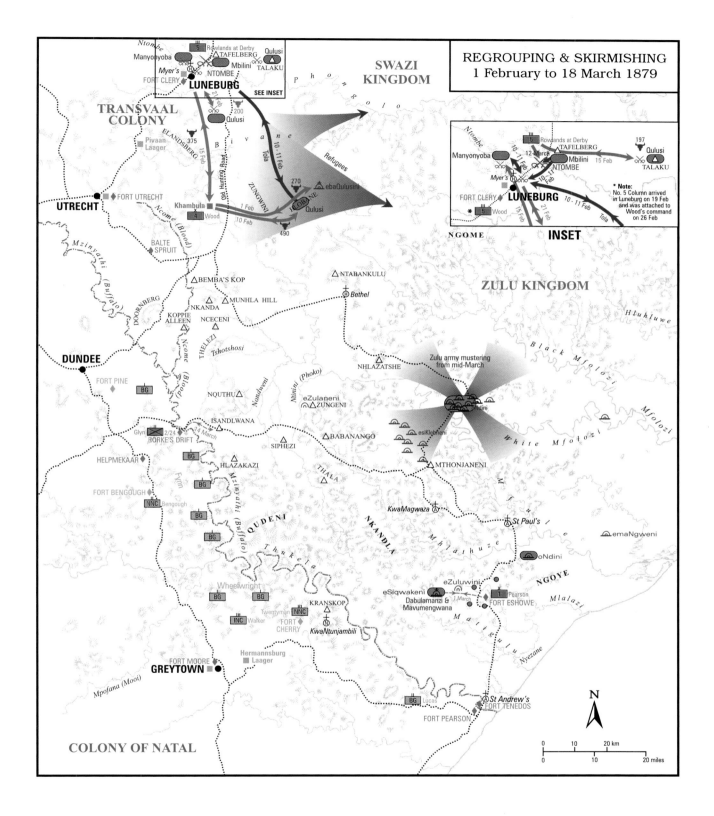

REGROUPING & SKIRMISHING
1 February to 18 March 1879

SWAZI KINGDOM

TRANSVAAL COLONY

ZULU KINGDOM

COLONY OF NATAL

INSET

* **Note:**
No. 5 Column arrived
in Luneburg on 19 Feb
and was attached to
Wood's command
on 26 Feb

the greatest threat, Cetshwayo decided to direct the army of 17 000 men against his base at Khambula. The army, under the command of Chief Mnyamana kaNgqengelele, began its march on 24 March, anticipating that it would be reinforced by a further 3 000 aba-Qulusi and other local irregulars as it advanced.

Coincidentally, Chelmsford had decided that the time was right to renew his offensive now that reinforcements were concentrated and sufficient transport had been assembled. However, before a second major thrust could be made into Zululand, it was necessary to relieve the beleaguered Eshowe garrison. On 23 March Chelmsford took command of the Eshowe Relief Column of 5 670 men assembled at Fort Pearson. To create a diversion in favour of the column's advance, Chelmsford ordered the forces stationed along the Thukela and Mzinyathi rivers to mount demonstrations, and to raid where feasible into Zululand. On 24 March Maj Twentyman demonstrated at Middle Drift, and raided across the Thukela on 2 April and again the following day. Capt Lucas demonstrated downstream on 27 March, along the lower Thukela. Noting this increased British activity, and realising that they might have to oppose an attempt to relieve Eshowe, the Zulu strengthened the forces investing the fort until there were some 10 000 men under the overall command of Somopho kaZikhala concentrated in the vicinity.

The Eshowe Relief Column began its advance into Zululand on 29 March. Chelmsford was determined to rectify the deficiencies that had led to the Isandlwana disaster. This time he organised effective forward reconnaissance and followed regular laagering procedures. He also marched closer to the coast than Pearson had to keep to more open terrain in order to avoid ambush.

While the Eshowe Relief Column was crossing the Thukela, Wood won the most hard-fought and decisive battle of the war at Khambula. Unaware that the main Zulu army was marching against him, Wood had continued to assert his local dominance. On 25 March another patrol from Khambula ravaged the Kubheka in the Ntombe valley. The next day Wood decided to clear Hlobane Mountain of the abaQulusi and Mbilini's people, who were using it as their base and a refuge for their livestock. Not only would this action create a diversion for the Eshowe Relief Column as Chelmsford required, but it might finally end resistance in that sector and bring in a great haul of cattle.

A force of mounted men and African auxiliaries under Wood left Khambula on 27 March for Hlobane. The following morning it succeeded in storming the mountain in a pincer movement, but it had fallen into a trap and was nearly cut off and destroyed by the abaQulusi and elements of the advancing Zulu army. The survivors fell back on the entrenched camp at Khambula, which the Zulu army attacked on 29 March. After a desperate battle lasting from midday to sunset, the Zulu were eventually thrown back and dispersed in a relentless mounted pursuit, their morale irreparably damaged. The abaQulusi and Mbilini's people withdrew from Hlobane on 3 April and moved north, raiding the Phongolo valley near Luneburg as they went. A British patrol killed Mbilini in a skirmish on 5 April, and the spirit of local resistance in north-western Zululand seemed temporarily to have died with him.

While Wood was mopping up after the decisive battle of Khambula, the Eshowe Relief Column continued its advance on Eshowe. On 1 April it formed an entrenched laager close to the burnt kwa-Gingindlovu *ikhanda*. The Zulu army concentrated on the hills beyond the Nyezane attacked it there on the morning of 2 April. It suffered the same fate as the army which had attempted to storm the Khambula camp, and confirmed that it was hopeless for the Zulu to attack fortified positions. Chelmsford relieved the Eshowe garrison on 3 April and evacuated it the next day to the Thukela. As the garrison withdrew, Chelmsford led out a patrol which destroyed Dabulamanzi's eZuluwini *umuzi*.

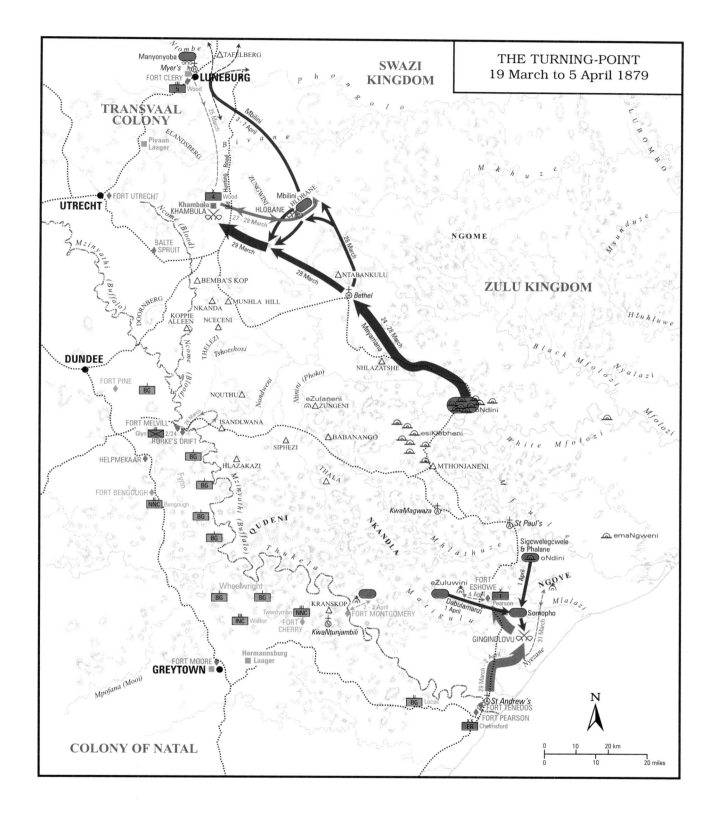

SWAZI
KINGDOM

TRANSVAAL
COLONY

Manyonyoba
Myer's
FORT CLERY
LUNEBURG
TAFELBERG
Wood
Mbilini
Elandsberg
Pivaan
Laager

FORT UTRECHT
UTRECHT
BALTE
SPRUIT
Khambula
KHAMBULA
Wood
HLOBANE
Mbilini
HLOBANE
NTABANKULU
Bethel
ZULU KINGDOM
NGOME

BEMBA'S KOP
MUNHLA HILL
NKANDA
KOPPIE
ALLEEN
NCECENI
DUNDEE
THELEZI
Tshotshosi
NHLAZATSHE

FORT PINE
BG
NQUTHU
Nondweni
eZulaneni
ZUNGENI
oNdini

FORT MELVILL
Glyn
ISANDLWANA
RORKE'S DRIFT
SIPHEZI
BABANANGO
esiKlebheni
White Mfolozi

HELPMEKAAR
BG
HLAZAKAZI
THALA
MTHONJANENI

FORT BENGOUGH
NNC Bengough
THALA
BG

QUDENI
NKANDLA
KwaMagwaza
St Paul's
emaNgweni
Sigcwelegcwele
& Phalane
oNdini

Wheelwright
BG
BG
KRANSKOP
FORT MONTGOMERY
Twentyman NNC
INC Walker
FORT CHERRY
KwaNtunjambili
eZuluwini
FORT
ESHOWE
Pearson
Dabulamanzi
Somopho
NGOYE
Mlalazi

FORT MOORE
Hermannsburg
Laager
GREYTOWN
GINGINDLOVU
Nyezane

COLONY OF NATAL
St Andrew's
FORT TENEDOS
FORT PEARSON
Chelmsford
Lucas
BG

N

COLONY OF NATAL

'Second in Zululand'. Maj-Gen Henry Hope Crealock, CB, the dandified and snobbish commander of the 1st Division, South African Field Force, caricatured by 'Spy' for Vanity Fair, *15 March 1879. Like his younger brother, Lt-Col J.N. Crealock, he was an accomplished artist with an acerbic tongue, which made him unpopular with his officers.*

One of the reasons why 'Crealock's Crawlers' of the 1st Division took so long to advance was the number of rivers in the Zululand coastal plain to be crossed. The engraving from the Illustrated London News *of 26 July 1879 shows a section of the trestle and pontoon bridge being constructed in May 1879 by the Royal Engineers over the lower Thukela. It is being brought into position under an escort of soldiers.*

The second invasion
6 April – 8 July

Chelmsford, conscious after the overwhelming victories at Khambula and Gingindlovu that his forces had entirely regained the initiative, determined to pursue the war to its conclusion. More than enough reinforcements had arrived in Natal for him confidently to resume the march on oNdini. Yet their very numbers meant increased strain on the Transport and Commissariat Department, highlighting its deficiencies, while Chelmsford seemed uncertain how best to deploy the excess of troops effectively. In the event, his new invasion strategy required two widely spaced columns to advance on oNdini from opposite directions, supposedly screening both Natal and the Transvaal from a Zulu counter-blow.

The Eshowe Relief Column, which had formed a new entrenched camp about a mile (1.6 km) south of the Gingindlovu laager on 6 April, a week later became the 2nd Brigade of the 1st Division under Maj-Gen Crealock. The 1st Brigade concentrated on the lower Thukela with Fort Pearson as its main depot. The entire 1st Division (which totalled 7 500 men) was to advance up the coastal plain to the Mhlathuze River, where it was to burn the emaNgweni and old oNdini *amakhanda*. The objective was to pressure Cetshwayo into dividing his forces to protect the *amakhanda* and the people of the coastal plain from British raids. But the over-methodical Crealock's advance proved painfully slow, and his lack of progress allowed Cetshwayo to

ignore his presence and to concentrate his forces to meet the other column's advance from the north-west.

April was spent bringing up convoys of supplies to the 1st Division, strengthening Forts Pearson and Tenedos, and building Forts Crealock and Chelmsford as advance posts. By mid-June the lower Thukela was spanned by a trestle and pontoon bridge; while a gunboat taking soundings at Port Durnford up the coast had established it as a feasible place for landing supplies once the Division advanced. On 20 June the 1st Division was finally concentrated at Fort Chelmsford where supplies had been accumulating. Overawed by all this activity, local chiefs began to negotiate their submission. The Division then advanced, threw a pontoon bridge across the Mlalazi River, and started Fort Napoleon on 25 June to cover the crossing. Mounted patrols raided between the foot of the Ngoye hills and the coast, and as far as the Mhlathuze River, burning many *imizi* and capturing much livestock. There was little, if any resistance, for the men were responding to Cetshwayo's summons to gather at oNdini to face the other column. By 1 July the 1st Division was encamped at Port Durnford where it was supplied by sea when the surf was not too heavy, or by convoy from Fort Chelmsford.

On 4 July Maj Barrow crossed the Mhlathuze with a mounted patrol and burned emaNgweni. No resistance was offered and many cattle were taken. On the same day, at Port Durnford, more local chiefs, responding to the favourable terms offered them, made their sub-

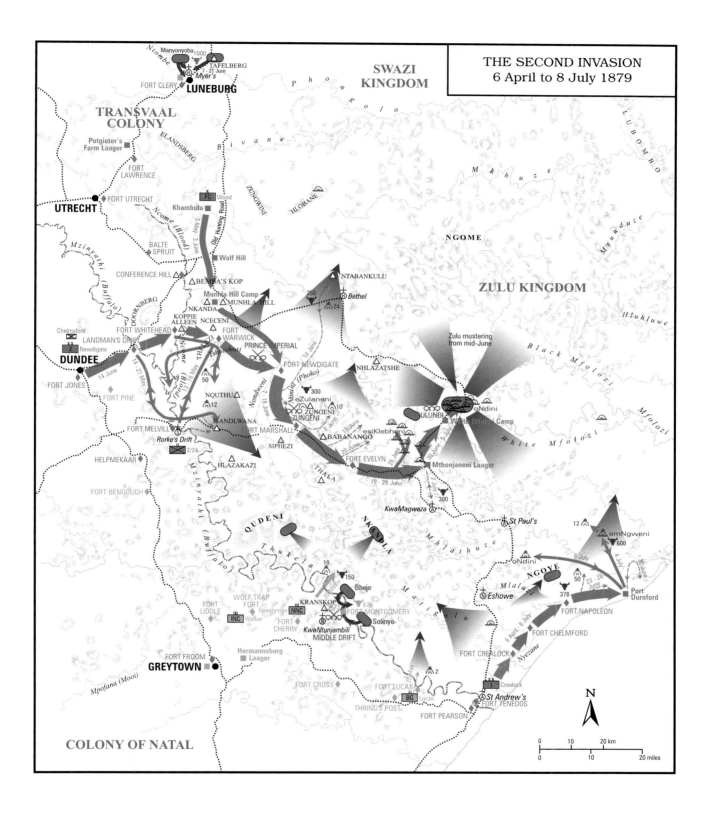

SWAZI KINGDOM

TRANSVAAL COLONY

ZULU KINGDOM

UTRECHT

DUNDEE

NGOME

COLONY OF NATAL

GREYTOWN

Manyonyoba 1000
TAFELBERG
Myer's
FORT CLERY
LUNEBURG
17 - 21 June

Potgieter's Farm Laager
FORT LAWRENCE
FORT UTRECHT
ELANDSBERG
Bivane
Ncome (Blood)
Phongolo

Khambula
Wood
FC
Old Hunting Road
5 May 3 June
ZUNGWIN
HLOBANE

BALTE SPRUIT
Wolf Hill
Mzinyathi (Buffalo)
DOORNBERG

CONFERENCE HILL
BEMBA'S KOP
Munhla Hill Camp
MUNHLA HILL
NKANDA
NTABANKULU
250
Bethel
24

Chelmsford
Newdigate
LANDMAN'S DRIFT
FORT WHITEHEAD
KOPPIE ALLEEN
NCECENI
FORT WARWICK
tshotshosi
PRINCE IMPERIAL
FORT NEWDIGATE (Phoko)
NHLAZATSHE

FORT JONES
FORT PINE
Ncome (Blood)
14 - 21 May
16 May
50
Nondweni
14 June
18 June
Ntinini (Phoko)
eZulaneni
ZUNGENI
300
10
8 June
19 June
esiKlebheni
ULUNDI
oNdini
White Mfolozi Camp
Zulu mustering from mid-June

NQUTHU
12
ISANDLWANA
FORT MARSHALL
BABANANGO
26 June
White Mfolozi
Mfolozi
Mfolozi

FORT MELVILL
Rorke's Drift
2/24
SIPHEZI
FORT EVELYN
30 June - 5 July
Mthonjaneni Laager
Black Mfolozi
Htuhluwe
Msunduze
LUBOMBO

HELPMEKAAR
HLAZAKAZI
THALA
20 June
19 - 29 June
300
KwaMagwaza
July

FORT BENGOUGH
Mzinyathi (Buffalo)
QUDENI
NKANDLA
St Paul's
oNdini
emNgweni
600
12 July

Thukela
19
150
Bheje
Mhlathuze
Eshowe
NGOYE
Mlalazi
50
378
4 July
6 July
23 - 26 June
Port Durnford

WOLF TRAP FORT
FORT LIDDLE
Tyentyman
Walker
NNC
INC
KRANSKOP
678
FORT MONTGOMERY
Solinye
KwaNtunjambili
MIDDLE DRIFT
Matigulu
FORT NAPOLEON
FORT CHELMFORD
Nyezane
6 April, 8 July

FORT CHERRY
Hermannsburg Laager
FORT FROOM
FORT CROSS
2
FORT LUCAS
Lucas
BG
THRING'S POST
FORT PEARSON
St Andrew's
FORT TENEDOS
Crealock
FORT CREALOCK

Mpofana (Mooi)

N

0   10   20 km
0   10   20 miles

The Zululand coast offered no secure anchorages or harbours. Supplies brought up for the 1st Division by sea were landed as depicted in the Illustrated London News *of 18 October 1879 on the beach at Port Durnford from lighters when the surf was not too heavy.*

mission. Crealock moved up the following day to a camp at the lower drift of the Mhlathuze, and there more of the most important coastal chiefs surrendered. Barrow led out another patrol on 6 June and burnt old oNdini, before returning to Port Durnford the next day. The 1st Division's objectives and been accomplished, but their actions had been essentially irrelevant – on 4 July the other column had scattered the Zulu army in the Mahlabathini plain and ended organised armed resistance.

Wood's forces at Khambula (3 200 men) had been restyled the Flying Column on 13 April, but remained under his independent command. The Flying Column was to co-operate in its advance from the north-west on oNdini with the 2nd Division (5 000 men) under Maj-

Officers of the Flying Column photographed in the field. Sitting, left to right: *Lt Henry Lysons, Orderly Officer; Brig-Gen Evelyn Wood, Officer Commanding; Lt-Col Redvers Buller, Commanding Mounted Troops.* Standing, from second from left: *Capt Lord William Beresford, Staff Officer; Maj Cornelius Clery, Principal Staff Officer; and Capt Edward Woodgate, General Staff Duties.*

Gen Newdigate. The 2nd Divison, which Chelmsford intended to accompany, was to be made up out of the balance of troops already in the Utrecht District, and from the reinforcements landed in Durban, including the Cavalry Brigade under Maj-Gen Marshall. The Division was to concentrate at Dundee, which Chelmsford selected over Helpmekaar as its main depot, because the roads were better by way of Ladysmith than by Greytown, and were less exposed to the Zulu border. Furthermore, Dundee was closer to the Orange Free State from which considerable supplies were being drawn. Most important of all, it avoided the disastrous road by way of Isandlwana and its still unburied British dead. But this meant that the 2nd Division would have to advance by a longer and unfamiliar route, which would require considerable and time-consuming reconnaissance.

On 28 April Fort Jones was begun at Dundee for the protection of the depot, and on 2 May an entrenched camp was established at Landman's Drift on the Mzinyathi River where the Division duly massed. Between 13 and 21 May the 2nd Division mounted extensive and repeated mounted raids with NNC support from Landman's Drift to secure their right flank and rear when they advanced, and to clear the Natal border of any lingering Zulu presence. Great numbers of huts were burned and cattle captured in an arc stretching east from the Mzi-

nyathi between Landman's and Rorke's Drifts towards Babanango Mountain. A reconnaissance-in-force to Isandlwana on 21 May, in co-operation with the Rorke's Drift garrison under Maj Dartnell (which on 9 April had made an extensive raid up the Batshe River to Isandlwana), at last began the long overdue burial of the dead. Meanwhile, to divert Zulu forces further to the east from his advance, Chelmsford required further raids to be mounted across the Thukela from Natal. On 20 May, Maj Twentyman made the border forces' most extensive incursion into Zululand. Capt Lucas also raided downstream on 28 May. Chelmsford believed the transborder raids helped maintain the strategic initiative, but they brought him into direct conflict with Sir Henry Bulwer, the Lt-Governor of Natal, who feared that they only set up a harmful cycle of raid and counter-raid.

This dispute between the civil and military authorities over the propriety of border raids was the last straw that decided the British cabinet on 26 May to replace Chelmsford with General Sir Garnet Wolseley. Cabinet had long lost confidence in Chelmsford's ability – or that of any other of its officials in South Africa – to bring the unacceptably expensive war to a speedy conclusion. Wolseley's appointment created a single, unified and effective command in southern Africa, which subordinated both Chelms-

'Handsome Fred', or Maj-Gen Frederick Marshall, was a famous cricketer and captain of the United Eleven of England, as well as the commander of the Cavalry Brigade attached to the 2nd Division. Lt-Col Crealock drew him at sunrise on campaign in Zululand, bundled up in his fur coat against the morning chill.

'A great deal of the sickness among the 1st Division may be ascribed to the effluvia which arises from the carcases of oxen in different stages of decomposition. These lie on the road where the troopers have to escort the convoys, and at every hundred yards this horrible atmosphere has to be breathed.'

(*Illustrated London News,* 26 July 1879)

ford and Bulwer and sidelined Frere, the High Commissioner. Chelmsford only learned of Wolseley's appointment on 16 June, and did not receive formal notice of it until 9 July. He consequently continued to act as if he were still in command in Zululand, though the knowledge that Wolseley was on his way spurred him on to bring the war to a successful conclusion before his hated replacement could arrive to take the credit.

Meanwhile, mounted reconnaissances undertaken during May from Landman's Drift established that the shortest route for the 2nd Division to follow to oNdini was across the Ncome River below Koppie Alleen, further south than originally intended. This necessitated creating a new depot, called Fort Whitehead, to replace the forward base Chelmsford had established to the north at Conference Hill, and relocating the stores. The whole Division advanced on Koppie Alleen, and on 31 May began to cross the Ncome into Zululand. Chelmsford's reputation immediately took another blow when the Prince Imperial of France (who was attached to his staff) was killed in a skirmish at the Tshotshosi River on 1 June. His death caused more consternation in Europe than the battle of Isandlwana. On 3 June the Division resumed its advance, establishing depots at Forts Newdigate, Marshall and (later) Warwick.

The same day the Flying Column effected its junction with the 2nd Division at the Tshotshosi River. Wood had begun his movement south on 5 May, and had marched by way of Wolf Hill and Munhla Hill, trusting the security of the Transvaal border to the garrisons he left behind. Not that they could do much outside their entrenchments if challenged. Between 7 and 21 June Zulu raiders in the region of Luneburg swept off thousands of cattle and sheep over the Phongolo and burned settlers' farms. The Zulu were assisted in their operations by disaffected Boers from the Wakkerstroom District of the Transvaal. However, these raiders were not such a threat that Wood was diverted from his march on oNdini.

On 5 June the mounted men of the Flying Column and the 2nd Division had an encounter at Zungeni Mountain with Zulu irregulars. The joint column continued the advance up the Ntinini River valley before halting from 7 to 17 June to escort convoys of supplies. Several raids went out to clear the area of Zulu, and Buller patrolled as far as Ntabankulu Mountain. The final joint advance on oNdini resumed on 18 June with the Flying Column in the van. It was laboured because Chelmsford had become overcautious. He would only move once cavalry had thoroughly reconnoitred the route ahead for any possible opposition, and the joint force formed laager every night when it halted. Moreover (as we have seen) it had to halt periodically to

During the second invasion, the advancing British systematically burned hundreds of imizi to break the spirit of Zulu resistance and to deny the Zulu forces opposing them adequate supplies in the field. The engraving from the Illustrated London News *of 6 September 1879 shows a patrol of the 17th Lancers of the Cavalry Brigade attached to the 2nd Division returning from their work of destruction.*

On 27 June 1879, three messengers from King Cetshwayo – Mgcwelo, Mtshibela and Mphokothwayo – carrying two tusks of ivory and driving a herd of 150 cattle as peace offerings, were intercepted by a British patrol. In this closely observed engraving from the Graphic of 30 August 1879, they are shown being brought into Chelmsford's camp on the Mthonjaneni heights. However, the message they carried failed to meet Chelmsford's stringent conditions for a peaceful settlement.

build fortified depots along its line of communication, and convoys had to be escorted back and forth to fill them with supplies.

For his part, Cetshwayo was uncertain how to prosecute the war further. He believed it to be already lost. He knew there were increasing defections along the British line of advance, especially to the 1st Division, but his *amabutho* were unwilling to give up before a further fight. So he compromised; he called up his *amabutho* for the last time to assemble in the Mahlabathini plain, and promised them he would fight if the British came on as far as oNdini. At the same time, he entered into intensified negotiations with the British. But, as he feared, Chelmsford was unwilling to negotiate seriously. He demanded crushing and impossible terms, thus ensuring that Zulu resistance would continue until he had achieved the overwhelming victory in the field he so desired.

Chelmsford's combined column thus continued its inexorable advance, on 22 June building a new depot at Fort Evelyn in sight of the Mahlabathini plain. The mounted men continued to patrol and raid. On 20 June there was a skirmish with 500 Zulu in the Mphembheni valley, and another in front of the column on 24 June. It was at that moment that the Zulu opposite Middle Drift made a last foray across the Thukela into Natal, evidently in retaliation for the earlier British raids. On 25 June about 1 000 Zulu ravaged the valley below Kranskop, with local border forces unable to prevent the incursion. But this isolated raid had no effect on Chelmsford's advance. On 26 June Wood led a strong patrol down into the emaKhosini valley on the south bank of the White Mfolozi, where it destroyed the many *amakhanda* clustered there. The joint column moved the following day to the Mthonjaneni heights, where a triple wagon laager in echelon was formed on 29 June.

With only a minimum of baggage Chelmsford marched his men down towards the Mahlabathini plain on 30 June, and on 2 July they formed a double laager and a fort on the south bank of the White Mfolozi. A mounted reconnaissance led by Buller on 3 July (which was nearly cut off by a well-laid Zulu ambush), established the ideal position for the coming battle of Ulundi. The British fought the next day in an infantry square which, although it provided all-round defence not unlike a laager, nevertheless possessed the moral force of not being an entrenched position. So when the Zulu broke before the concentrated firepower of the square and fled from a mounted counter-attack, they knew that they had been defeated in the open field

'Until the King sends an Ambassador and complies with the preliminary conditions, the army under my command in every part of Zululand has orders to advance and make raids.'
(Lord Chelmsford, 16 June 1879)

The British advance on the White Mfolozi on 1 July 1879, as shown in the Illustrated London News *of 30 August 1879. Note the Flying Column's wagon laager in the centre middle distance. On 2 July the 2nd Division parked its wagons next to it, and the fort commanding the double laager was built on the little hill shown to the left. The Mahlabathini plain is in the distance, where a number of* amakhanda *can be seen.*

> 'The army is now thoroughly beaten, and as we were beaten in the open, it will not reassemble or fight again.'
>
> (Ndungungunga kaNgengene, 4 July 1879)

and that further resistance was futile. The Zulu army consequently dispersed, and King Cetshwayo fled north, his power irrevocably broken.

The victorious British burnt all the *amakhanda* in the Mahlabathini plain before retiring to the Mthonjaneni heights. Rain between 6 and 8 July prevented any further movement, though Buller raided south towards kwaMagwaza capturing many cattle. Chelmsford was criticised for withdrawing to his base at Mthonjaneni instead of advancing to consolidate his victory. His decision was influenced by his shortage of supplies and lack of adequate shelter, as well by as his conviction that organised resistance by the Zulu army was over. But he was also motivated by his desire to resign his command now that Wolseley had at last reached the front. Between 2 and 4 July Wolseley had tried in vain to land through heavy surf at Port Durnford to take up his command, before riding into Port Durnford from Durban on 7 July.

Pacification and withdrawal 9 July – 22 September

Wolseley proceeded to St Paul's on 15 July to inspect Wood's Flying Column which had begun retiring there on 9 July by way of kwaMagwaza (where it started Fort Albert on 11 July) preparatory to being broken up officially on 31 July. On 26 July Lt-Col Baker Russell was put in command of the reduced Flying Column, which would be required for the

final pacification of Zululand, and the units not needed returned to Natal and the Transvaal. Supplies were brought up to St Paul's from Port Durnford by 1 000 Africans of the Carrier Corps, and a fort was begun on 28 July to protect them.

Meanwhile, on 10 July the 2nd Division began its march back to Natal from Mthonjaneni by the way it had come. The Division was formally broken up on 26 July near Fort Marshall. Some units remained in garrison at various posts in Zululand until convoys could bring out all the unconsumed supplies, and others were detached to construct Fort Cambridge, a half-way post to Luneburg. The rest returned to Durban for embarkation.

Wolseley received the formal surrender of the coastal chiefs on 19 July at his temporary camp on the lower drift of the Mhlathuze near the burned-out ema-Ngweni *ikhanda*. But he realized that it was still necessary to obtain the submission of the other great chiefs of Zululand, and to capture the fugitive Cetshwayo to ensure a final peace. He therefore decided to re-occupy the Mahlabathini plain to force compliance. To that end, on 23 July he broke up the 1st Division, and formed Lt-Col Clarke's Column out of the units he did not send back to Natal. The following day, Clarke's Column marched for oNdini. On 7 August it built Fort Victoria at the foot of the Mthonjaneni heights, where Wolseley joined it. Wolseley formed camp on 10 August at kwaSishwili, close to the

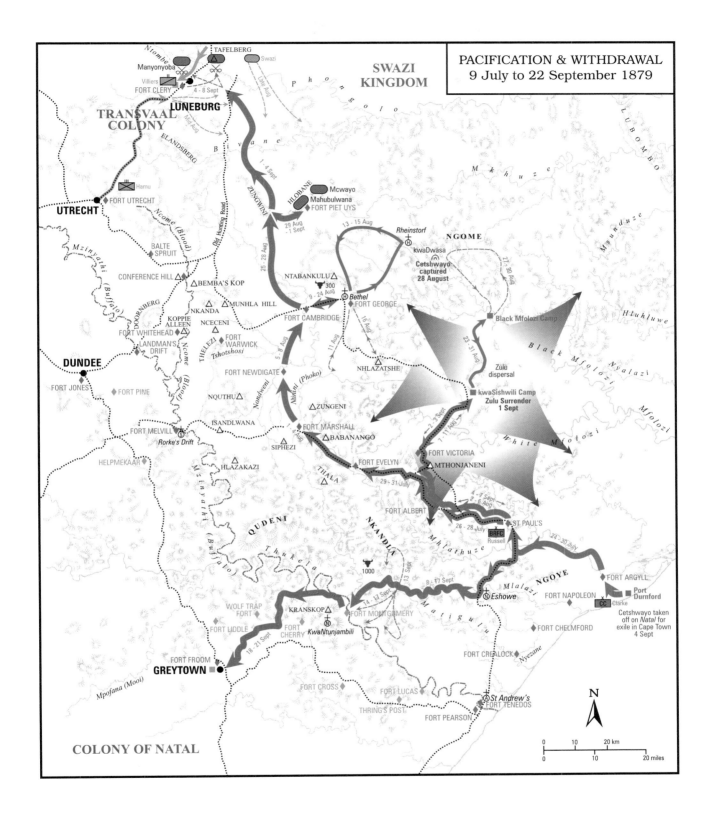

PACIFICATION & WITHDRAWAL
9 July to 22 September 1879

On 1 September 1879, at his camp at kwaSishwili, close by the burned-out oNdini, Gen Sir Garnet Wolseley announced to the assembled Zulu notables which thirteen of them would be favoured with independent sovereignties now that the Zulu kingdom was to be broken up. In this engraving of the occasion for the Graphic *of 25 October 1879, Chief Gawozi kaSilwana Mpungose is shown putting his cross to the treaty on the table. John Shepstone, Acting Secretary for Native Affairs in Natal, guides his hand and Wolseley stands facing him, left hand on hip.*

destroyed oNdini. Between 14 and 26 August most of the most important chiefs of central and northern Zululand who had not yet submitted came into Wolseley's camp to do so. In south-western Zululand the chiefs had also decided that the struggle was over, and on 20 August they surrendered at Rorke's Drift to H.F. Fynn, the Resident Magistrate of the Umsinga Division.

However, it remained imperative to take Cetshwayo to prevent him renewing resistance and stirring up those regions still unpacified. The chiefs also realised this, especially those who had made their peace with the British and stood to gain from the new order. So Mnyamana, the king's former chief councillor, gave the information necessary for a patrol under Maj Marter to capture Cetshwayo at the kwaDwasa *umuzi* deep in the Ngome forest. Cetshwayo passed through Wolseley's camp under escort on 31 August, and on 4 September was taken off at Port Durnford on the *Natal* for exile in the Cape. With the king's capture, the chiefs were able with a clear conscience publicly to accept, on 1 September, Wolseley's terms for a settlement. The monarchy was suppressed and the military system abol-

ished. Britain did not annex Zululand, but left it fragmented under 13 independent chiefs appointed by Wolseley and under the nominal supervision of a British Resident. The settlement was the recipe for the devastating civil war soon to follow, but at the time it seemed to answer the immediate requirements of ensuring the security of Zululand's neighbours and sparing Britain any new responsibilities and administrative burdens. His task complete, Wolseley and his staff left oNdini for Utrecht on 4 September.

Meanwhile, Baker Russell's Flying Column left St Paul's on 26 July for Fort Cambridge, which it reached on 5 August. Russell's objective was the pacification of north-western Zululand, where Wolseley feared the abaQulusi and Kubheka might attempt a last-ditch resistance. Patrols were sent out, and the Flying Column moved forward across the White Mfolozi to construct Fort George on 10 August. Between 13 and 15 August, Baker Russell patrolled across the Black Mfolozi to its headwaters to overawe the local population, but no resistance was offered. Further patrols went out, and between 11 and 25 August the Mdlalose people all surrendered.

However, the abaQulusi were reported to be mustering near Hlobane.

While the Flying Column was at Fort George, Lt-Col Villiers approached from Derby in the north with a force of Mounted Burghers, Hamu's adherents and Swazi allies. His purpose was to catch the people of the north-west between his and Russell's forces, but his African allies and auxiliaries had little stomach for any action but looting, and comprehensively devastated the country between the Phongolo and the Bivane rivers. Fortunately for him, Villiers met with no resistance before he reached Luneburg on 25 August with his motley force. On the same day, Russell moved his column back to Fort Cambridge and then on to Hlobane, where he camped on 29 August under its southern slopes. There on 30 August he built Fort Piet Uys to protect the stores brought up from Fort Cambridge. The abaQulusi, learning of Cetshwayo's capture, decided there was no further point in resisting. Between 30 August and 3 September they submitted piecemeal to the Flying Column as it advanced towards Luneburg. On 4, 5 and again on 8 September Russell's men and the Luneburg garrison mercilessly attacked Manyonyoba's caves in the Ntombe valley, finally blowing some up with women and children inside. Kubheka resistance collapsed, and on 8 September Villiers's ill-disciplined force was broken up and sent home. Baker Russell's Column was ordered to Lydenburg in the Transvaal on 10 September to join in the renewed operations against the Pedi. Manyonyoba, though he had evaded capture in the Ntombe caves, finally surrendered on 22 September.

Clarke's Column left oNdini for Natal on 5 September by way of St Paul's, eNtumeni and Middle Drift, which he reached on 20 September. Clarke's mission was to accept the surrender of the chiefs of the inaccessible central border region, the only ones who had not yet formally submitted. He sent out patrols to confiscate firearms and to levy cattle fines from the recalcitrant chiefs. One by one – at Camp Entumeni on 12 September, Camp Nogolo (13–14 September), at Nobiya's kraals (15–17 September), Middle Drift (18–20 September) and Camp Amathalati on the Natal side of the border (21 September) – the border chiefs made their grudging peace with the victors. With their final submission and the evacuation of the last British troops from Zululand, the war was over.

Mahubulwana kaDumisela was the principal induna *of the abaQulusi and King Cetshwayo's last commander in the field in the north-west. He was unswervingly loyal to the royal cause, and only submitted on 1 September 1879 to Lt-Col Baker Russell once he had received a secret order, sent by Cetshwayo after his capture on 28 August, to disband his men still under arms. He is shown in a photograph of c. 1882 standing next to the short and dapper Mfunzi, a principal royal messenger, who had repeatedly conveyed Cetshwayo's futile peace overtures to the British in 1879.*

A facsimile published by the Illustrated London News *on 12 July 1879 of the sketch by their special artist, Melton Prior, made on the Isandlwana battlefield when it was revisited on 21 May by Maj-Gen F. Marshall in command of a column of British cavalry, Mounted Volunteers and African auxiliaries. Nearly four months after the battle the dreadful stench of decay had largely dissipated, but desiccated bodies and wreckage lay all around. While horses were harnessed to the best preserved wagons to take them away, troops wandered over the site, collecting relics and identifying some of the dead. Although the colonial troops began the burial of their own dead, the bodies of the men of the 24th Regiment were left untouched until they could be interred by their own comrades.*

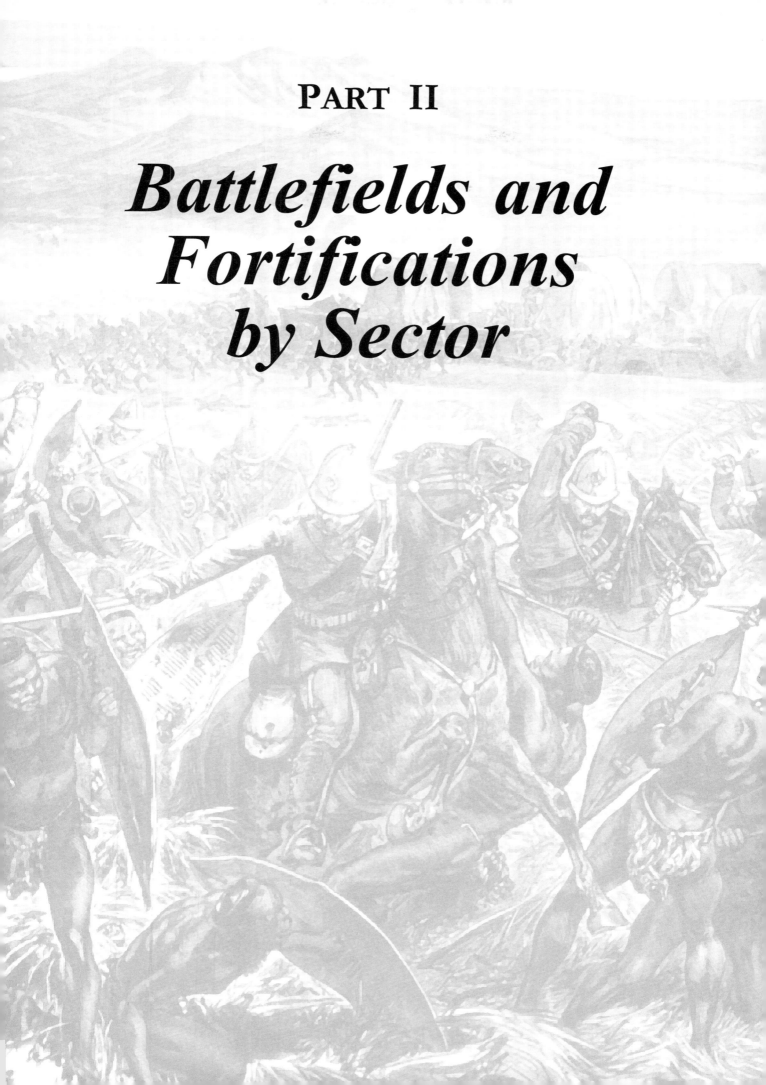

PART II
Battlefields and Fortifications by Sector

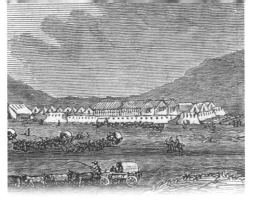

Classification and Depiction of Sites

The maps and diagrams in this book are the fruits of a combination of skills: archival research; field work; sketching and mapping by traditional methods; and the enhancement of the results through computer graphics.

Battlefields

The dispositions of the combatants portrayed in the maps of the battles and more significant skirmishes have been based on contemporary British reports, accounts and maps, on Zulu recorded oral testimony and on personal examination of the terrain. Recent interpretative studies by other historians of the Anglo-Zulu War have been consulted, and in many cases have proved most valuable.

Fortifications

The fortifications depicted in this book have been located through study of contemporary descriptions, and the comparison of war-time and a few later nineteenth-century maps with modern survey maps and, in some cases, aerial photographs. Once a site was determined, its remains were mapped using a prismatic compass for directions and pacing for dimensions. Afterwards, the detailed field sketches were drafted into diagrams and checked against photographs of the site. A cartographer gave the maps their final polish.

There are two fundamental categories of fortifications: permanent and temporary (fieldworks). Both are represented here, the first usually comprising colonial works, and the second imperial ones. In neither case are the works as elaborate as would have been necessary in Europe because the Zulus had no artillery or scaling ladders, were inadequately equipped with firearms and were unable to support close or prolonged sieges because of their own problems of supply and discipline. All that was required for defence, therefore, was a closed work a few yards high, surrounded by a ditch and possibly an abattis (defences made of felled trees and bushes), with a clear, all-round field of fire extending several hundred yards. Other important considerations were ground sufficiently level and drained for encampment, and easy access to good water, grazing and adequate supplies of firewood.

Permanent fortifications

Permanent fortifications are simply works built to last. The colonial government or the settlers erected almost all such fortifications in time of peace for security during periods of danger, and indiscriminately called them 'laagers'. The government bore the expense of those constructed in the towns, in addition to providing the specifications and negotiating the building contracts. But it would only undertake to pay half the cost of those erected in the countryside, the other half being carried by the local white farming community. These settlers would elect a committee to supervise the building, which they would normally carry out themselves. On occasion, if the need seemed pressing, they would proceed with a laager even without receiving government sanction or assistance.

Such fortifications were made of dressed stone and mortar in the form of a square enclosure, about 10 feet (3 m) high, with bastions at two opposite corners. Some of the rural settler structures could be rather more rough and simple, and some, like the Ermelo Fort, had a sod parapet surmounting the dry-stone wall. All were large enough to accommodate the white settler families of the vicinity (and often their servants), as well as their wagons, which provided them with shelter.

Remains of these stone laagers are numerous, although only Bester's and the Strydpoort laagers have much of their walls still standing. Fort Pine is a special case since

Fort Pine, built by the Natal government in 1878 for the protection of the Mzinyathi (Buffalo) River valley, was the headquarters of the Buffalo Border Guard, shown in this photograph of early 1879 drawn up in front of its stone walls. Local settlers took refuge there in the panic following Isandlwana.

it was begun by the government as a post for the Natal Mounted Police, but not completed as such by the time of the war when it was used as a settler refuge and garrisoned by Volunteer units. After the war it was altered and added to, and then served its original purpose. Perhaps in consequence of this and its relatively recent abandonment, it is still remarkably complete despite its ruinous state.

Where laager walls were added to, or connected existing government buildings such as magistrate's offices, courtroom or gaol, the trace of the laager might be rectilinear or even L-shaped. Only one such government laager can be depicted – that at Oliviershoek which, as it happens, is of the standard square shape – for the others (such as at Richmond, Stanger and Umzinto) have all been incorporated in existing police stations, gaols or military post, and are thus of restricted access. Fort Durnford, a blockhouse at Estcourt, is an altogether exceptional structure – its trace is square and bastioned, but it is double-storied and roofed.

Remains of one other kind of permanent fortification survive; namely, the temporary fortification that became permanent through the established presence of British garrisons. The 'Old Fort' at Durban and Fort Napier at Pietermaritzburg both began as fieldworks but durable brick barracks and other buildings were soon erected. Forts Buckingham and Williamson may be regarded as aborted examples of the same process, while in 1879 Fort Amiel at Newcastle was in the early stages of becoming a permanent military station.

Temporary fortifications
Temporary fortifications are fieldworks thrown up in the course of a war, either deliberately to secure some strategic place, or hastily for a tactical purpose and usually under battle conditions. Almost all such fortifications in 1879 were the work of the imperial forces. Strategic fieldworks in Natal were meant to provide frontier bases, and those in Zululand to protect lines of supply and to guard storage depots. Most

Fort Pearson, an earthen redoubt built in November 1878 to command the lower drift across the Thukela, was sketched in late February 1879 by Lt-Col Crealock.

The camps and laagers of the 2nd Division and Flying Column drawn by Lt-Col Crealock on 22 June 1879 from the commanding heights of Fort Evelyn on the Babanango ridge. The Mahlabathini plain is visible in the far distance below, though it is not possible to make out oNdini itself.

were made of earth, strengthened with stone, though some were built of stone only. Such works vary considerably in form and style, though all were characterized by a low but formidable parapet, ditch and abattis. Some (such as Fort Eshowe) take in a large area because their garrisons were of battalion strength. Others (such as the redoubt at St Paul's) have a short perimeter because they would have accommodated no more than half a company. The areas of most, however, fall between these two extremes and would have held garrisons of one to two companies. The traces of some (such as Fort Pearson) are irregular owing to the contour of the hill on which they were built, while others (like Fort Montgomery) are irregular despite the level ground. In contrast, many others are square or pentagonal and (as with Fort Marshall) have a remarkable symmetry. Later in the war paired redoubts (such as Fort Cambridge) were built, between which a large force or convoy could improvise a hasty defence. In at least two cases (Fort George and Conference Hill) the redoubts were linked by ramparts. Expertise and imagination probably also influenced design. To a contemporary, Fort Lawrence seemed an aesthetic as well as an engineering feat; in contrast, Forts Cross and Liddle were simply prosaic copies of the plans of Durban's 'Old Fort' and those of Fort Napier.

There seem to be no remains of tactical fieldworks in the form of the many march laagers which the imperial forces made at their halts in Zululand. These works were a modification of the wagon laager, whose effectiveness had long been proved by the Boers. The wagons were normally parked in echelon (front wheels abreast of the rear wheels of the next vehicle), rather than end to end, because it took too much time and labour to manoeuvre them into that position. If time and space allowed, formations of three mutually supporting laagers were formed; otherwise, when a column moved daily, a single square or oblong laager was formed, divided into compartments for the animals, soldiers and headquarters. Experience showed the British that with a large force and a moderate convoy of wagons, the defensive line to be held (as at Gingindlovu) was a shelter trench outside the wagon laager, in which the draft-animals were corralled. The trench would be manned two deep during an engagement, leaving enough space between it and the wagons for officers, ammunition boxes and black auxiliaries. On the other hand, with a small force and a large convoy, the perimeter had to be shorter to concentrate the firepower available. It was therefore the line of wagons rather than the surrounding trench that was held. Earth from the trench dug very close to the wagons was packed underneath them, and five men would fire through the loopholes left between the spokes of a wagon's wheels, while another five fired from the wagon itself. It was normal to clear the bush and burn the grass within 125 yards (114 m) of a laager to prevent the enemy from using it as cover, or from setting it alight to endanger the camp, or to provide a smoke-screen for attack.

There were also fieldworks which were tactical, in that they were thrown up in conjunction with march-laagers and abandoned when the force moved on; and yet which were strategic too, in that they were well sited and could easily be re-occupied and strengthened. Such works were usually called 'entrenched camps' (as at Wolf Hill), and occasionally 'laagers' (such as Walker's Laager). They were often anchored on a strong redoubt, such as 'Fort Nolela', which was built to command Chelmsford's double laager on the eve of the battle of Ulundi.

Improvised fortifications

At certain places within Natal where laagers had not been built, or where there were too few settlers to defend one, posts such as magistrates' offices, churches, sheds or stables provided rallying points for local settlers, who made them defensible by barricading and loopholing. At two large farmsteads stockades were also erected. In Pietermaritzburg and Durban numerous buildings, both public and private, were made defensible through barricading, loopholing and sandbagging. In Pietermaritzburg these fortified buildings were connected by makeshift barricades to form an enclosure, styled the city's 'laager'; but in Durban, in accordance with the principles for the defence of an open town, they were not, although a more typical defensive position was created by erecting a palisade across the Point. None of these defensive improvisations survives. But some of the buildings which were fortified still stand, such as the old courthouses in Pietermaritzburg and Durban.

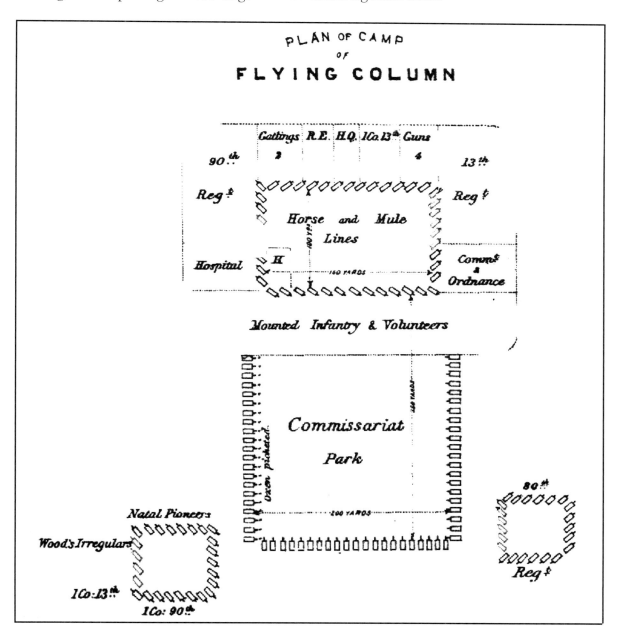

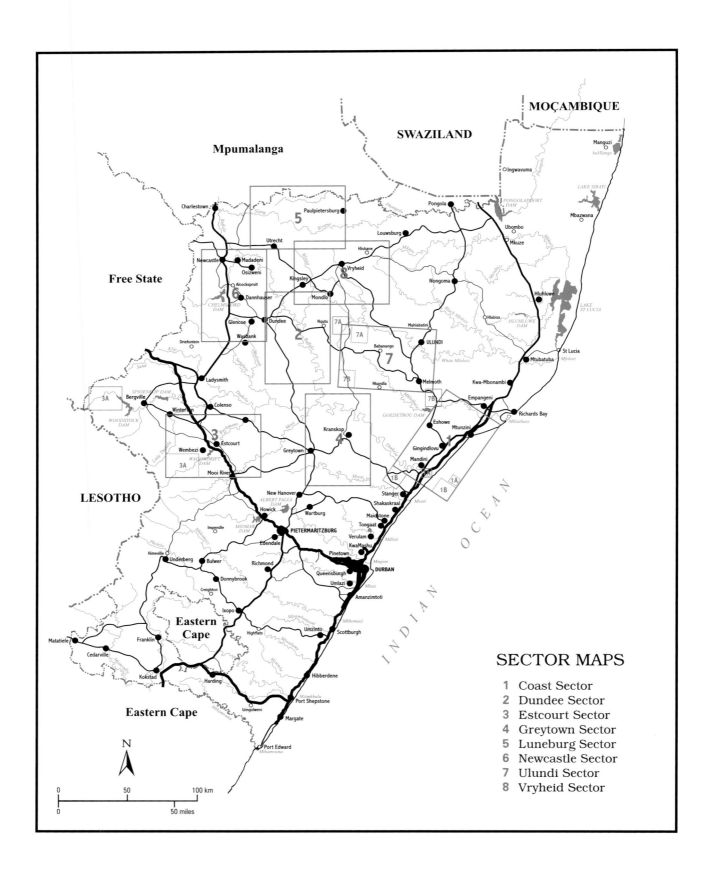

SECTOR MAPS

1 Coast Sector
2 Dundee Sector
3 Estcourt Sector
4 Greytown Sector
5 Luneburg Sector
6 Newcastle Sector
7 Ulundi Sector
8 Vryheid Sector

Introduction to the Maps

The maps and diagrams of the battle-fields and fortifications which follow are grouped according to sector: **Coast, Dundee, Estcourt, Greytown, Luneburg, Newcastle, Ulundi, Vryheid, Pietermaritzburg** and **Durban**. In each sector (with the exceptions of Pietermaritzburg and Durban) a modern sector map shows towns, roads and museums, as well as game and nature reserves, and locates the battlefields and fortifications of its area. Each sector also includes a section providing brief descriptions and diagrams of its fortifications, which is followed by maps of battlefields (whenever applicable), accompanied by accounts of the battles.

The diagrams of the fortifications depict features as they are today. However, forts for which contemporary diagrams have survived are included for comparison. The maps of the Durban and Pietermaritzburg laagers show features as they were at the time of the war. In the case of battlefields, the dispositions of forces have been superimposed on maps depicting the terrain as it was in 1879, and modern roads, railways and buildings have been excluded.

Not all fortifications received official or even standard appellations. In each case we have chosen what seemed the oldest and most descriptive name. Un-named forts are referred to by the names of the historic farms on which they stand, or of historic buildings nearby.

Key to Symbols
IN MODERN SECTOR MAPS

Anglo-Zulu War sites

battlefield	⚔
fortification site with remains	◆
fortification site with doubtful remains	◇
fortification site without remains	+
possible fortification site	○

Features

secondary road	D56
main road	R625
arterial road	R74
freeway	N3
bridge	)(
drift	⊹
pass	∷
town	▭ □ ●
museum	🏛
monument	⚐
mission station	⚐
farmstead	■
mountain	△
boundary	▬ ‥ ▬ ‥ ▬

COAST SECTOR

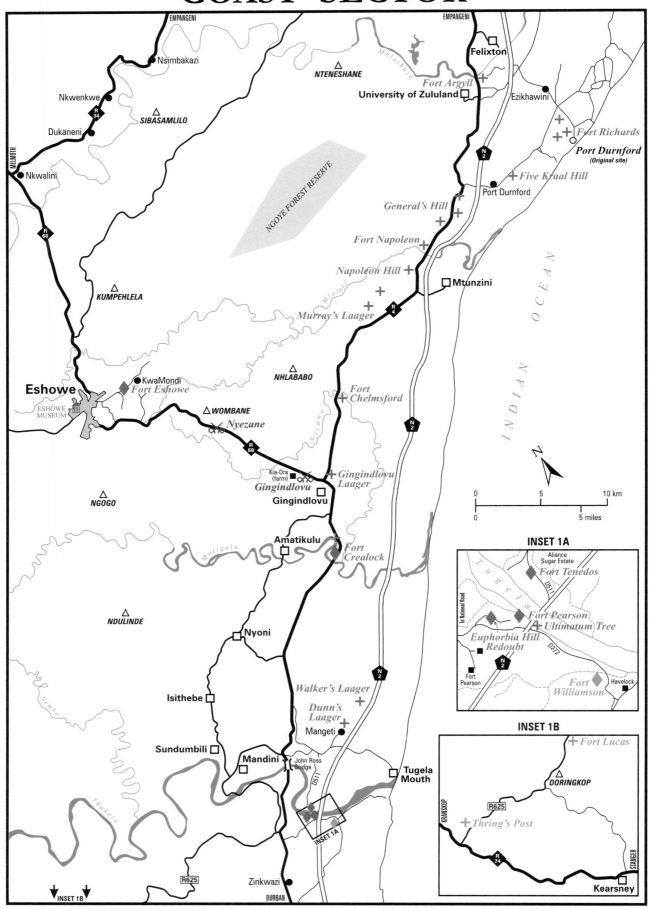

EMPANGENI

EMPANGENI

Felixton

Nsimbakazi

NTENESHANE

Fort Argyll

University of Zululand

Ezikhawini

Nkwenkwe

R34

Fort Richards

SIBASAMLILO

Dukaneni

Port Durnford
(Original site)

Five Kraal Hill

Nkwalini

Port Durnford

NGOYE FOREST RESERVE

General's Hill

R68

Fort Napoleon

KUMPEHLELA

Napoleon Hill

Mtunzini

R4

Murray's Laager

NHLABABO

Fort Chelmsford

Eshowe

KwaMondi
Fort Eshowe

ESHOWE
MUSEUM

△*WOMBANE*

Nyezane

N2

I N D I A N   O C E A N

R68

Kia-Ora
(farm)

Gingindlovu
Laager

Gingindlovu

Gingindlovu

NGOGO

Amatikulu

*Fort
Crealock*

NDULINDE

Nyoni

Isithebe

Walker's Laager

N2

*Dunn's
Laager*

Sundumbili

Mangeti

Mandini

John Ross
Bridge

D511

**Tugela
Mouth**

R625

Zinkwazi

DURBAN

INSET 1B

0   5   10 km

0   5 miles

INSET 1A

Aliance
Sugar Estate

Tugela

Fort Tenedos

D511

To National Road

Fort Pearson

Ultimatum Tree

*Euphorbia Hill
Redoubt*

D272

N2

Fort
Pearson

*Fort
Williamson*

Havelock

INSET 1B

Fort Lucas

KRANSKOP

DORINGKOP

R625

Thring's Post

STANGER

R74

Kearsney

COAST SECTOR
Fortifications

*The 1st Division building up supplies along the track below Fort Pearson
preparatory to crossing the lower Thukela for the second invasion of Zululand.*

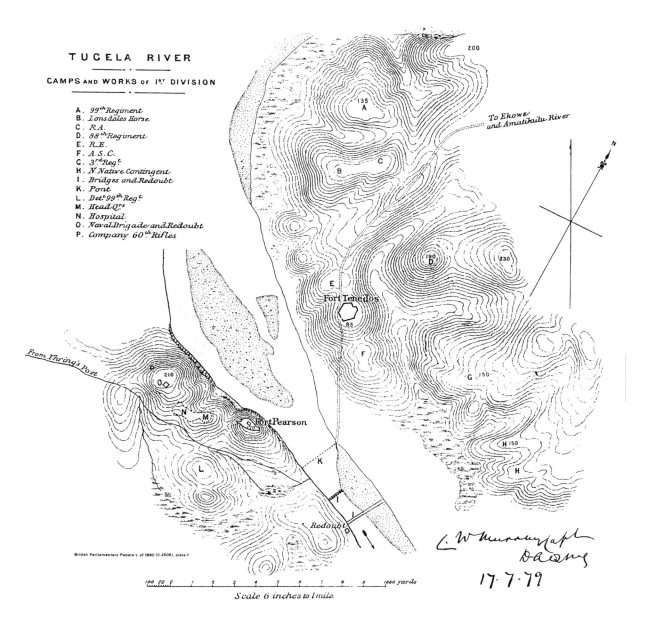

TUGELA RIVER

CAMPS AND WORKS OF 1ST DIVISION

A. 99th Regiment
B. Lonsdale's Horse
C. R.A.
D. 88th Regiment
E. R.E.
F. A.S.C.
G. 3rd Regt
H. N. Native Contingent
I. Bridges and Redoubt
K. Pont
L. Dett 99th Regt
M. Head Qrs
N. Hospital
O. Naval Brigade and Redoubt
P. Company 60th Rifles

To Ekowe
and Amatikulu River

Fort Tenedos

From Thring's Post

Fort Pearson

Redoubt

100 50 0   1   2   3   4   5   6   7   8   9   1000 yards

Scale 6 inches to 1 mile

17·7·79

◆ Along the lower Thukela are the remains of several fortifications. **Fort Williamson,** begun in 1861 and in disrepair by 1870, was designated in October 1878 to receive a garrison from the 2/3rd Regiment (East Kent. The Buffs); however, in November two companies of The Buffs built and garrisoned **Fort Pearson** instead. One of the two small reboubts built near Fort Pearson survives on **Euphorbia Hill,** where the Naval Brigade encamped.

FORT WILLIAMSON

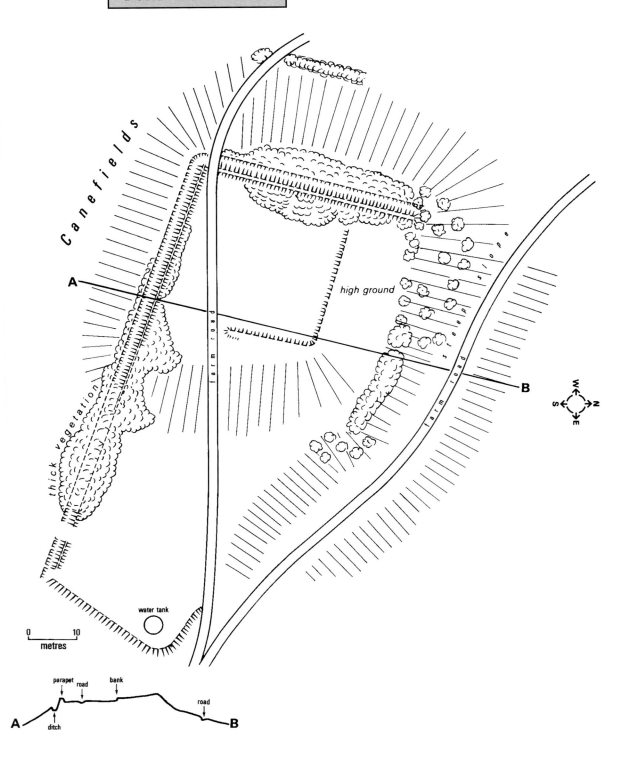

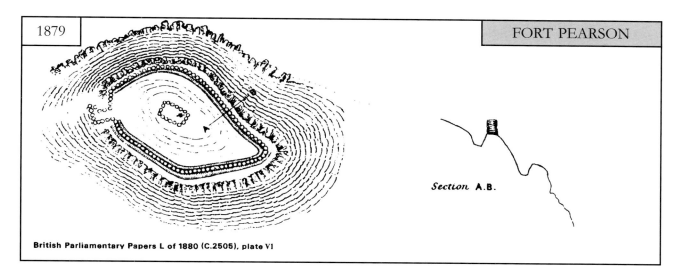

1879

FORT PEARSON

Section A.B.

British Parliamentary Papers L of 1880 (C.2505), plate VI

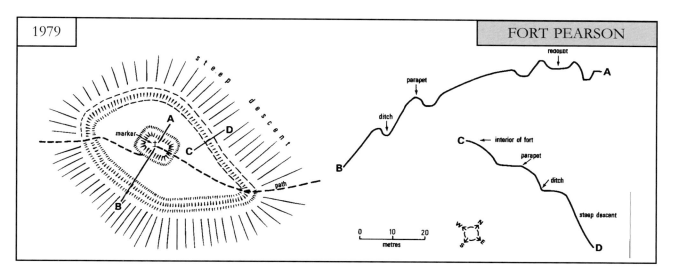

1979

FORT PEARSON

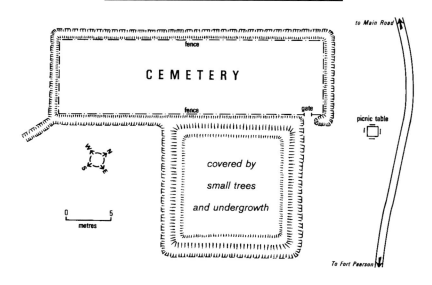

EUPHORBIA HILL REDOUBT

◆ Between 13 and 17 January 1879, No. 1 Column built **Fort Tenedos**. It was subsequently modified and garrisoned by a company of the 99th (Duke of Edinburgh's Lanarkshire) Regiment, followed by two companies of The Buffs from 26 January to 28 March. Contingents of the Naval Brigade also helped in the construction of Forts Pearson and Tenedos, and garrisoned them after the advance of the Eshowe Relief Column. Fort Tenedos was abandoned in July, but a company of the 99th remained at Fort Pearson until the end of September. During April, No. 8 Battery, 7th Brigade, Royal Artillery was stationed at Fort Pearson, and during May at Fort Tenedos.

The earthwork Fort Tenedos, built in January 1879 on the Zulu bank of the Thukela, surrounded by its wire entanglements. Fort Pearson and the camp of the 1st Division can be seen on the bluff across the river.

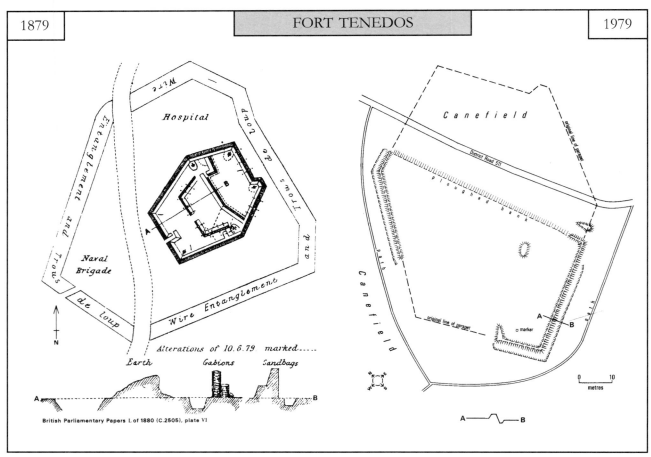

1879   FORT TENEDOS   1979

Fort Eshowe was built by No. 1 Column between 23 and 30 January at the site of the Norwegian mission, and remained under blockade until early April when Lord Chelmsford relieved the garrison. The fort was abandoned on 4 April, but a detachment of the 88th Regiment (Connaught Rangers) was stationed at Eshowe from mid-July to early August.

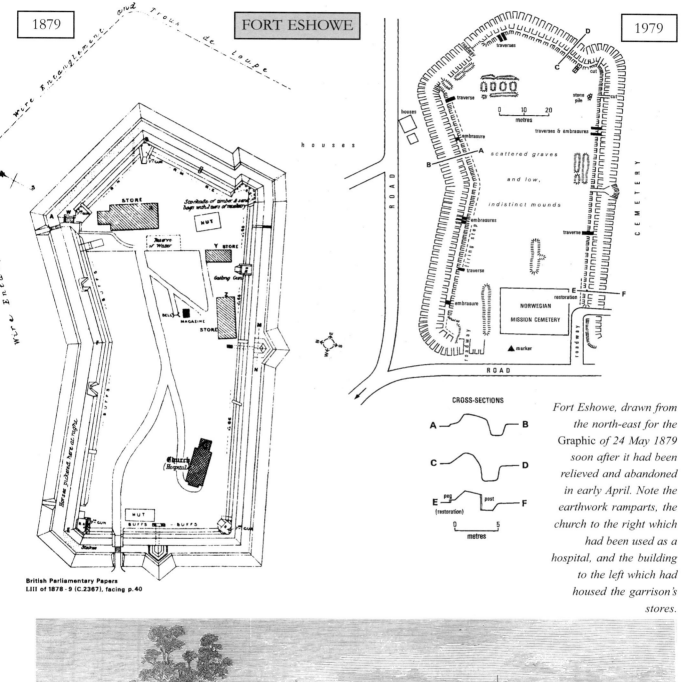

1879

FORT ESHOWE

1979

British Parliamentary Papers
LIII of 1878 - 9 (C.2367), facing p.40

CROSS-SECTIONS

Fort Eshowe, drawn from the north-east for the Graphic *of 24 May 1879 soon after it had been relieved and abandoned in early April. Note the earthwork ramparts, the church to the right which had been used as a hospital, and the building to the left which had housed the garrison's stores.*

Fort Crealock was built on 23 April 1879 by men of the 1st Brigade, 1st Division, South African Field Force as a depot on the Division's line of advance. It was garrisoned by men of the 5th Battalion, Natal Native Contingent; from mid-June by three companies of the 99th; and from late July to early August by No. 8 Battery, 7th Brigade, RA, and a detachment of the 88th.

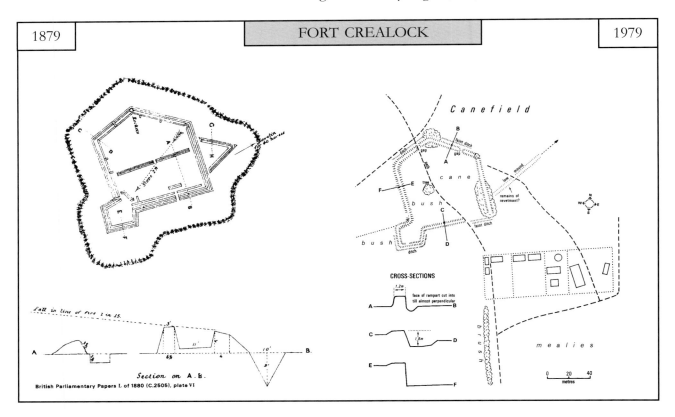

| 1879 | FORT CREALOCK | 1979 |

British Parliamentary Papers L of 1880 (C.2505), plate VI

The earthwork fort at Thring's Post can be made out on the skyline. Men of Capt G.A. Lucas's Border Guard are formed up in column by companies, screened by a line of skirmishers: a classic disposition much easier to maintain on parade than in combat, especially with raw troops.

There are no discernible remains at the site of **Fort Richards**, begun on 1 July by men of the 1st Brigade, 1st Division, but apparently never completed. The erection of pylons has obliterated **Fort Argyll**, an advance post built and garrisoned by troops of the 91st Regiment (Princess Louise's Argyllshire Highlanders) from 24 August to 14 September 1879. The other fortifications constructed by the Eshowe Relief Column and the 1st Division during their advances along the coast have been destroyed by sugar cane and wattle cultivation. The forts were **Chelmsford**, begun on 29 April by the 2nd Brigade, 1st Division, and **Napoleon**, a square redoubt begun on 25 June. The rest were small redoubts (such as the one built on 11 June to defend the semi-permanent trestle and pontoon bridge across the lower Thukela drift), and march-laagers or entrenched camps, of which only a few (**Napoleon Hill** and **Dunn's**, **Murray's**, **Walker's** and the **Gingindlovu** laagers) even received names. **Fort Lucas** and the fort at **Thring's Post**, built during May by the Border Guard, have both disappeared.

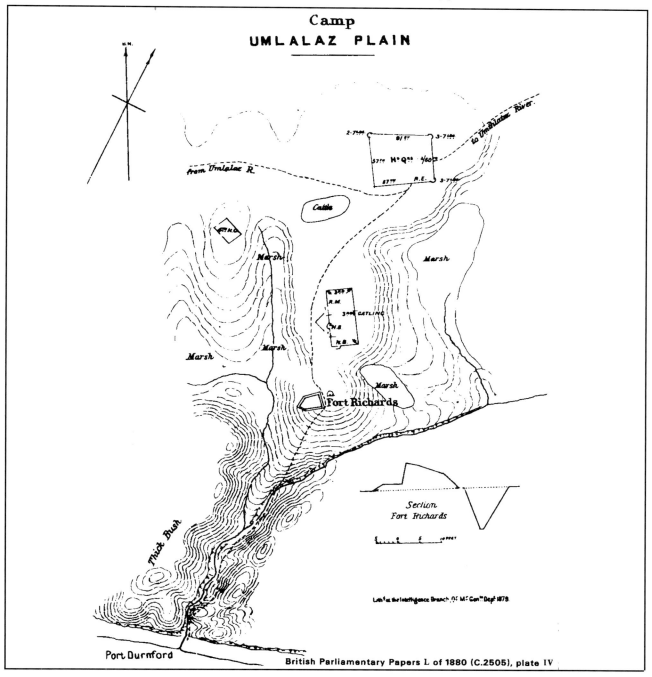

Camp
UMLALAZ PLAIN

British Parliamentary Papers L of 1880 (C.2505), plate IV

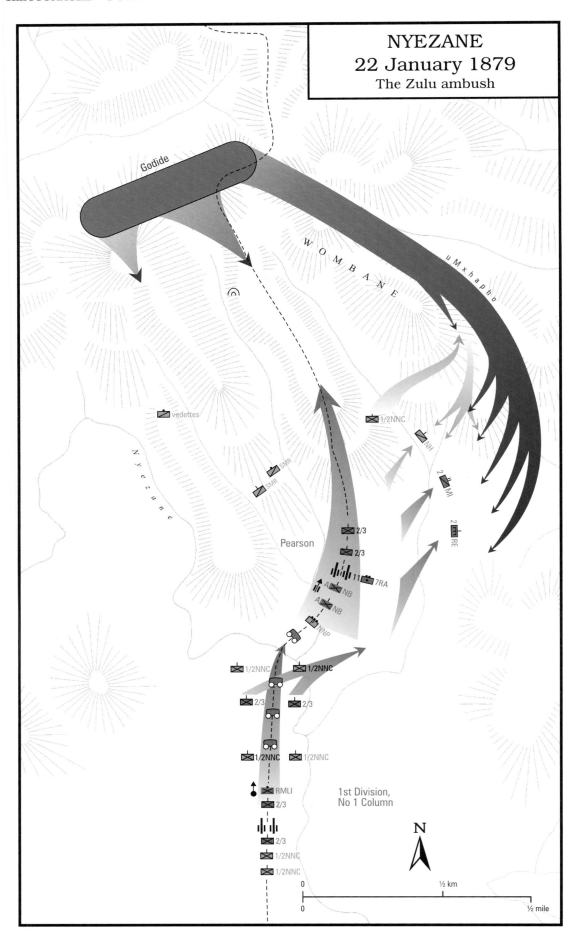

NYEZANE
22 January 1879
The Zulu ambush

Godide

WOMBANE

uMxhapho

Nyezane

vedettes

1/2NNC

SMR

NH

SMR

2 MI

Pearson

2/3

2/3

2 RE

11   7RA

A NB

A NB

NNP

1/2NNC   1/2NNC

2/3   2/3

1/2NNC   1/2NNC

RMLI

2/3

1st Division,
No 1 Column

2/3

1/2NNC

1/2NNC

N

0   ½ km

0   ½ mile

COAST SECTOR
Battle of Nyezane

O n 22 January 1879 (the same day as the battle of Isandlwana) a running fight occurred when No. 1 Column fought through a Zulu ambush laid in the hills to the north of the Nyezane River. The British, advancing from the south, called it the battle of Nyezane, but the Zulu knew it as the battle of Wombane, after the hill that was the key to their position.

The Zulu ambush
The British No. 1 Column under Col Pearson advanced on Eshowe in two divisions. Early on 22 January, the 1st Division halted between the Nyezane River and a range of hills to the north to allow the straggling convoy of 50 wagons and their escort to close up, and to give the men and oxen time to be rested and fed. The 2nd Division was some way to their rear. The British were unaware that the Zulu, under Godide's command, were lying in wait over the skyline of the hills, ready to engage the column in front while sweeping round both flanks to envelop it when it moved along the track following the crest of a low spur running up the heights. On either side of this track the ground fell away steeply to narrow valleys covered with bush, before rising again to high spurs that commanded the route.

At about 08h00 vedettes observed Zulu scouts on Wombane, the eastern of the flanking two hills, and Pearson ordered

a company of 1/2nd NNC forward to disperse them. This movement dislocated Zulu plans, for the uMxhapho *ibutho*, who made up the left horn, were provoked into rushing into the attack before the Zulu of the chest and right horn were ready to commit themselves. The Zulu left horn routed the NNC and then ran down Wombane in five distinct streams straight at the British column. Setting up a heavy, but inaccurate fire, they skirmished in extended order to within 90 yards (100 m) of the dismounted Mounted Infantry and Natal Hussars,

British forces
No. 1 Column
Col C.K. Pearson commanding.

1st Division, No. 1 Column, Col Pearson commanding:
No. 11 Battery, 7th Brigade, Royal Artillery (two 7-pounder guns).
Section of the Royal Marine Light Infantry with two 7-pounders, a Gatling gun and a 24-pounder rocket tube.
No. 2 Company, Royal Engineers.
Naval Brigade's contingent from *HMS Active*.
Six companies of the 2nd Battalion, 3rd Regiment (East Kent. The Buffs).
No. 2 Squadron Mounted Infantry; Natal Hussars; Stanger Mounted Rifles; Victoria Mounted Rifles.
Seven companies of the 1st Battalion, 2nd Regiment, Natal Native Contingent; half a company of No. 2 Company, Natal Native Pioneer Corps.

2nd Division, No. 1 Column (detachment), Lt-Col W.H.D.R. Welman commanding:
Two companies of the 2nd Battalion, 3rd Regiment (East Kent. The Buffs); one company of the 99th (Duke of Edinburgh's Lanarkshire) Regiment.

Total: 73 officers and 2 047 men, of whom 860 were black.

Zulu forces
The crack element of the Zulu force was the major portion of the uMxhapho *ibutho*, which had set off from oNdini on 17 January, accompanied by smaller contingents from the uDlambedlu and izinGulube *amabutho*. On their way through the coastal region they were reinforced by small local elements of the iNsukamngeni, iQwa, uDududu, iNdabakawombe and other *amabutho* still clustered at the coastal *amakhanda*, as well as by numbers of local irregulars. The latter made up about a fifth of the combined Zulu force, which probably numbered close to 6 000 men. Chief Godide kaNdlela of the Ntuli was in command, and his lieutenants included Chief Matshiya kaMshandu of the Nzuzu, Masegwane kaSopigwasi, Cetshwayo's *inceku* (personal attendant and advisor) Mbilwane kaMhlanganiso, *induna* of the nearby kwaGingindlovu *ikhanda*, and Phalane kaMdinwa, *induna* of the Hlangezwa.

British casualties
Killed: 2 white officers, 5 white NCOs and 5 black troops of the NNC; 3 white troops.
Wounded: 1 NNC officer, 13 white troops and an unrecorded number of black NNC troops.

Zulu casualties
The British estimated that about 300 Zulu were killed, though the number could well have been in excess of 400.

'We could distinctly watch the course of the smoking shells, as they flew over the enemy's bush cover and exploded among the trees. Skirmishers, too, peppering away at a terrific rate . . . infantry firing away, piff-piff and faster and faster it went, and then a volley and another volley; not much indication of the enemy's whereabouts by return fire.'

(*Natal Mercury*, February 1879)

and the Royal Engineers who were deployed to repel them in a skirmishing line. Meanwhile, the Zulu chest began to move forward cautiously.

The British counter-attack

Pearson sent forward the troops at the head of the column, consisting of two companies of The Buffs, two companies of the Naval Brigade with their rocket tube, the two Royal Artillery 7-pounder guns and the Natal Native Pioneers. They were joined from the rear of the column by a third company of The Buffs and the Royal Marines section with their Gatling gun. They took up position on a knoll lying to the right of the track a third of the way up the central spur. From there the whole Zulu position could be raked with fire. Meanwhile, the convoy continued to close up and park. When it was sufficiently concentrated, Pearson directed two further companies of The Buffs to deploy to the right of the Royal Engin-eers, leaving a company of The Buffs and the NNC to guard the parked wagons.

The Zulu left horn rapidly withdrew in an orderly manner before the British skirmishing line facing Wombane, but were subjected to damaging fire from the knoll when they were flushed out of the bush on to the open hillside. The Royal Engineers, Mounted Infantry and Natal Hussars moved forward to intercept Zulu attempting to retire across the Nyezane. They were supported from over the river by two companies of The Buffs and one of the 99th, which Col Welman had ordered

forward from the still distant Second Division.

Soon after the retreat of their left horn, the Zulu began belatedly and rather tentatively to advance their right to outflank the British on the opposite side, and occupied the high hill to the west of the road, and an *umuzi* about 440 yards (402 m) from the knoll. There they were pinned down by the Stanger and Victoria Mounted Rifles and a small party of vedettes, while the *umuzi* was set alight by rocket fire. The Naval Brigade, supported by a company of The Buffs, and with a body of the NNC to their left, charged the Zulu concentrated at the burning *umuzi*. After a temporary check and several casualties, they succeeded in gaining possession of the high ground to the west of the Eshowe road, dispersing the Zulu right horn. The Naval Brigade and The Buffs next proceeded to clear the heights beyond the *umuzi* still held by the Zulu chest, and then to take the dominating crest of Wombane. The loss of Wombane, the key to their position, caused the Zulu to disperse rapidly, in comparatively good order, down the far side. British gun and rocket fire broke up any groups that attempted to re-form, and the last shots died away about 09h30.

Zulu non-combatants had watched the battle from the surrounding hills, and the majority of the defeated Zulu force gathered on a hill 4 miles (6.4 km) from the battlefield and remained there while the British halted to attend to their casualties. They dispersed at noon when the British column resumed its advance on Eshowe.

'The battle was so fierce that we had to wipe the blood and brains of the killed and wounded from our heads, faces, arms, legs and shields after the fighting.'

(Chief Zimema of the uMxhapho *ibutho*, 22 January 1929)

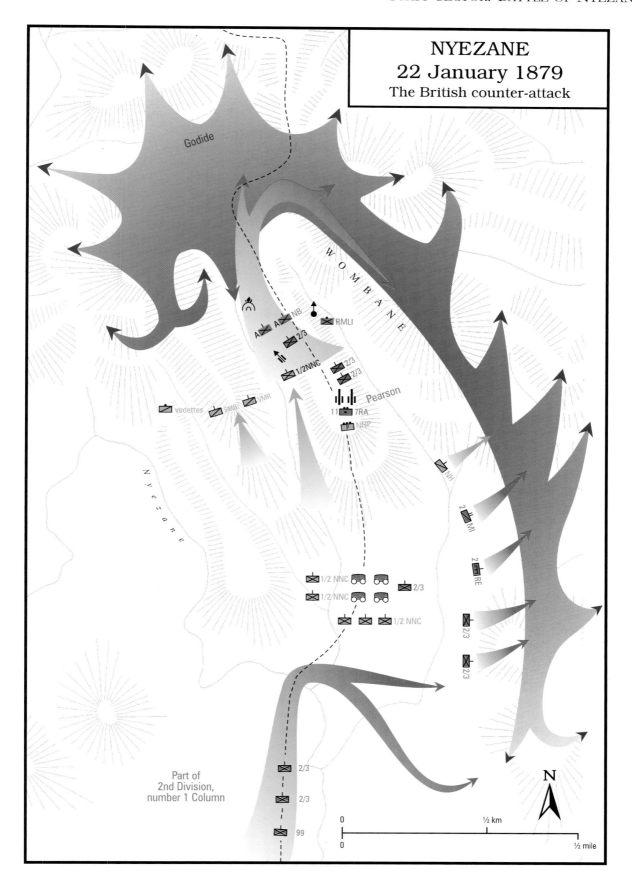

NYEZANE
22 January 1879
The British counter-attack

Godide

W O M B A N E

N y e z a n e

NB
A A
RMLI
2/3
1/2NNC
2/3
2/3
vedettes SMR VMR
Pearson
11 7RA
P NNP
NH
2 MI
2 RE
1/2 NNC
1/2 NNC 2/3
1/2 NNC
2/3
2/3

Part of
2nd Division,
number 1 Column

2/3

2/3

99

N

0 ½ km
0 ½ mile

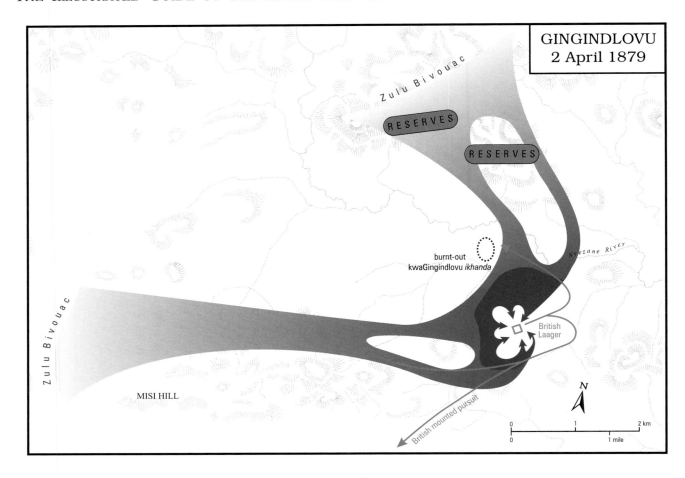

GINGINDLOVU
2 April 1879

Zulu Bivouac

RESERVES

RESERVES

Nsezane River

burnt-out
kwaGingindlovu *ikhanda*

British
Laager

Zulu Bivouac

MISI HILL

N

British mounted pursuit

0   1   2 km

0   1 mile

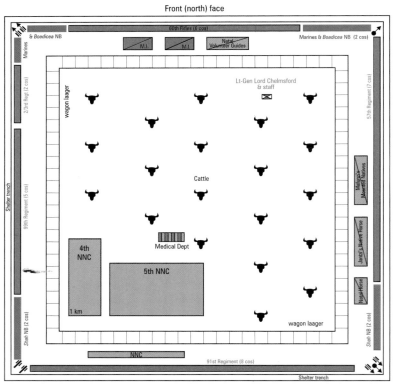

Front (north) face

60th Rifles (6 cos)

& *Boadicea* NB

Marines & *Boadicea* NB (2 cos)

Marines

M.I.   M.I.   Natal
Volunteer Guides

wagon laager

2/3rd Regt (2 cos)

Lt-Gen Lord Chelmsford
& staff

57th Regiment (7 cos)

Shelter trench

99th Regiment (5 cos)

Cattle

Mafunzi's
Mounted Natives

Jantzi's Mounted Horse

Medical Dept

Natal Horse

4th
NNC

5th NNC

1 km

wagon laager

Sheh NB (2 cos)

Sheh NB (2 cos)

NNC

91st Regiment (8 cos)

Shelter trench

THE BRITISH LAAGER

COAST SECTOR

Battle of Gingindhlovu

In a set piece battle on 2 April 1879 near the burned-out kwaGingindlovu *ikhanda*, the Eshowe Relief Column, secure within its wagon laager, repulsed an attack by the Zulu forces that had been blockading the British garrison in Eshowe.

The British laager

On 1 April the Eshowe Relief Column constructed a wagon laager on a slight knoll south of the Nyezane River. It was about 130 yards (119 m) square to give sufficient room inside for the 2 000 oxen, 300 horses and 2 280 black troops. During combat the 3 390 white troops would man two-deep the enclosing shelter-trench, which was about 156 yards (143 m) square and about 15 yards (14 m) in front of the wagons, and marksmen would be stationed along the tops of the wagons. The corners were reinforced by the 9-pounder guns, Gatling guns and rocket tubes.

The Zulu deployment

That night, the Zulu forces previously bivouacked around Eshowe steadily concentrated in the vicinity of the laager. The British stood to arms at 04h00 on 2 April, and at 05h45 the Zulu were reported to be advancing to the attack. At 06h00 the Zulu on the far side of the Nyezane, and on top of Misi Hill to the west, came in sight of the laager. Swarms of skirmishers drove in the British picquets and mounted scouts. A strong Zulu column crossed the

British forces
Eshowe Relief Column
Lt-Gen Lord Chelmsford commanding.
1st Brigade, Eshowe Relief Column, Lt-Col F.T.A. Law commanding:
Naval Brigade Artillery from *HMS Shah* and *Tenedos* (two 9-pounder guns, two 24-pounder rocket tubes and one Gatling gun).
Naval Brigade's contingents from *HMS Shah* and *Tenedos*.
91st Regiment (Princess Louise's Argyllshire Highlanders); two companies of the 2nd Battalion, 3rd Regiment (East Kent. The Buffs); five companies of the 99th (Duke of Edinburgh's Lanarkshire) Regiment.
4th Battalion, Natal Native Contingent.

Total: 1 770 white officers and men and 800 black troops.

2nd Brigade, Eshowe Relief Column, Lt-Col W.L. Pemberton commanding:
Naval Brigade Artillery from *HMS Boadicea* (two 24-pounder rocket tubes and one Gatling gun).
Naval Brigade's contingent from *HMS Boadicea*; detachments of Royal Marines from *HMS Boadicea* and *Shah*.
57th (West Middlesex) Regiment; six Companies of the 3rd Battalion, 60th Regiment (The King's Royal Rifle Corps).
5th Battalion, Natal Native Contingent.

Total: 1 470 white officers and men and 1 200 black troops.

Divisional Troops, Maj P.H.S. Barrow commanding:
Mounted Infantry; Jantzi's Native Horse; Mafunzi's Mounted Natives; No. 1 Troop, Natal Horse; Natal Volunteer Guides.
Native Foot Scouts.

Total: 150 white mounted troops, 130 black mounted troops and 150 Foot Scouts.

Zulu forces
Individual Zulu units' positions have not been ascertained. The overall commander was Somopho kaZikhala, *induna* of the emaNgweni *ikhanda*, and the force numbered between 10 000 and 11 000 men, or 180 *amaviyo*. It comprised several elements that had been concentrated in the vicinity of Fort Eshowe. Somopho personally commanded a contingent of 3 000 irregulars, made up mainly from Tsonga and neighbouring people from up the coast in the region of St Lucia Bay, as well as 1 500 of the coastal elements of *amabutho* connected to the kwaGingindlovu *ikhanda*. They had been bivouacked along the Nyezane River. Sigcwelegcwele kaMhlekehleke, *induna* of the iNgobamakhosi *ibutho*, and Phalane kaMdinwa, *induna* of the Hlangwezwa, were Somopho's principal lieutenants, and had joint command over the 3 000 members of the iNgobamakhosi, uMcijo, uNokhenke and uMbonambi *amabutho* who had been barracked at the old oNdini *ikhanda*, and also over 1 500 of the iNdulyengwe at the isinPuseleni *ikhanda* nearby. Prince Dabulamanzi kaMpande brought the 1 000 local warriors that had been stationed at eNtumeni, and commanded the right horn during the battle. Other local notables were present, including Masegwane kaSopigwasi, and Mbilwane kaMhlanganiso (both commanders at Nyezane), Chief Mavumengwana kaNdlela of the Ntuli, and Sintwangu, Cetshwayo's *inceku* and messenger.

British casualties
Killed: 2 officers, 7 white troops and 5 black troops.
Wounded: 4 officers, 26 white troops and 17 black troops.

Zulu casualties
Some 470 Zulu were buried within 500 yards (457 m) of the laager, 250 of them who had fallen in front of the western and southern faces. A further 200 dead were found nearby. Many more lay within a radius of 5 miles (8 km), along the Zulu line of flight, especially along the banks of the Nyezane where the wounded had been abandoned to the NNC by their fleeing comrades. It seems probable that the Zulu lost nearly 1 200 men.

Lt-Col Crealock was slightly wounded in the battle of Gingindlovu on 2 April 1879. His sketch of the engagement shows the Zulu advancing across the Nyezane River from the hills to the north. Note the crush of oxen within the laager.

Nyezane, the left division (or left horn) advancing at the north-east corner of the laager, where it could take advantage of some dead ground, and the right (or chest) at its northern face. Slightly later, a somewhat weaker column (the right horn) came forward from north of Misi Hill, one part confronting the western face of the laager and the other the southern. The Zulu deployed in open order and at the double, while two large bodies of reserves waited on the hills beyond the Nyezane. Once the enveloping Zulu crescent was in position, the Zulu broke into three distinct lines and advanced on the laager in knots of 5 to 10 men, taking every advantage of the cover. At a distance of about 750 yards (686 m) they opened up a brisk but ineffective fire.

The attack on the laager

The Gatling guns began the engagement at 1 100-yard (1 006-m) range, and firing became general when the Zulu were within 350 or 450 yards (320 or 411 m) of the laager. Despite several desperate charges, the Zulu were unable to break through the concentrated British fire – even though this was not nearly as effective and accurate as it might have been because of the inexperience of many of the troops – and never came closer than 20 yards (18 m) of the shelter trench.

The men of the 60th Rifles manning the north face wavered badly under attack, and had to be rallied. The crisis passed, and at 06h40 the Zulu chest confronting them began to retire into the long grass. Chelmsford ordered Barrow's Mounted Infantry and Natal Volunteer Guides out of the north side of the laager

in pursuit, but the Zulu rallied and drove them back. The chest then circled to their right to reinforce the left division of the right horn attacking the laager's western face. Meanwhile, at 07h00, the right division of the right horn began a determined assault on the laager's southern face under Dabulamanzi's leadership. Chelmsford ordered two companies of the 60th out of the north face in support of the hard-pressed 91st. Dabulamanzi's attack stalled under the heavy fire, rolling around for a brief and unsuccessful attempt at the eastern face of the laager.

The British sortie and pursuit

With the Zulu pinned down everywhere, Chelmsford directed Barrow and all the mounted men to sortie out of the laager's unengaged eastern face to push them into a retreat. Barrow, with half the Mounted Infantry and the Natal Native Horse in support, charged the flank of the wavering Zulu right horn causing it to retreat. Barrow kept up pursuit for about 1.5 miles (2.4 km) towards Misi Hill and southwards towards the Matigulu River. Meanwhile, the rest of the Mounted Infantry and the Natal Volunteer Guides wheeled left to attack the Zulu retiring from the north face of the laager, and followed them up towards the burnt-out kwaGingindlovu *ikhanda* and the flooded Nyezane beyond. At 07h15 the NNC advanced out of the southern side of the laager to mop up behind the mounted men, and kill the Zulu wounded. In case the Zulu retreat was a feint, Chelmsford ordered all the other troops to remain in the laager. But the Zulu had suffered enough. Their reserves on the hills be-

yond the Nyezane also retreated when they saw their army in flight, and fire from the 9-pounders dispersed those from the right horn who attempted to rally on Misi Hill. An hour and a half after the Zulu were first sighted across the Nyezane, Chelmsford ordered the ceasefire sounded.

In S. Durand's portrayal of the battle of Gingingdlovu for the Graphic *of 17 May 1879, soldiers of the 91st Highlanders are shown moving out of the wagon-laager to reinforce the firing-line. Colonial wagon-drivers, many of whom were experienced hunters, are firing with telling accuracy at the Zulu from the wagons over the heads of the troops.*

DUNDEE SECTOR

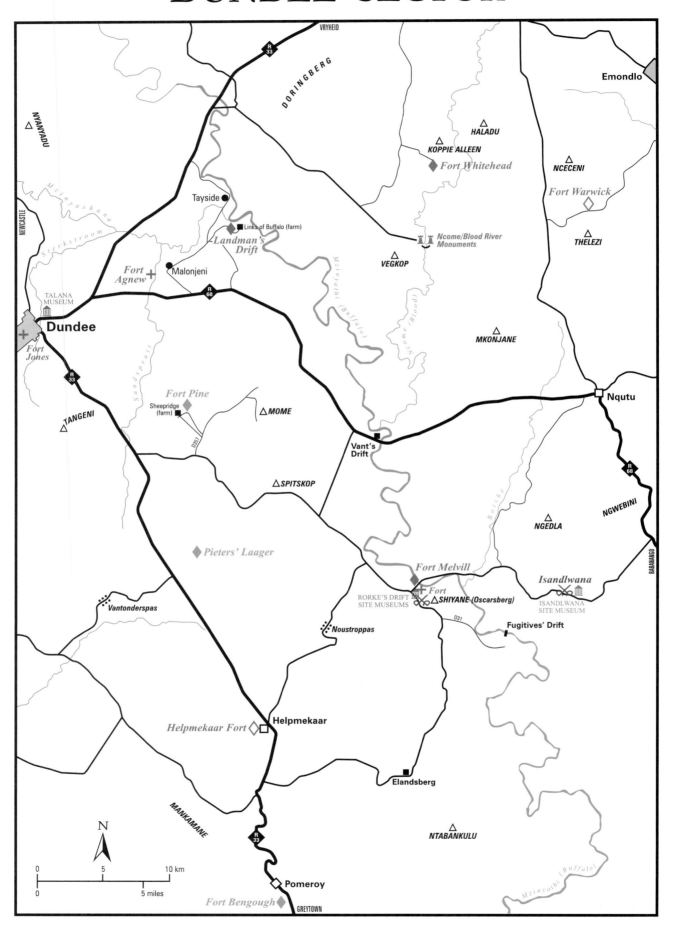

DUNDEE SECTOR
Fortifications

◆ **Fort Pine**, was initially called the Dundee Laager, and was intended as a post for the Natal Mounted Police. When the Buffalo Border Guard made it their headquarters it was named after a former lieutenant-governor of Natal, Sir Benjamin Pine. Its construction in 1878 took nine months, although the interior buildings had still to be completed when the war broke out. Settlers began to come in then, and after Isandlwana the fort was entirely filled with Boer wagons and tents. There were insufficient men among the occupants to guard the walls effectively, and these the local field cornet found difficult to organize. So on 7 February 1879 the Buffalo Border Guard and the Newcastle Mounted Rifles were sent to garrison the fort. They remained there until July, though by May most of the settlers had abandoned it. The war-time fort was described as 'an open square, with walls 14-ft (4.2-m) high, with loopholes'. After the war much was added, as the diagram indicates.

> ' The laager at Fort Pine . . . is entirely filled with Boer wagons and tents; and with such a lot of people, including children of all ages, and every family slaughtering their own meat, you can imagine what sort of place it is.'
> (*Natal Colonist*, 20 Feb 1879)

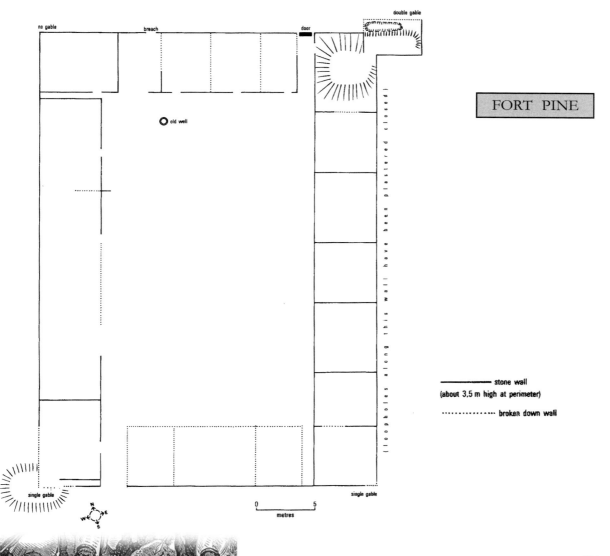

FORT PINE

——— stone wall
(about 3,5 m high at perimeter)

·············· broken down wall

Pieters' Laager (sometimes called the Paddafontein Laager) was built before the end of 1877 by local farmers, though its walls still needed to be heightened and loopholed. Reports of 1878 are not clear on whether these finishing-touches were made. At the outbreak of the war there were at least 12 wagons at the laager, but no report has been found of it's use subsequently. After the war it was apparently known as 'Klipkraal Laager'.

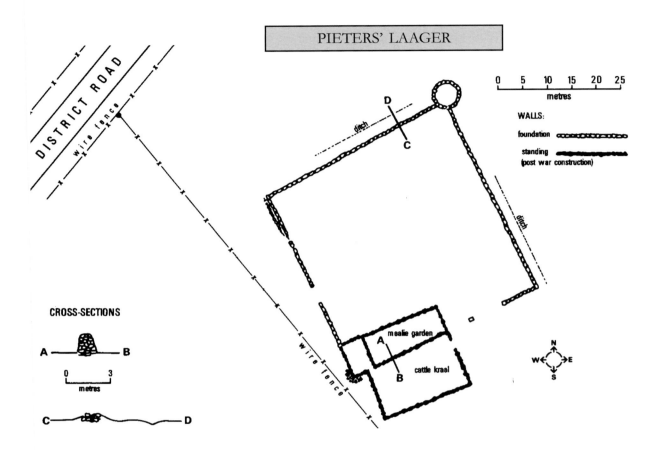

Fort Bengough was built during the fortnight after Isandlwana and garrisoned by the 2nd Battalion, Natal Native Contingent, commanded by Maj H.M. Bengough. The central, square section was the magazine. The white officers camped in one of the flanking sections, their black troops in the other.

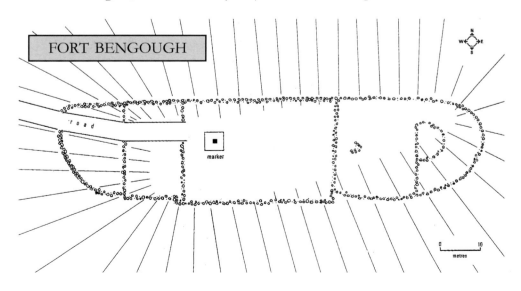

◆ **Fort Melvill**, built between March and May 1879 by detachments of the 2/24th (2nd Warwickshire) Regiment and the 2nd Battalion, NNC, under the direction of Lt R.daC. Porter, RE, superseded the fortified mission station as the Rorke's Drift base. It was named after Lt Teignmouth Melvill of the 1/24th, who had fallen during the Isandlwana rout while attempting to save the Queen's Colour from capture. Various companies of the 2/24th under Lt-Col W. Black garrisoned the fort until August, when a company of the 99th (Duke of Edinburgh's Lanarkshire) Regiment took the post.

FORT MELVILL

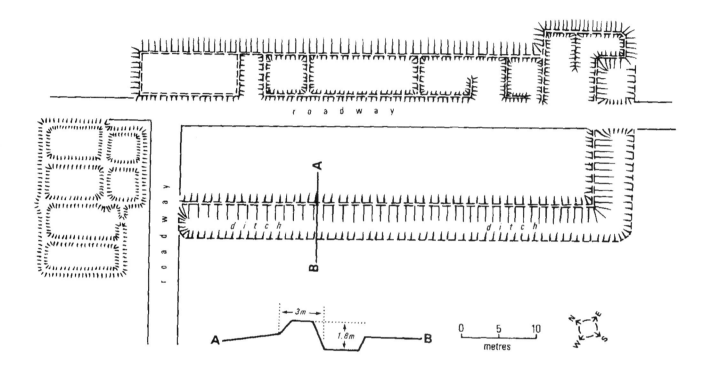

r o a d w a y

ditch   ditch

← 3m →

1.8m

0   5   10
metres

Fort Melvill photographed in about 1879 and showing its commanding position above the pont over the Mzinyathi (Buffalo) River.

At **Landman's Drift**, where the 2nd Division, South African Field Force, massed in May 1879 and formed a depot, three earthen forts were built end to end to each other, in a kind of echelon with about 50 yards (46 m) between each. Only one has survived. However, there is another feature nearby which may be the remains of a small redoubt, possibly built later by a detachment of the 2/24th, which garrisoned the post until September.

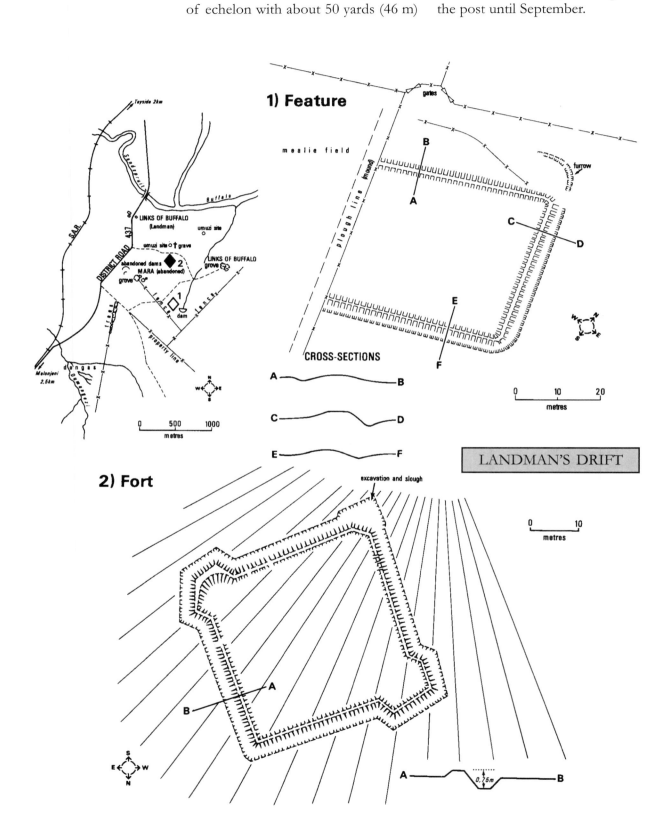

1) Feature

CROSS-SECTIONS

2) Fort

LANDMAN'S DRIFT

At Koppie Alleen, to which the 2nd Division advanced late in May, the 58th (Rutlandshire) Regiment began **Fort Whitehead,** named after their colonel, on 28 May. After the 2nd Division moved on, companies of the 2/24th garrisoned the fort.

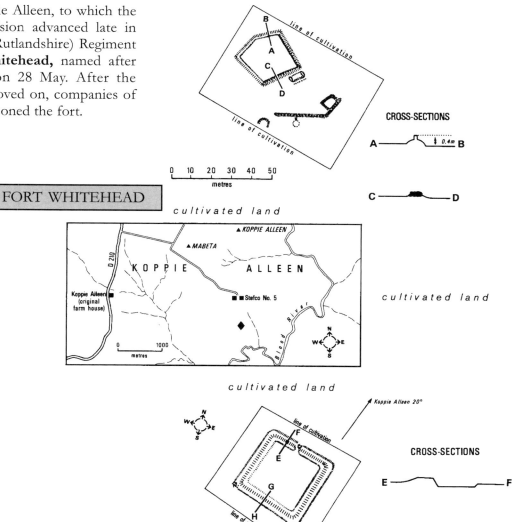

FORT WHITEHEAD

CROSS-SECTIONS

Fort Warwick, a small and now apparently very mutilated earthwork on the advancing 2nd Division's line of communication to Koppie Alleen, was built in June 1879 by a company of the 2/24th, under Capt J.J. Harvey.

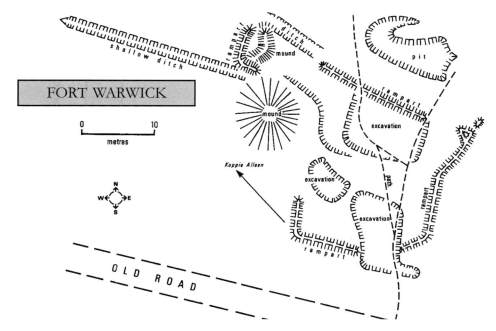

FORT WARWICK

◇ The depot of the Centre Column during the first invasion of Zululand was at **Helpmekaar.** An entrenched laager formed there on the night of Isandlwana was replaced during the following few weeks by a strong earthwork fort, built by the 5th Company, Royal Engineers, under Capt W. Parke Jones, and men of the 2/4th (King's Own Royal) Regiment. It was garrisoned throughout the war by companies of the 1/24th and a variety of other units. There still seem to be some traces of this fort.

HELPMEKAAR FORT

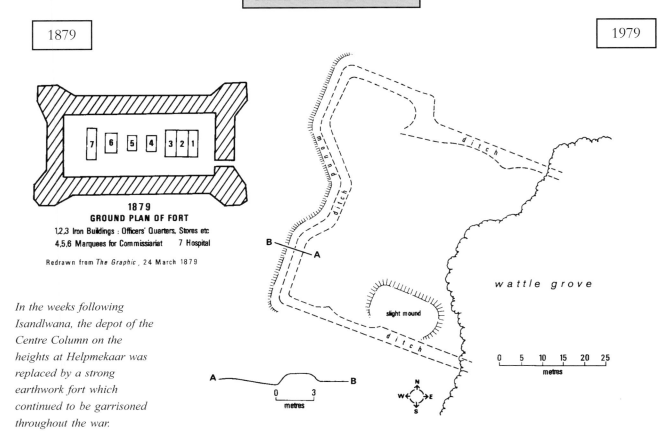

1879

1979

1879
GROUND PLAN OF FORT
1,2,3 Iron Buildings : Officers' Quarters, Stores etc.
4,5,6 Marquees for Commissariat   7 Hospital

Redrawn from *The Graphic*, 24 March 1879

In the weeks following Isandlwana, the depot of the Centre Column on the heights at Helpmekaar was replaced by a strong earthwork fort which continued to be garrisoned throughout the war.

Fort Jones, built early in May for the protection of the 2nd Division's depot at Dundee, was garrisoned by companies of the 2/24th, under Lt-Col H.J. Degacher, has disappeared with the expansion of the town. **Fort Agnew**, which appears on a wartime map, was probably never built. No mention of it in 1879 has been found and no traces of a fort exist on the site. The improvised defences that were thrown up at the mission station at **Rorke's Drift** before the battle, were replaced within a few weeks by a stone-walled and loopholed enclosure connecting the remains of the mission buildings and the cattle-kraal. It was built by companies of the 2/24th who garrisoned it until they removed to Fort Melvill. Within three years of the war no readily recognisable vestiges of the fortifications were to be seen.

Fort Jones and the camp of the 2nd Division at Dundee, sketched by Melton Prior for the Illustrated London News *of 12 July 1879. Note the three galvanised iron commissariat sheds within the fort. They had been removed from the fort at Helpmekaar when, with the mounting of the second invasion in April, it had ceased to be an important depot. The* umuzi *in the foreground has been very accurately observed.*

DUNDEE SECTOR

Battle of Isandlwana

The most commemorated battle of the war was fought at Isandlwana where, on 22 January 1879, the Zulu army outmanoeuvred the British Centre Column and gained a great victory.

British and Zulu movements
21 January

On 20 January the British No. 3 Column reached its campsite at the eastern base of Isandlwana Hill. The position was difficult to defend in that it was overlooked by a spur of the Nyoni hills some 1 000 yards (914 m) to the north, and the layout of the camp was overly extended. But since Lord Chelmsford regarded the camp as temporary, and considered no Zulu attack likely, no attempt was made to entrench it, nor to laager the wagons, which were required to bring up supplies from Rorke's Drift. On the same day the Zulu army bivouacked at Siphezi Hill, 12.5 miles (20 km) east of Isandlwana. Chelmsford had no idea of the whereabouts of the Zulu army. He believed that Chief Matshana kaMondisa of the Sithole was gathering a force to the southeast in the region of the Qudeni bush and the Mangeni River to interrupt his column's line of supply once it advanced further into Zululand. Accordingly, on 21 January he sent out a reconnaissance-in-force in that direction consisting of most of the Natal Mounted Police and half the Natal Mounted Volunteers (150 men) under Maj Dartnell, and 16 companies (about 1 600 men) of the

British forces

No. 2 Column (detachment), Brev Col A.W. Durnford, RE, commanding:
No. 11 Battery, 7th Brigade, RA (Rocket Battery: three 9-pounder rocket-troughs): Brev Maj F.B. Russell, RA.
Natal Native Horse: Capt G. Barton:
No. 1 Troop Sikali's Horse, Lt C. Raw; No. 2 Troop Sikali's Horse, Lt J.A. Roberts; No. 3 Troop Sikali's Horse, Lt R.W. Vause; Edendale Troop, Lt H.D. Davies; Hlubi's Troop, Lt A.F. Henderson.
1st Battalion, 1st Regiment Natal Native Contingent:
D Company, Capt C. Nourse; E Company, Capt W.R. Stafford.

No. 3 Column (detachment), Brev Col H.B. Pulleine, 1/24th Foot, commanding:
N Battery, 5th Brigade, RA (division of two 7-pounder guns): Brev Maj S. Smith.
5th (Field) Company, RE (advance party).
1st Battalion, 24th (2nd Warwickshire) Regiment: Capt W. Degacher (Acting Major):
A Company, Lt C.W. Cavaye; C Company, Capt R. Younghusband; E Company, Lt F.P. Porteous; F Company, Capt W.E. Mostyn; H Company, Capt G.V. Wardell.
2nd Battalion, 24th (2nd Warwickshire) Regiment:
G Company, Lt C.D.A. Pope.
Details of 90th Regiment (Perthshire Volunteers Light Infantry) (attached 1/24th); Army Service Corps; Army Hospital Corps.
No. 1 Squadron Mounted Infantry.
Natal Mounted Police.
Natal Volunteer Corps: Natal Carbineers, Lt F.J.D. Scott; Newcastle Mounted Rifles, Capt C.R. Bradstreet; Buffalo Border Guard, Quartermaster D. McPhail.
1st Battalion, 3rd Regiment, Natal Native Contingent:
No. 6 Company, Capt R. Krohn; No. 9 Company, Capt J.F. Lonsdale;
2nd Battalion, 3rd Regiment, Natal Native Contingent:
No. 4 Company, Capt E. Erskine; No. 5 Company, Capt A.J. Barry.
Natal Native Pioneer Corps: No. 1 Company (details).

Total: 67 officers; 1 707 men, of whom approximately half were African.

Zulu forces

Nearly 20 000 Zulu under Chief Ntshingwayo kaMahole of the Khoza and Chief Mavumengwana kaNdlela of the Ntuli attacked the British camp at Isandlwana, while a further 3 000 to 4 000, who made up the reserve and were not engaged, went on to attack Rorke's Drift. In combat the army was deployed as follows: right horn – uDududu, iSangqu, iMbube and uNokhenke; centre – uMcijo and uMxhapho; left horn – uMbonambi, iNgobamakhosi and uVe; reserve – uThulwana, iNdluyengwe, iNdlondlo and uDloko.

British casualties

Killed: 52 officers; 739 white troops; 67 white NCOs of the NNC. 471 black troops (including non-combatants) were recorded as killed, though the number was probably closer to 500.

Zulu casualties

The Zulu either removed their dead from the battlefield, or buried them in dongas, antbear holes or the mealie-pits of nearby *imizi*. Most of the wounded who reached their homes would have died of their bullet-wounds. It is therefore not known precisely how many Zulus died, but the number was probably no less than 1 000. A great many men of high status were among the fallen.

A photograph believed to be of Chief Ntshingwayo kaMahole Khoza, induna *of the kwaGqikazi* ikhanda *and senior of the two commanders of the Zulu army at Isandlwana.*

'We saw a small body of Volunteers . . . gallop up to within eight hundred yards of them [about 1 000 Zulu massed on Magogo], when instantly, and with beautiful precision, two companies of the enemy opened out into skirmishing order, the flanks at the double, and tried to surround the party.'

(*Natal Mercury*, supplement, January 1879)

'Every field glass was levelled at the camp. The sun was shining brightly on the white tents but all seemed quiet. No signs of firing or an engagement could be seen, and although bodies of men moving about could be distinguished, yet they were not unnaturally supposed to be our own troops. The time was now 1.45 p.m. and not the faintest idea of disaster had occurred to us.'

(Charles Norris-Newman, 1880)

two battalions of the 3rd Regiment, Natal Native Contingent, under Cmdt R. Lonsdale. A Zulu force of up to 2 000 men under Matshana skilfully retired eastwards before the joint force, and by evening were massed on the Magogo heights. When Dartnell's mounted troops attempted to approach them, the Zulu deployed into two horns in skirmishing order, and the mounted men had to withdraw to avoid being enveloped. To forestall an advance by this Zulu force on Isandlwana, Dartnell's joint force bivouacked for the night in a square on the Hlazakazi heights, across the valley from the Magogo heights.

The Zulu commanders, Chiefs Ntshingwayo and Mavumengwana, who had originally considered a flank march down the Mangeni valley to the Mzinyathi River to cut off Chelmsford from Natal, apparently decided to take advantage of Chelmsford's division of his forces. They detached more men to reinforce Matshana, and during the evening of 21 January moved the main army from Siphezi to the Ngwebeni valley, which was concealed from Isandlwana by the Nyoni heights 9 miles (14 km) to the southwest. The Zulu moved in small units, taking every advantage of the terrain so that British mounted patrols did not grasp that a whole army was on the move. They bivouacked along the Ngwebeni with the uNokhenke, uMcijo, uDududu, iSangqu

and iMbube *amabutho* on the right facing Isandlwana. The iNgobamakhosi, uVe and uMbonambi formed the centre, and the uDloko, uThulwana, iNdluyengwe and iNdlondlo the left. The *amabutho* were fresh for they had advanced slowly and were adequately fed.

Chelmsford's forces' movements 22 January

Around midnight on 21/22 January there was a panic among the NNC of the British reconnaissance force on Hlazakazi, and Dartnell sent Chelmsford a note – which the General received at 01h30 – urgently requesting support. Col Glyn, accompanied by Chelmsford, accordingly advanced at 04h30 on 22 January with four out of the six guns of the battery, six companies of the 2nd Battalion of the 24th (2nd Warwickshire) Regiment, Mounted Infantry and Pioneers. Chelmsford left the camp with a garrison of two guns, five companies of the 1/24th and one of the 2/24th, the remainder of the mounted troops and four companies of the 3rd NNC. He also ordered up Col Durnford from Rorke's Drift with the available men of the No. 2 Column to reinforce the camp. Until he arrived, Lt-Col Pulleine would be the senior officer at Isandlwana, and his orders (it seems) were to act strictly on the defensive.

When Glyn's force reached Hlazakazi at about 06h00, the main body of Zulu on Magogo had moved onto the Phindo and Silutshana heights, and Dartnell's men soon became involved in a heavy skirmish on the Phindo heights where Matshana had his stronghold. The Zulu, though, were generally making an orderly withdrawal north-east towards Siphezi, with the consequence that Chelmsford's forces were being drawn ever further from the threatened camp at Isandlwana. Meanwhile, Chelmsford used the morning to find a suitable new campsite for his column on the Mangeni. At 09h30 he received a message from Pulleine that Zulu were advancing on the camp. Lt Milne of his staff studied the camp through a telescope but saw nothing untoward (the shoulder of Silutshana cut off the view of the plain east of Isandlwana). Satisfied

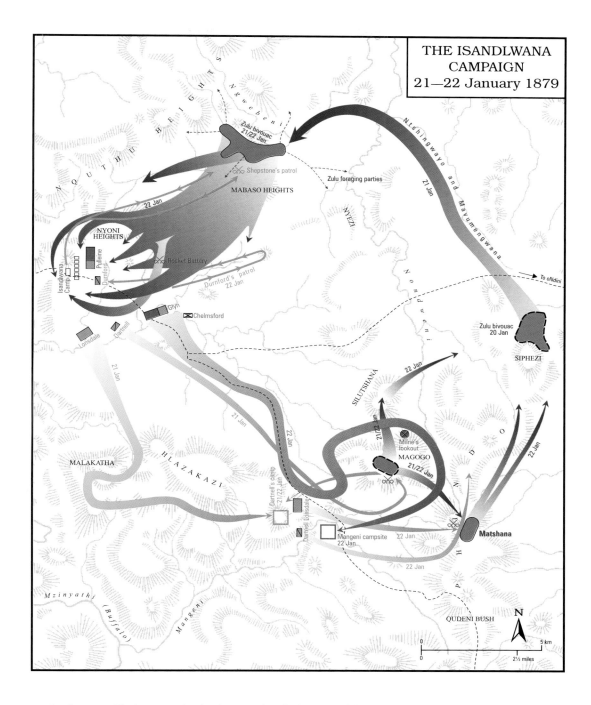

THE ISANDLWANA
CAMPAIGN
21—22 January 1879

that the camp was not in danger, Chelmsford rode off between 10h30 and 12h30 to scout the area, and almost all subsequent messages relating to Isandlwana failed to find him. Having settled on a suitable campsite on the Mangeni, he ordered Glyn's force to concentrate there. From the campsite Chelmsford and his staff examined the Isandlwana camp with their field glasses and assumed that the Zulu attack (if there had been one) had been successfully beaten off. It was only at 14h45 that the General eventually decided to return to Isandlwana with a small escort to investigate, and on the way he was informed that in his absence the Zulu had overrun the camp. Convinced at last, he ordered the forces concentrating at the Mangeni campsite to march to the relief of the Isandlwana

Isandlwana Hill and the camp of No. 3 Column sketched on 20 January 1879 by Lt-Col Crealock. Note the fresh green of the grass, grown high after the late summer rains. Isandlwana means 'something like a small house', which in how the Zulu perceived the mountain. To the British, it resembled the sphinx on the bulge of the 24th Regiment.

'A small herd of cattle came past our line from the right, being driven by some of our scouts, and just when they were opposite the uMcijo regiment a body of mounted men appeared on the hill to the west, galloping up, evidently trying to cut them off. When several hundred yards off they saw the uMcijo and dismounting . . . fired one volley at them and retired. The uMcijo at once jumped up and charged.'

('Zulu Deserter', February 1879)

garrison 7 miles (11 km) away. It was only by 18h30 that Chelmsford was able to gather all his scattered forces within 3 miles (5 km) of Isandlwana. He advanced in darkness with the mounted men in front, the guns in the centre with three companies of the 2/24th on either side of them, and the NNC on the flanks. Chelmsford halted his column half a mile (0.8 km) from the camp and fired shrapnel over the nek. But the fighting around Isandlwana was over, and the Zulu gone. So Chelmsford continued on to the camp, where at about 20h30 his men bivouacked among the dead.

Initial encounter
22 January
Meanwhile, during the morning of Wednesday, 22 January, stragglers had continued to come into the Zulu *umnyama* bivouac along the Ngwebeni, while parties of foragers were out rounding up livestock and gathering mealies. The Zulu commanders knew it was unlikely the army could remain unnoticed by the British for much longer, or that the favourable division of the British forces could continue. Consequently, despite it being a time of darknesss (*umnyama*) because the moon was new and evil influences more potent, they decided to fight later that day once the army had been

ritually prepared for battle. (The inauspicious time did not prevent the Zulu engaging the British at Nyezane and Rorke's Drift either.) However, before the Zulu army was ready, a British patrol stumbled on their position and precipitated the battle.

At 08h00 a Zulu force was reported approaching the Isandlwana camp. Pulleine recalled most of his picquets and formed the infantry in column facing the Nyoni heights to the north. No. 5 Company (Capt Barry) of the 2nd Battalion of the 3rd Natal Native Contingent stayed where it was on the Nyoni heights, and No. 9 Company (Capt Lonsdale) of the 1st Battalion remained between the camp and Tutshane, a conical hill to the east, where Lt Scott's detachment of the Natal Carbineers was posted as vedettes. After an hour, when no Zulu appeared in appreciable numbers, the troops fell out. Firing was heard from the direction in which Chelmsford had gone, and it was presumed that he was engaged with the Zulu and that there was no threat to the camp.

At about 10h30 Col Durnford arrived from Rorke's Drift in response to Chelmsford's orders with a part of No. 2 Column (about 500 men) and immediately assumed command of the camp. At 11h00 he sent out Capt G. Shepstone of

his staff with a detachment of the Natal Native Horse (Nos. 1 and 2 Troops, Sikali's Horse) to clear the Nyoni heights of any Zulu who might be there. Barry's company of NNC was already on the escarpment and supported Shepstone's men; and A Company (Lt Cavaye) of the 1/24th occupied Barry's former position at the western end of the picquet line. The troops in front of the camp had their dinner.

Soon afterwards, scouts to the north of Isandlwana informed Durnford that a large Zulu column was moving eastwards towards Chelmsford's force. Although the orders were to defend the camp, Chelmsford had also requested Durnford to co-operate in his action against Matshana's force. Durnford decided that the priority must be to prevent Chelmsford from being attacked in the rear. So at about 11h30 he rode out of the camp with the Hlubi and Edendale Troops of the Natal Native Horse to prevent their presumed junction with Matshana. D Company (Capt Nourse), 1/1st NNC and the Rocket Battery under Maj Russell followed in support. Durnford ordered Shepstone and his mounted men to co-operate in an encircling movement to cut off the Zulu column, and reportedly required Pulleine to come to his support with the troops that had been left

guarding the camp, should he get into difficulties.

While moving along the Nyoni heights, Shepstone's patrol – operating in two separate groups, one along the ridge and the other in the valley beyond – intercepted a group of Zulu foragers driving a small herd of cattle, and pursued them north-east towards the Ngwebeni. At about midday the patrol came

Brevet Col Anthony William Durnford, Royal Engineers, commander of No. 2 Column. Chelmsford ordered him up from Rorke's Drift on 22 January to reinforce the camp at Isandlwana.

Brevet Lt-Col Henry Burmester Pulleine, commander of the 1/24th Regiment with No. 3 Column. Chelmsford left him in command of the camp on 22 January.

> 'At about 10.30 the Zulus were seen coming over the hills in thousands. They were in most perfect order, and seemed to be in about 20 rows of skirmishers one behind the other. They were in a semi-circle around our two flanks.'
>
> (Lt H.L. Smith Dorrien, 25 January 1879)

over the Mabaso heights, just where the uMcijo were concentrated, and the concealed valley, filled with the Zulu army, was suddenly revealed. The patrol dismounted, fired a volley and retired. The uMcijo charged after them, supported by the uNokhenke, uDududu, iSangqu and iMbube on their right, and the uMbonambi, iNgobamakhosi and uVe on their left. In this way the Zulu left, as it had been in the bivouac, became the extreme right, while the right became the centre, and the centre the left. The commanders tried to hold back the impulsive younger *amabutho*, but succeeded only with the more experienced uThulwana, iNdluyengwe, iNdlondlo and uDloko. They formed them into a circle where they underwent the ritual preparations for battle. The reserve, which these *amabutho* had become, then moved off far behind the rest of the army along a shallow valley running the length of the Nyoni heights, out of sight of the British below.

The battle before the camp

Shepstone's mounted troops retired steadily before the Zulu, but Barry's supporting NNC broke and fell back towards the camp. Shepstone himself advised Pulleine at about 12h15 of the Zulu advance. At precisely the same moment Pulleine received orders from Chelmsford to strike camp and move on to the Mangeni site. Pulleine disregarded this singularly inappropriate order and immediately ordered No. 3 Troop, Sikali's Horse and E Company (Capt Stafford) of the 1/1st NNC to support Shepstone's retiring mounted troops. On the left, A Company (Lt Cavaye) was reinforced with F Company (Capt Mostyn) of the 1/24th, all in skirmishing order, while the Native Horse and Stafford's company of the NNC eventually formed on their left. To prevent the Zulu centre from massing in the dead ground before the camp and cutting off outlying detachments, Pulleine advanced his two 7-pounder guns under Maj Smith to a rocky knoll facing the Nyoni heights several hundred yards beyond the left front of the NNC camp. He deployed E Company (Lt Porteous) and H Company

(Capt Wardell) of the 1/24th in skirmishing order some distance to their right. No. 4 Company (Capt Erskine) of the 2/3rd NNC, which had been in reserve before the camp, advanced to E Company's left, where it bolstered Barry's retreating No. 5 Company, 2/3rd NNC. Capt J. Lonsdale's No. 9 Company of the 1/3rd NNC maintained its position to H Company's right. G Company (Lt Pope) of the 2/24th extended along the front of the camp to protect it, and No. 6 Company (Capt Krohn) of the 1/3rd NNC also remained in reserve to their left before the camp. Meanwhile, to the left rear, C Company (Capt Younghusband) of the 1/24th covered the steady retreat of A and F Companies, and of the Native Horse. In moving his troops so far forward, and by forming a long firing line in open skirmishing order, Pulleine was throwing away the advantage of concentrated fire-power delivered from a tight, all-round formation. Moreover, the extended deployment made it difficult to bring up reserve ammunition and nothing was done to organise an efficient supply. Consequently, many units were in constant danger of running out of ammunition, and this certainly reduced their effectiveness. But Durnford's sortie had made it impossible for Pulleine to concentrate on the camp if he were effectively to support Durnford's withdrawal.

The main part of the Zulu army advanced along the Nyoni heights at a fast walking pace, already deployed in their classic bull's horns formation. As they came under fire from the camp they extended their concentrated formation into loose lines of skirmishers, one behind the other, and came on in rushes, making good use of cover. The right horn was thin, consisting of no more than five ranks, but increased towards the chest and left horn to between 220 and 325 yards (201 and 297 m) in width, or up to 20 ranks deep, with between 10 and 12 ranks being the mean. The Zulu spread out methodically along the British front. The chest went steadily against the left centre of the camp, while the horns attempted to outflank and envelop the

> 'The guns fired hard at the uMcijo first, they fired sufficient times for this regiment to lie down like grass in a strong wind.'
>
> (Luke Sofikasho Zungu of the iNgobamakhosi *ibutho*, 17 December 1935)

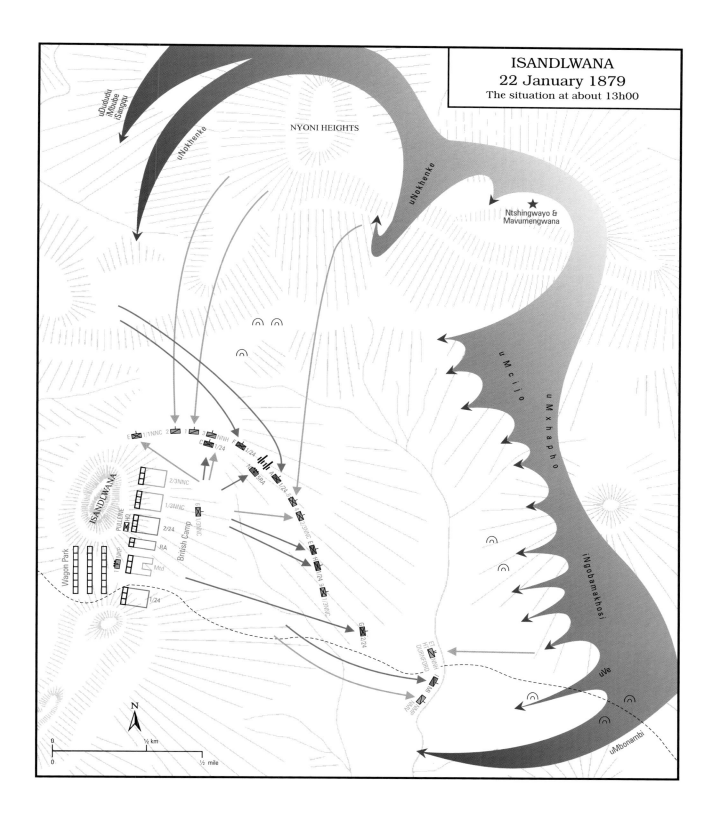

ISANDLWANA
22 January 1879
The situation at about 13h00

'When the soldiers retired on the camp, they did so running, and the Zulu were then intermixed with them. Things were then getting very mixed and confused what with the smoke and dust.'

(Mehlokazulu kaSihayo, February 1880)

'I saw a line of soldiers near the tents who were in a line shoulder to shoulder and I was afraid to go to attack them as they had chucked away their guns which were broken by using them as clubs and were standing with those small spears that they carried at their sides. I saw them like a fence holding hands against the attackers.'

(Luke Sofikasho Zungu, 17 December 1935)

defenders. Those Zulu with firearms kept up a continuous but inaccurate fire.

As the Zulu attack unfolded, fortunes varied between the two horns and the chest. Some 5 miles (8 km) out of camp, towards the Nyezi hill, Durnford encountered the rapidly deploying iNgobamakhosi and uVe and began a fighting retreat towards the camp. On the way he picked up the handful of survivors from his Rocket Battery, which had wheeled left up the Nyoni heights below Itusi hill in support of Shepstone's patrol, and had been overwhelmed by an advance guard of the uMbonambi. Meanwhile, the Natal Mounted Police, Natal Mounted Volunteers and Mounted Infantry had moved out of camp to a donga to the east. Durnford's retiring force formed line on their left and were joined by Scott's vedettes from the conical hill. Here the dismounted force of nearly 200 men held up the Zulu left horn as it attempted to encircle the camp. The young uVe, who were in the van, were repulsed and retired until reinforced by the iNgobamakhosi. These too were pinned down by fire from the donga, and by shelling from the two 7-pounders. One of the guns was temporarily moved to the right to fire on the uMbonambi, and the Zulu responded by opening their ranks still further. The uMbonambi began a lateral movement to their left and pushed forward behind and beyond the iNgobamakhosi to complete the turning movement around Durnford's force. Their advance forced the British to reinforce their right at the expense of their centre, and Pope's company of the 2/24th, which had been moving up from the camp to cover Wardell's right, began to hurry even further across to support Durnford and to plug the gap between his men and Lonsdale's company of the NNC.

Meanwhile, on the Zulu right, the uNokhenke had tried to come down from the Nyoni heights on the British left flank, but had come under heavy fire. They scattered but then regrouped on the high ground and continued their flanking movement. The uDududu, iMbube and iSangqu, who had not been diverted from

their intention of sweeping around the camp to take it from the rear, raced ahead of them. The reserve proceeded stolidly in the right horn's wake. It was the Zulu centre, which consisted of the uMcijo, elements of the uMxhapho and some of the reserve that had refused to be restrained, which suffered the heaviest casualties of the day. In the hollow between the Nyoni heights and the rocky knoll they were exposed to British fire at its most concentrated, and by 13h00 their attack had stalled as they tried to take cover. The situation was saved by the uMbonambi on the Zulu left driving a herd of cattle before them to distract the British. They finally outflanked Durnford's position and began to pour into the camp, joined by the uVe. Durnford, running out of ammunition and about to be cut off, was compelled to retire on the camp. Pope's company, advancing to reinforce him at the donga, fell back to rising ground behind it. The Zulu pursuing Durnford outflanked Lonsdale's NNC to his left, who also retreated towards the camp. Erskine's and Barry's companies of the NNC at the centre of the line then broke and fled, exposing the flanks of the British companies on either side to the advancing iNgobamakhosi.

At much the same time the right horn completed its turning movement. The uNokhenke began to enter the camp from the north-west, while the other *amabutho* of the right horn passed behind Isandlwana, seeking to join up with the those of the left horn already in the camp. Realising that his flanks were turned and that his line was collapsing, at 13h15 Pulleine tried to pull his men back to concentrate on the camp. Krohn's reserve company fled without fighting to join other elements of the NNC, Pioneers and Native Horse, as well as the wagon conductors and other non-combatants, in attempting to take flight across the nek south of Isandlwana and down the wagon track to Rorke's Drift.

The Zulu storm the camp
The Zulu commanders were stationed on a slight eminence on the Nyoni

heights directly north of the uMcijo. When the British began to fall back on the camp, they sent down senior officers to encourage the centre to advance and support the horns' encirclement. The centre resumed the attack with steady determination, and at about 130 yards (119 m) from the British they charged home at the double. They became intermingled with the British as they drove them back, and the *amabutho* themselves lost formation as they carried the camp. The uNokhenke seized the base of Isandlwana while the uDududu, iMbube and iSangqu drew themselves into long lines between the camp and the river, cutting the wagon road and British line of retreat to Rorke's Drift. However, they were unable to surround the British en-

tirely because many of the left horn had been diverted in pursuit of the mounted units and NNC already in flight towards the Mzinyathi, and a narrow gap in the encirclement was left open south-south-west of Isandlwana. Mounted men, cut off from the direct route to Rorke's Drift by the Zulu right horn, led the way down what became known as the 'Fugitives' trail' to Sothondose's Drift downstream. The uDududu, iMbube and iSangqu of the right horn, supported by the iNdlu-yengwe from the reserve, joined the iNgobamakhosi, uVe and uMbonambi of the left in pursuing them as far as the Mzinyathi. The Zulu reserve had arrived only in time to see the camp already being overrun. It did not therefore intervene but, after detaching the iNdluyenge

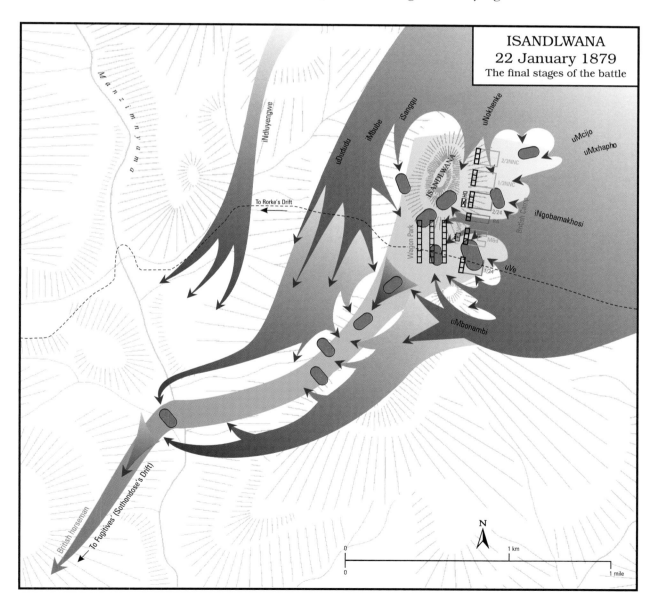

Chelmsford returned with his force to the stricken camp at Isandlwana on the evening of the battle to find it looted by the victorious Zulu, and the corpses of its defenders ritually disembowelled. This engraving, published in the Graphic of 29 March 1879, was taken from a sketch done on the spot by Trooper N. Nelson of the Natal Mounted Police. In the original drawing, the corpses of the British were accurately shown stripped naked with their abdomens slit wide open. The staff artists of the Graphic could not bring themselves to reproduce the grisly reality when they prepared the engraving.

'I saw quite a lot of white men escape on horseback soon after we attacked, they rode off on horseback to Jim's place . . . They were cowards to leave their brothers behind.'
(Luke Sofikasho Zungu December 1935)

to join in general pursuit, swept the country in open order in the direction of the drifts upstream of Sothondose's.

Numbers of the mounted fugitives were killed along the trail, and the 7-pounder guns soon overturned in a donga and were abandoned. Others drowned in the swollen Mzinyathi as they attempted to cross, or died on the Natal bank where the Qungebe people of Gamdana kaXongo and some Natal Africans co-operated with the pursuing amabutho in cutting them off. Many of the British regulars, who fought their way hand-to-hand through the camp, managed to rally at the nek south of Isandlwana where the 1/24th had its camp, as did Durnford's men. They seem finally to have been overwhelmed by about 14h00. Younghusband's company made a last stand on the southern shoulder of Isandlwana, and some smaller groups held out for some time on the north-western side of the mountain. Resistance continued until late afternoon, the scenes

of horror magnified by a partial eclipse of the sun, which reached its greatest phase at 14h29, making the dull, cloudy day darker still.

However, not all the regulars made a last stand at the camp, but attempted a disciplined fighting withdrawal towards the Mzinyathi through the narrow gap in the Zulu encirclement. Shepherded on their left by the Zulu who held the ridge parallel to the line of retreat, and bounded on their right by steep dongas, groups of up to half-company strength were systematically cut off and killed in desperate, hand-to-hand fighting. The furthest any of these groups got was to the far bank of the Manzimnyama stream.

The victorious Zulu comprehensively looted the captured camp. As darkness fell they saw Chelmsford's force approaching in battle order and prudently fell back over the Nyoni heights, with their booty, to their bivouac at the Ngwebeni.

 Pte S. Wassall, 80th Regiment
There was no provision in 1879 for the posthumous award of the VC, but in 1907 the families of Lt N.J.A. Coghill and Lt T. Melvill, both of the 1/24th Regiment, were sent the decoration when this was authorised.

DUNDEE SECTOR

Battle of Rorke's Drift

In an epic action during the afternoon and night of 22 January and the early hours of 23 January 1879, the small British garrison at Rorke's Drift fought off repeated assaults by Zulu forces who had not been engaged with the rest of their army at Isandlwana. The Zulu referred to it as the battle of kwaJimu (Jim's place) after James Rorke who had originally established his trading store at the drift.

Afternoon

When the Centre Column advanced across the Myinyathi River on 11 January 1879, it left behind a small garrison, consisting of a company of the 2/24th Regiment, a company of the 2/3rd NNC and various detached personnel to secure its depot at Rorke's Drift. Not anticipating a Zulu attack, the British neglected to fortify the Swedish mission church and house at the place, which had been converted respectively into a commissariat store and hospital.

Shortly after 15h00 on 22 January, Hlubi's Troop of the Natal Native Horse, and other mounted fugitives from Isandlwana, brought word that a large Zulu force was heading towards Rorke's Drift. Lt Chard, RE, the senior officer present, resolved that the garrison must hold the post, and hastily established a defensive perimeter consisting of a breast-high barricade of mealie bags connecting the loopholed store and hospital, two wagons and the stone-walled cattle-kraal.

The approaching Zulu force consisted

of the reserve of mature *amabutho* who had not been engaged with the rest of Zulu army at Isandlwana. The iNdlu-yengwe *ibutho*, who had split off from the main body and joined in the pursuit of the British fugitives towards Sothondose's (or Fugitives') Drift, forded the Mzinyathi just above the drift. The remainder of the reserve crossed further upstream, where the Batshe runs into the Mzinyathi. The Zulu were not making a serious incursion into Natal, but were intent merely on ravaging the plain between the Mzinyathi and Helpmekaar heights to prove their prowess and to compensate for missing much of the fighting at Isandlwana. The poorly guarded British post at Rorke's Drift – filled with tempting supplies – seemed an easy prize to be snatched during the course of their punitive raid.

Around 16h20 the Hlubi Troop, who were keeping watch on the river crossings, reported the Zulu approach to Chard and then galloped off to the safety of the entrenched British base at Helpmekaar, followed by the demoralised company of NNC. Deprived at a stroke

---

British forces

No. 3 Column (detachment), Lt J.R.M. Chard, RE, commanding:
2nd Battalion, 24th (2nd Warwickshire) Regiment: B Company, Lt G. Bromhead.
Detached personnel from the Royal Artillery, the Royal Engineers, the 2nd Battalion, 3rd Regiment (East Kent. The Buffs), the 1st Battalion, 24th (2nd Warwickshire) Regiment, the 90th Regiment (Perthshire Volunteers Light Infantry), the Commissariat, Medical and Chaplain's Departments, the Natal Mounted Police and Natal Native Contingent; also a ferryman.

Total: 8 officers, 131 men, of whom 35 were sick.

Zulu forces

The Zulu attackers under the command of Prince Dabulamanzi kaMpande were the reserve that had not been engaged with the rest of the army at Isandlwana, They comprised the main elements of the uThulwana, iNdlondlo, iNdluyengwe and uDloko *amabutho* – a force of between 3 000 and 4 000.

British casualties

Killed: 17 men.
Wounded: 1 officer and 7 men.

Zulu casualties

The British buried 351 Zulu who had been killed close to the post, and a further 200 or so bodies were 'found' further off – some of which were those of the wounded whom the British finished off on the morning after the battle. For months after, the garrison kept coming across bodies of the wounded who had crept away to die, but kept no tally. An unknown number of the wounded also drowned crossing the Mzinyathi, and on their way home. In all, the Zulu lost an estimated minimum of 600.

PAGE 109

Prince Dabulamanzi kaMpande, King Cetshwayo's half-brother, led the Zulu assault on Rorke's Drift. He is shown in the photograph of 1873 on horseback in conversation with the hunter-trader John Dunn, King Cetshwayo's white chief and erstwhile adviser, who cannily joined the British at the beginning of the war.

of about 200 of its defenders, the perimeter of the post at Rorke's Drift was now too long to be held by the remaining garrison, and Chard ordered it halved by building a barricade of biscuit boxes across the enclosure. The barricade was still incomplete when the Zulu attacked, and since all the sick had not yet been evacuated form the hospital, the depleted garrison was forced to hold the entire original perimeter.

The Zulu assault on Rorke's Drift was poorly co-ordinated and reflected their belief that the post would be easily overrun. Between 500 and 600 of the iNdluyengwe came around the southern side of Shiyane (the Oskarsberg) at about 16h30. They formed into a crescent-shaped fighting line extending from Shiyane towards Siqindi hill to its south-east, and advanced at a steady trot against the southern perimeter of the post. At about 60 yards (55 m) the heavy crossfire proved too much for them. Some remained pinned down and occupied the cookhouse ovens and took advantage of the cover afforded by banks and ditches. The majority swerved to their left and attacked the hospital building and the north-western line of mealie bags where there was less chance of being caught in a crossfire, and where plenty of cover was available. They succeed in advancing right up to the barricades, and the defenders

forced them back in hand-to-hand fighting. Repulsed, the iNdluyengwe took cover in the mission's mealie garden and orchard, and in the sunken road and surrounding bush.

The remaining 3 000 or so *amabutho*, mainly the uThulwana, now came up around the southern shoulder of Shiyane and, finding the iNdluyengwe fully committed, had no choice but to attack in support. Some positioned themselves along the rocky ledges and caves on the mountainside overlooking the post, and kept up a constant harassing fire. Fortunately for the defenders below, this proved inaccurate and ineffective because of the inferior nature of most of the Zulu firearms and the extent of the range – 300 yards (274 m) or more. Besides, the Zulu were shooting into the late afternoon sun. The majority, however, reinforced the iNdluyengwe and launched a series of desperate assaults on the hospital and line of mealie bags from the north-west. Because of the limited length of the defensive perimeter, it was never possible for the Zulu to bring more than a fraction of their forces to bear, and these were exposed to fire at point-blank range. The garrison repulsed each charge in intense hand-to-hand fighting, and on each occasion the Zulu fell back to the cover of the bush and orchard and regrouped for a fresh attempt.

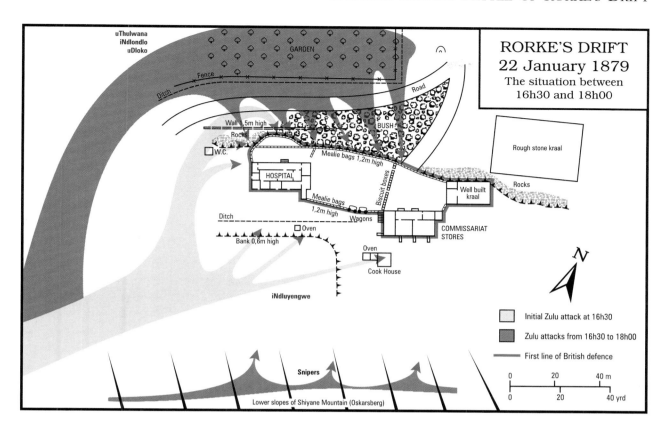

RORKE'S DRIFT
22 January 1879
The situation between
16h30 and 18h00

Initial Zulu attack at 16h30

Zulu attacks from 16h30 to 18h00

First line of British defence

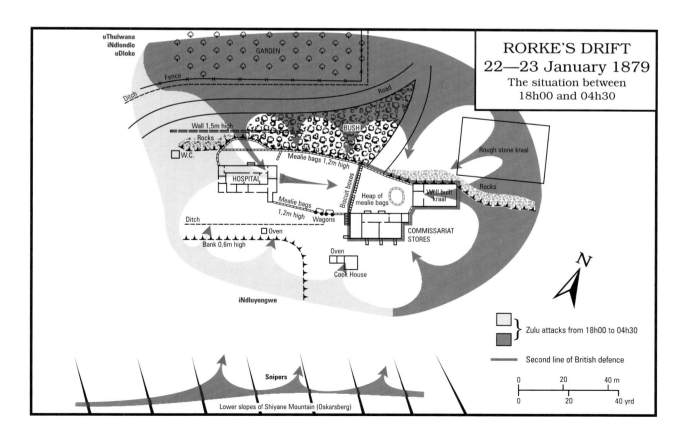

RORKE'S DRIFT
22—23 January 1879
The situation between
18h00 and 04h30

Zulu attacks from 18h00 to 04h30

Second line of British defence

'Presently the uThulwana said, "O! Let us go and have a fight at Jim's!" The white men had by this time made their preparations . . . The Zulu arrived at Jim's house. They fought, they yelled, they shouted, "It dies at the entrance! It dies in the doorway!" They stabbed the sacks; they dug with their assegais. They were struck; they died.'

(Munyu of the uThulwana *ibutho*, 1884)

Dusk and darkness

At length, at about 18h00, as dusk shrouded their movements, the Zulu began to extend their attack further to their left beyond the cover of the bush. Chard, increasingly fearful of a Zulu break-in, and concerned at the mounting casualties from the snipers on Shiyane, decided he must withdraw to the shorter perimeter behind the line of biscuit boxes. As the defenders fell back, the Zulu immediately occupied the abandoned line of mealie bags, set the roof of the hospital alight and burst into the building. The hospital garrison retired room by room, and in desperate fighting brought out all the sick that they could.

Greatly encouraged, the Zulu tried to set fire to the roof of the storehouse, and began an assault on the stone cattle-kraal which formed the eastern perimeter. Believing that the reduced line of defences was also about to be breached, the British began converting two heaps of mealie bags into a sort of redoubt to provide an elevated line of fire and a final defence. The blaze from the hospital (which only died down about midnight) probably saved the British because it silhouetted the attackers, and by illuminating the whole battlefield foiled attacks from unexpected quarters.

Even so, the Zulu managed after several repulses to clear half the cattle-kraal and to take possession of the wall across its middle. Yet this success marked the turning of the tide. The Zulu were unsettled by the knowledge that two companies of the 1/24th had marched down from Helpmekaar to within 3 miles (5 km) of Rorke's Drift before withdrawing on seeing the hospital in flames, and were apprehensive of further movements by British troops. This, coupled with the uncertainties of darkness (the Zulu did not normally make night attacks), heavy casualties, and failure to carry the post after persistent attempts, made them increasingly reluctant to attempt another full-scale assault. Consequently, they did not again charge up in a body after about 21h00, but maintained their positions and kept up a heavy fire from all sides. After midnight they contented themselves with desultory fire from Shiyane and the bush on the op-

A photograph taken in late 1879 of the remains of Rorke's storehouse and the loopholed stone walls that were erected in the weeks following the battle to enclose the position. Fort Bromhead, as it was sometimes known, was abandoned in May 1879 for Fort Melvill built nearby to command the drift across the Mzinyathi (Buffalo) River. After the war, the Revd Otto Witt re-established the Swedish mission at the site. He demolished the storehouse and fort walls and used the stone to build a new house and church.

posite side of the post, and even this ceased at about 04h00.

Morning

The British garrison, not knowing that the Zulu had given up the assault, feverishly strengthened their defences against renewed attack. But by daybreak most of the Zulu had retired around the southern shoulder of Shiyane. At 07h00 the garrison saw numbers of Zulu concentrated

on Siqindi Hill, but these too melted away as the surviving portion of the Centre Column (which had spent the night on the deserted Isandlwana battlefield) came into sight of Rorke's Drift at about 08h00. Members of the relieving British force systematically killed all the Zulu wounded or exhausted they found lying or hiding away in the vicinity of Rorke's Drift.

The gallant defence of Rorke's Drift diverted public attention from the British disaster at Isandlwana. In this cartoon of 22 March 1879, Mr Punch congratulates Lt John Rouse Merriott Chard, RE, the senior officer present, and Lt Gonville Bromhead, who had been left in command of the detachment of the 24th Regiment at the post.

Lt J.R.M. Chard, Royal Engineers
Lt G. Bromhead, 2/24th Regiment
Surgeon J.H. Reynolds, Army
    Medical Dept
Acting Asst Commissary J.L.Dalton,
    Commissariat & Transport Dept
Cpl W.W. Allen, 2/24th Regiment
Cpl F.C. Schiess, Natal Native Contingent
Pte F. Hitch, 2/24th Regiment
Pte A.H. Hook, 2/24th Regiment
Pte R. Jones, 2/24th Regiment
Pte W. Jones, 2/24th Regiment
Pte J. Williams, 2/24th Regiment

Clr Sgt F. Bourne, 2/24th Regiment
Cpl M. McMahon, Army Hospital Corps
2/Cpl F. Attwood, Army Service Corps
Wheeler J. Cantwell, Royal Artillery
Pte W. Roy, 1/24th Regiment

ESTCOURT SECTOR

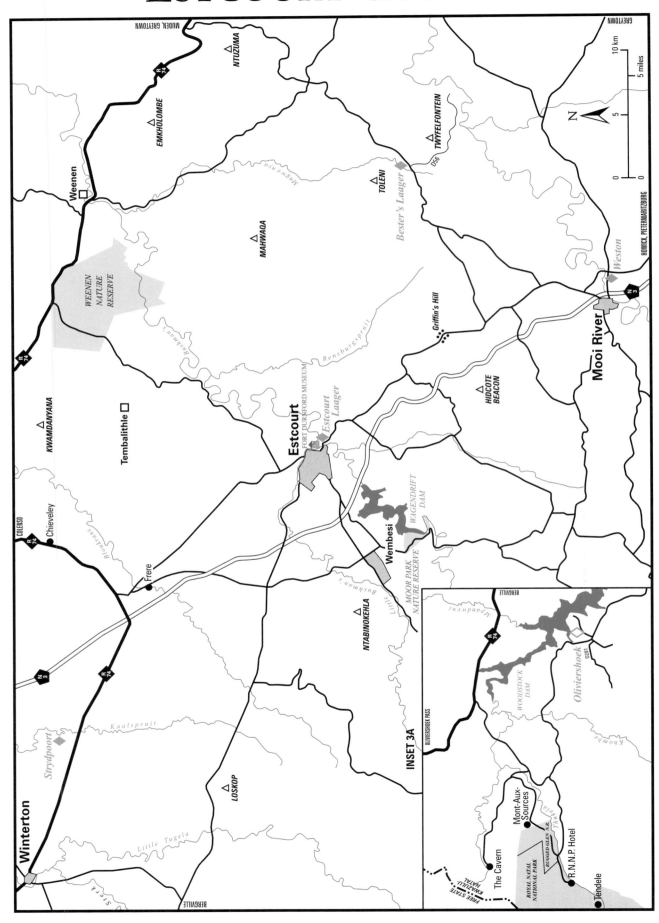

completed, apparently for lack of funds. At the end of 1878 it was considered as a defensive post for local settlers, but was finally abandoned because it could be subjected to rifle fire from the adjacent rising ground.

ESTCOURT SECTOR

Fortifications

◆ **Bester's Laager**, on the farm Twyfelfontein, was started some 20 years before the war and presumably named after P.M. Bester, the farm's owner from 1858 to 1872. It was not

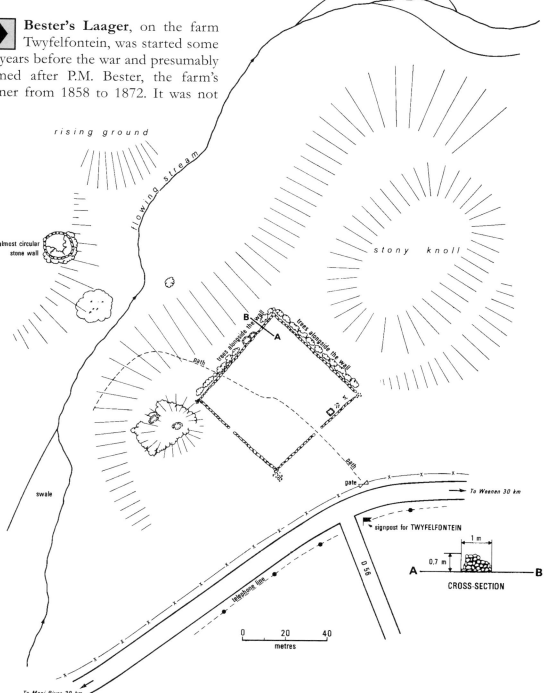

rising ground

flowing stream

almost circular
stone wall

stony knoll

trees alongside the wall

B
A

path

trees alongside the wall

path

swale

gate

To Weenen 30 km

signpost for TWYFELFONTEIN

D 56

telephone line

1 m

0,7 m

A ———————————— B

CROSS-SECTION

0   20   40
metres

To Mooi River 20 km

◆ In early January 1879, prior to the outbreak of the war, the **Estcourt Laager** was proclaimed the central post of defence for the settlers in Weenen County. It consisted of a blockhouse (Fort Durnford, begun in 1874), three guardhouses and a stables block built in 1876 for the Natal Mounted Police stationed there. All these buildings had been connected by a stone wall in 1878 to form the laager, which was then further strengthened and improved during the war, in spite of being too large for defence by the number of settlers expected to resort to it. The Estcourt Museum is now housed in the blockhouse. While post-war alterations have occurred in the old laager wall, much of the original can still be easily traced.

ESTCOURT LAAGER

The Estcourt Laager photographed from the north-east. Fort Durnford, the blockhouse begun in 1874, is on the right, and the stable block, built in 1876 for the Natal Mounted Police, is on the left. The strong stone wall begun in 1878 to connect these buildings can be clearly seen, as can the loopholed guardhouses at the corners. This ambitious fortification was never attacked in 1879 and was, in any case, far too large for defence by the number of settlers expected to take refuge there.

The **Strydpoort Laager** (later called 'Fort Eldorado' from the name of a sub-division of the old Strydpoort farm) was also built before the war, but precisely when is not clear. References to it in 1878 indicate that it was already complete. Throughout the war it was the base of the Upper Tugela Defence Corps of between 40 and 70 men, under the command of A.I.E. Pretorius.

St John's Church at **Weston** was designated as a post of defence in February 1879. Arrangements were made to loophole the walls and to erect a sod enclosure in the graveyard; however, these alterations were to be made only in an emergency, which never arose.

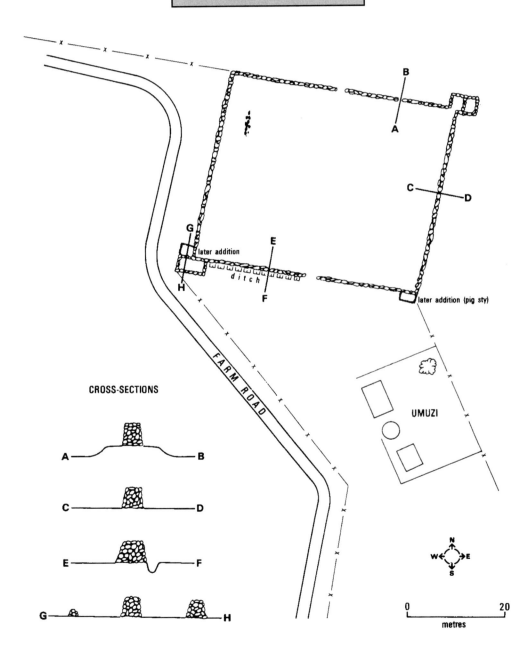

STRYDPOORT LAAGER

At **Oliviershoek** the construction of a 'proper laager' began in March 1879, incorporating the magistrate's office and the gaol. After the war the laager became a police post. The remains of two walls on one face suggest a rebuilding or repairing of the original stonework. Since the establishment of a new police station nearer the main road, the old buildings have been derelict and the laager walls have fallen into ruin.

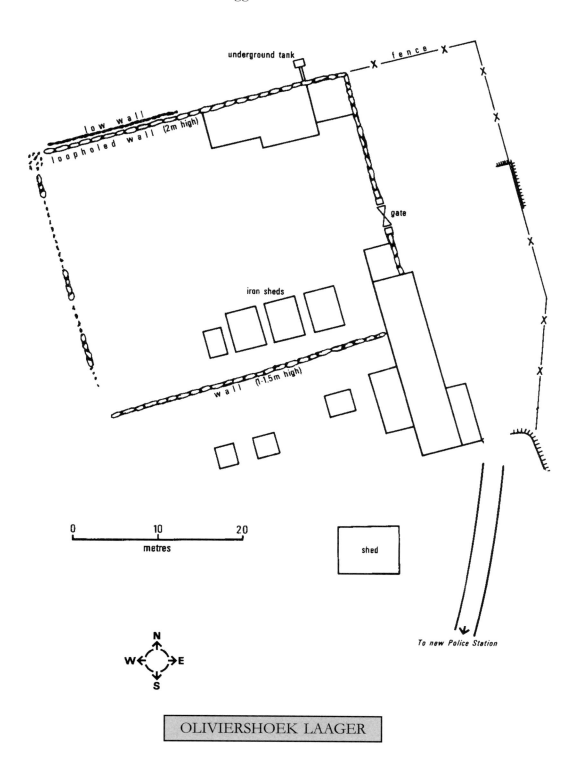

OLIVIERSHOEK LAAGER

GREYTOWN SECTOR

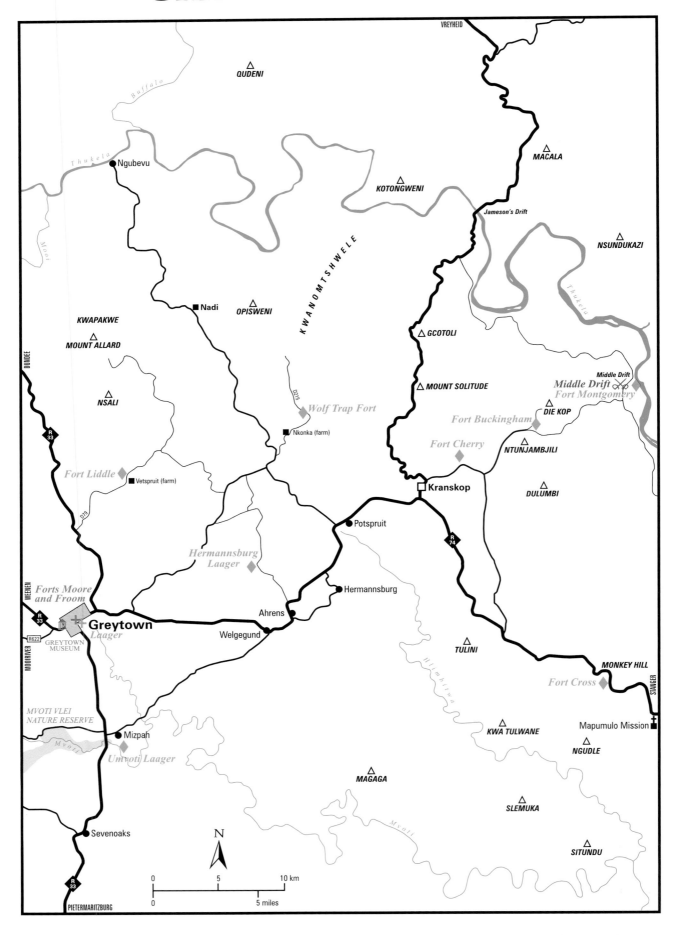

QUDENI

Buffalo

VREYHEID

MACALA

KOTONGWENI

Thukela

Ngubevu

Jameson's Drift

NSUNDUKAZI

K W A N O M T S H W E L E

Thukela

Mooi

Nadi

OPISWENI

KWAPAKWE

MOUNT ALLARD

GCOTOLI

DUNDEE

NSALI

D215

MOUNT SOLITUDE

Middle Drift

Middle Drift
Fort Montgomery

DIE KOP

Wolf Trap Fort

Fort Buckingham

R
33

Nkonka (farm)

Fort Cherry

NTUNJAMBJILI

Fort Liddle

D79

Vetspruit (farm)

Kranskop

DULUMBI

Potspruit

R
74

Hermannsburg
Laager

WEENEN

Forts Moore
and Froom

R
33

Ahrens

Hermannsburg

R622

Greytown
Laager

Welgegund

TULINI

GREYTOWN
MUSEUM

MOORIVER

MONKEY HILL

STANGER

Fort Cross

MVOTI VLEI
NATURE RESERVE

Mizpah

Mvoti

Umvoti Laager

Mapumulo Mission

KWA TULWANE

NGUDLE

MAGAGA

Himbiwa

Sevenoaks

R
33

N

SLEMUKA

Mvoti

SITUNDU

0   5   10 km

0   5 miles

PIETERMARITZBURG

GREYTOWN SECTOR

Fortifications

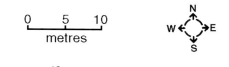

◆ There are the remains of two colonial fortifications in this sector. The **Hermannsburg Laager** (known locally as 'Fort Ahrens'or 'Fort Perseverance') was built in 1878 by the local Dutch-speaking settlers. They took shelter in it from January until mid-April 1879 and furnished a mounted force of between 50 and 80 men, who used the laager as a headquarters and base for patrols of the vicinity.

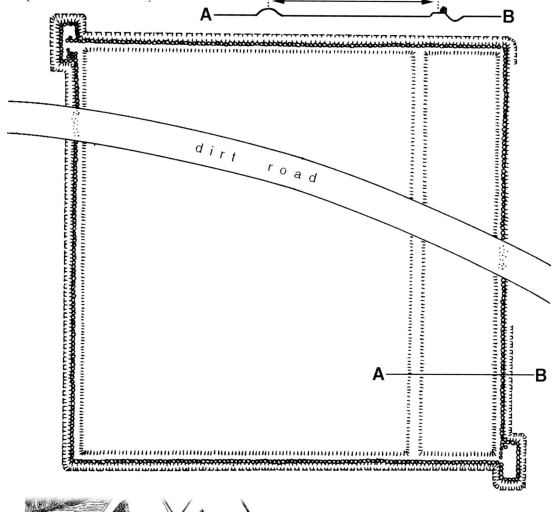

HERMANNSBURG LAAGER

The **Umvoti Laager** (called 'Fort Mizpah', 'Fort Menne' and 'Menne's Laager') was also built in 1878 by local farmers. It was briefly occupied in January 1879, but then abandoned early in February for want of sufficient defenders. The unusual trace of a parallel wall outside the stone enclosure suggests a subsequent reduction in the size of the laager, possibly when it was reportedly used during the 1906 Rebellion. All the fortifications of the imperial troops in the area have survived.

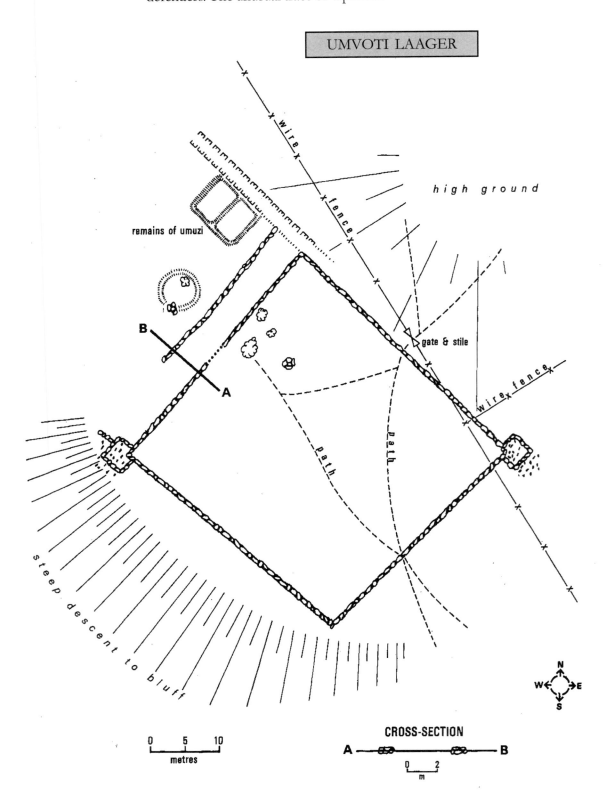

UMVOTI LAAGER

remains of umuzi

high ground

gate & stile

path

path

wire fence

wire fence

B

A

steep descent to bluff

0   5   10
metres

CROSS-SECTION

A ——————— B

0   2
m

N
W   E
S

The oldest, **Fort Buckingham**, built in 1861, modified in 1863–4 and abandoned after 1868, was in ruins by the time of the war. The fort was never manned then, although it may have been used as an outpost (its remains suggest alterations, possibly during subsequent military occupations in 1901 and 1906).

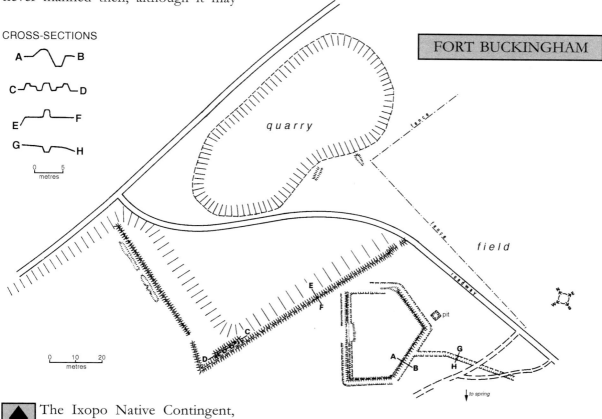

FORT BUCKINGHAM

The Ixopo Native Contingent, which arrived in the area in March 1879 and was later distributed to important defensive positions, built the **Wolf Trap Fort**, probably in May.

WOLF TRAP FORT

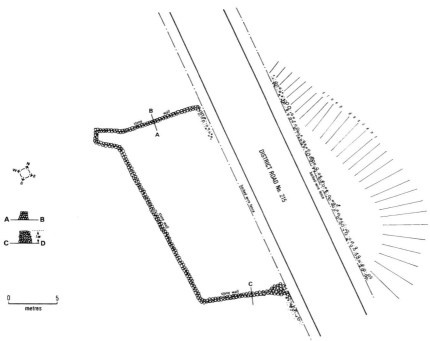

◆ **Fort Cherry** took its place as the most important advanced base in the area. Hastily constructed in the panic following Isandlwana and greatly strengthened thereafter, it was garrisoned by the 1st and 3rd Battalions of the Natal Native Contingent under the command of Capt C.E.LeM. Cherry.

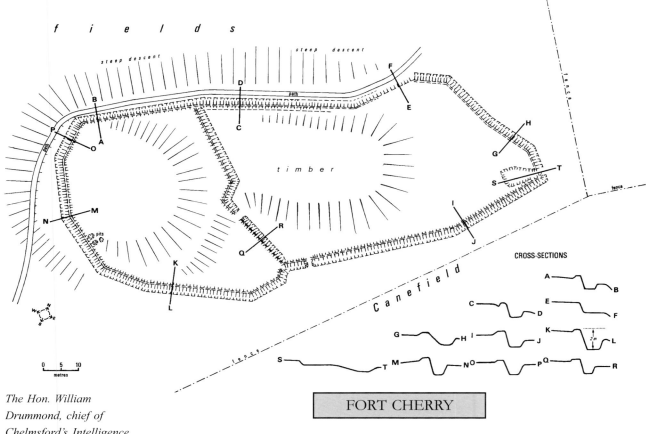

FORT CHERRY

The Hon. William Drummond, chief of Chelmsford's Intelligence Department, confronting Mfunzi and Nkisimana, two senior messengers from King Cetshwayo, who were seeking to open peace negotiations. The interview, as depicted in the Illustrated London News *of 31 May 1879, took place on 15 April in d'Almaine's fortified farmhouse, used by the garrison of Fort Cherry on the hill close by as a store-house (note the mealie-bags and tins of meat). Maj A.C. Twentyman, commander of the imperial troops in Defensive District No. VII, is seated by the table. The Hon. A. Burke, correspondent for the* Daily Telegraph, *looks on, hands in pocket.*

Fort Montgomery was thrown up in front of Middle Drift by men of the 1st Battalion, NNC during the demonstration at the end of March 1879 in favour of Lord Chelmsford's advance to relieve Eshowe, and was named after the battalion commander, Cmdt A.N. Montgomery. The fort was then left unoccupied until after the Zulu had raided the Natal bank of the Thukela on 25 June, when Cherry sent down a detachment of the NNC, who made it 'strong enough to be held against a large Zulu force'.

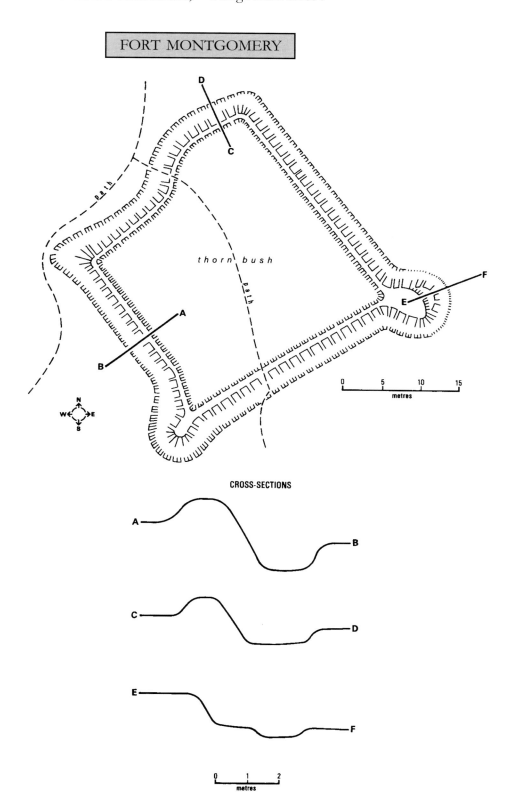

FORT MONTGOMERY

CROSS-SECTIONS

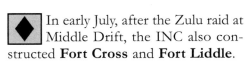 In early July, after the Zulu raid at Middle Drift, the INC also constructed **Fort Cross** and **Fort Liddle**.

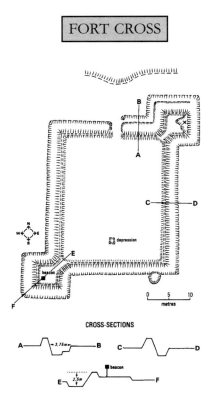

FORT CROSS

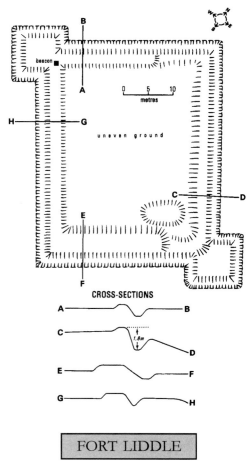

FORT LIDDLE

The Ixopo Native Contingent were raised in late February 1879 in Defensive District No. IV in the south of Natal, and were sent north to reinforce the troops guarding Defensive District No. VII. During July, when the Zulu raided at Middle Drift, they were garrisoning Forts Cross and Liddle on the heights above the Thukela valley. The INC were made up of about 800 foot and 500 mounted men. Two of the latter are depicted in the Graphic of 17 May 1879, riding very typically with only the big toe in the stirrup.

There are no remains of the **Greytown Laager**, which the Natal government began in 1854 and improved during 1877–8. The settlers of Greytown and the surrounding area took refuge there after Isandlwana and again after the Zulu raid at Middle Drift. Nothing is left of the adjoining **Fort Moore**, built during January 1879 by the two companies of the 2/4th (King's Own Royal) Regiment which garrisoned the town, nor of **Fort Froom**, erected in its place in May by the succeeding garrison of two companies of the 94th Regiment.

The settlers of Greytown and Umvoti County took refuge after Isandlwana in the Greytown Laager, which dated from 1854.
The adjoining Fort Moore was built by the military in January 1879. This sketch from the Graphic *of 26 April 1879 illustrates the difference between the tall, loopholed stone walls of the typical settler laager, and the low earthwork parapet, ditch and abattis of the standard fieldwork.*

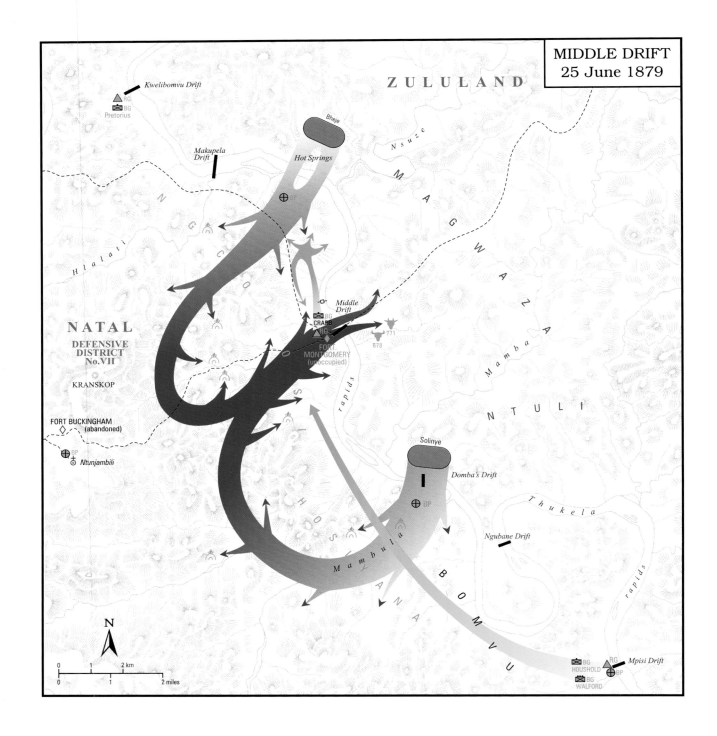

GREYTOWN SECTOR

Raid at Middle Drift

An extensive and successful Zulu raid across the Thukela River into Natal took place at Middle Drift on 25 June 1879 in retaliation for earlier raids into Zululand by colonial troops stationed along the middle Thukela.

For months rumours had been reaching the Border Police stationed along the Natal side of the middle Thukela that the Zulu intended raiding the valley between the river and Kranskop in retaliation for the British cross-border incursions of April and May 1879. Nevertheless, when it did eventually occur, the Middle Drift raid took the colonial and imperial forces guarding the border completely by surprise.

Under cover of early-morning mist, two large parties of Zulu, who had concentrated at Bheje's *umuzi*, crossed the Thukela in the vicinity of Hot Springs, killing one of the two Border Police standing guard. The two groups then joined up and, some 500 strong, set off in the direction of Kranskop, guided under duress by local people. The Ngcolosi people of Chief Hlangabeza bolted for the thick bush and tried to drive their cattle out of the reach of the raiders, but the Zulu pushed on as far as the foot of Kranskop, setting fire to all the *imizi* as they went and killing all in their path, women and children included. Driving herds of cattle and livestock before them, and with some captive women in tow, they rounded the eastern base of Kranskop.

Meanwhile, at Middle Drift, D. Crabb, the levy leader stationed there, was alerted by the sound of gunfire. He called out his force of levies and set off towards Hot Springs. But the Zulu were already to his left and rear, and Crabb dispersed his outnumbered men with orders to save the lives and belongings of the Ngcolosi.

When the Zulu reached the hill below the KwaNtunjambili mission, they turned back towards the river. On the way they were joined by a second force under Solinye, which had crossed into Natal at Domba's Drift, below Middle Drift, where the Mambulu stream runs into the Thukela. The mist hung very densely until 09h00, giving every advantage to the 500 raiders. They brushed aside the feeble opposition of the local River Guard and set about burning the *imizi* of Chief Homoyi's Bomvu and Chief Ndomba's Hosiyana, and driving off their cattle. Some fight was put up by Sgt Sibaya and two Border Policemen and six River Guards, but this pocket of resistance was easily bypassed. Having devastated the Mambulu valley, Solinye's men moved up the Thukela to their

'There had been sunlight that day, but as the *impi* went forward a thick fog spread all over that part, and in this fog the impi went from kraal to kraal, killing people . . . After recrossing into Zululand the mist cleared. It was the Cubes who are said to have caused the mist, which enabled them to massacre their enemy as they had done.'

(Mpatshana, 30 May 1912)

British forces
Defensive District No. VI, Sub-District No. 2
Border Guard (E. Walford, levy sub-leader).

Total: 70 men

Defensive District No. VII
Border Police.
River Guard, Station No. 5 (D. Crabb, levy leader).
River Guard, Station No. 7 (W.F. Houshold, levy leader).

Total: approx. 70 men

Zulu forces
About 1 000 men from the Zulu border population were involved, primarily the Magwaza people of Chief Qethuka kaManqondo, the Ntuli people of Chief Mavumengwana kaNdlela, and the Cube people of Chief Sigananda kaSokufa. However, numbers of the Ngcolosi people from Natal were with them. They had crossed over to Zululand in November 1878, and Bheje and Solinye, the leaders of the two raiding parties, were prominent among them.

British casualties
Killed: 1 Border Policeman; 2 River Guards; 30 Africans of the border population.

Zulu casualties
About 10 killed or wounded, and perhaps a few drowned.

View from Kranskop across Middle Drift and the Thukela River into Zululand, drawn by Lt-Col Crealock in October 1878. This was the valley ravaged by the Zulu in the raid of 25 June 1879.

rendezvous below Kranskop with the first force of Zulu from upstream. Together, they ravaged the country down to Middle Drift. Seeing they were intent on retiring, Crabb rallied his scattered levies and some Border Police and harried the Zulu flanks, recapturing some cattle. The Zulu burnt the ferryman's huts at Middle Drift and crossed back into Zululand at about 11h30.

A party of about 100 Zulu lagged with their booty behind Solinye's force. W. Houshold, the levy leader downstream at Mpisi Drift, took his 35 levies of the Cele and Hlongwa people (the rest had gone to Kranskop to pay the hut tax), augmented by 70 levies supplied by E. Walford, the levy leader at the next drift downstream, and intercepted them. A sharp little skirmish ensued, with casualties on both

NOTE JUST COME IN FROM CHERRY—"ZULUS HAVE CROSSED THE RIVER, GET UP AND LOOK SHARP"

' Mr Houshold, in charge of the Border Guard at Impino, hearing the firing . . . arrived on the scene in time to intercept one party of Zulus, several of whom were killed and wounded as they re-crossed the river. He recaptured a small herd of cattle that they were driving off. Mr Crabbe at Middle Drift had a narrow escape; being surrounded by the Zulus, he had to conceal himself for a short time.'

(*Natal Mercury*, 2 July 1879)

sides. The Zulu beat a hurried retreat across the river, and abandoned a small herd of captured cattle.

All the Zulu had retired across the Thukela with their loot before the 800 men of the 1st and 3rd Battalions, NNC, stationed at Fort Cherry on the heights above the valley, could be prepared for action. All the other levies and Natal Mounted Volunteers in the vicinity went on to the alert, but none took the field. The Zulu got away with 678 cattle and 771 goats, and took some 40 prisoners. They also looted £170 intended by the locals for paying the hut tax. They left behind 73 burnt *imizi*, destroyed food stores and 30 of the border population dead. The arrangements for the defence of the Natal border against a Zulu raid had been tested and found inadequate.

LUNEBURG SECTOR

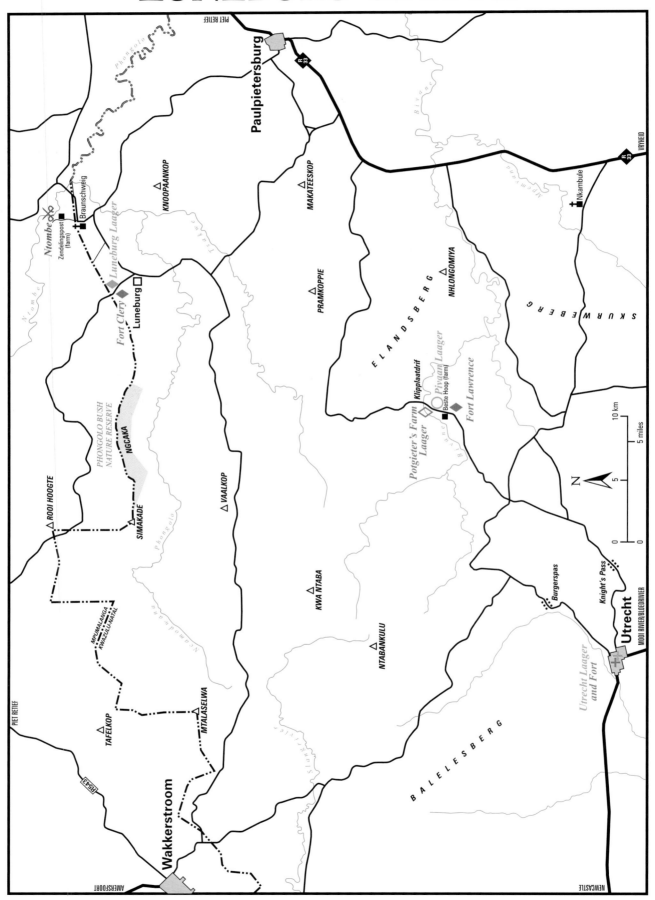

PIET RETIEF

Paulpietersburg

VRYHEID

Phongolo

KNOOPAANKOP

MAKATEESKOP

Bivane

Nkambule

Braunschweig

Ntombe

Zendelingspost
(farm)

Luneburg Laager

PRAMKOPPIE

NHLONGOMIYA

SKURWEBERG

Fort Clery

Luneburg

ELANDSBERG

PHONGOLO BUSH
NATURE RESERVE

NGCAKA

Klipplaatdrif

Pivaan Laager

Beste Hoop (farm)

Fort Lawrence

ROOI HOOGTE

Porgieter's Farm
Laager

SIMAKADE

VAALKOP

Phongolo

10 km

5 miles

N

KWA NTABA

Ndwandwe

MPUMALANGA
KWAZULU/NATAL

NTABANKULU

Burgerspas

Knight's Pass

TAFELKOP

MTALASELWA

Utrecht Lager
and Fort

MOOI RIVIER/BLOEDRIVIER

Utrecht

PIET RETIEF

R543

BALELESBERG

Wakkerstroom

AMERSFOORT

NEWCASTLE

LUNEBURG SECTOR

Fortifications

◆ Since 1869 a community of German settlers of the Hermannsburg Mission Society had been established in the valley between the Phongolo and Ntombe rivers, deep within the Disputed Territory. As this was an area claimed by the Zulu king, the settlers had built for their protection the stone-walled **Luneburg Laager** around their church in the tiny settlement of that name. Twice, in November 1877 and in May 1878, they took refuge there for fear of

Zulu attack. A further scare in October 1878 persuaded Sir Bartle Frere to instruct that troops be sent from the Utrecht garrison in the Transvaal to protect the settlers. On 19 October 1878, two companies of the 90th Regiment (Perthshire Volunteers Light Infantry), under Maj C.F. Clery, arrived to strengthen the laager and fortify the adjoining graveyard. In December two companies of the 1/13th Regiment (1st Somersetshire) Prince Albert's Light Infantry and the dismounted Kaffrarian Rifles became the garrison, succeeded on 9 February 1879 by five companies of the 80th Regiment (Staffordshire Volunteers) under Maj C. Tucker. They were relieved on 9 April by two companies of the 2/4th (King's Own Royal) Regiment under Maj W. F. Blake. There was apparently some doubt that the latter were sufficient to man the fortifications, so the Kaffrarian Rifles were sent back, apparently in June, when the graveyard wall was taken down.

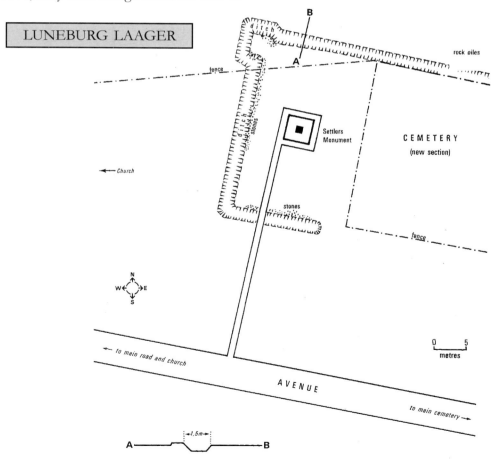

LUNEBURG LAAGER

The earthwork **Fort Clery** outside the Luneburg Laager was built during November 1878 by the detachment of the 90th. Subsequently, the fort was manned by the Kaffrarian Rifles and then by troops of the 80th, who mounted two 6-pounder guns during their stay. They were relieved by a detachment of the 2/4th, followed once more by the Kaffrarian Rifles.

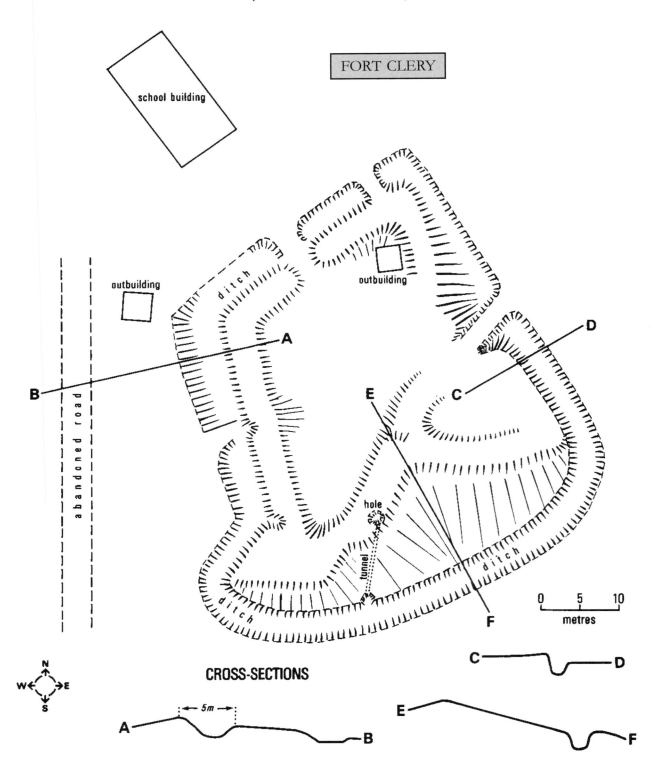

FORT CLERY

school building

outbuilding

outbuilding

abandoned road

A

B

D

C

E

hole

tunnel

ditch

ditch

ditch

F

0   5   10
metres

CROSS-SECTIONS

N
W   E
S

← 5m →

A

B

C

D

E

F

Fort Lawrence was built on 8 May by a company of the 2/4th, under Capt H.B. Lawrence, stationed from May 1879 at the Widow Potgieter's farm. A *Natal Mercury* correspondent described it on 5 June as 'a perfect model fortification', enhanced by covered ways below ornamental arches set on pillars of cut sandstone. These decorative features have not survived.

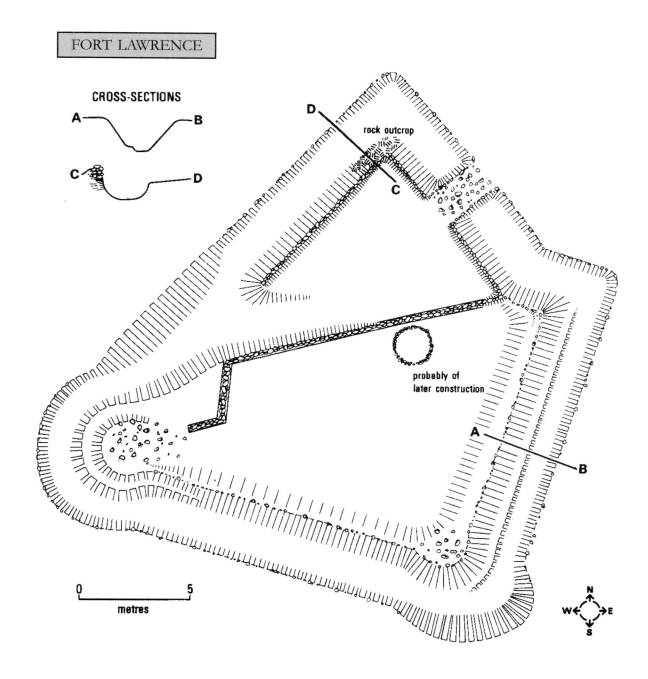

FORT LAWRENCE

CROSS-SECTIONS

A — B

C — D

rock outcrop

D

C

probably of
later construction

A

B

0 ___ 5
metres

N
W E
S

◇ The **Potgieter's Farm Laager** was built by a detachment of one company each of the 1/13th and 90th, which moved there on 21 April 1879 from Wood's Camp at Khambula with 28 wagons to mine coal from an exposed seam. They reportedly built 'a circular stone laager' for their wagons. After sending off some 40 wagon-loads of coal for use as fuel by Wood's force, the detachment rejoined the column on or about 8 May, when Lawrence's company of the 2/4th arrived in the area.

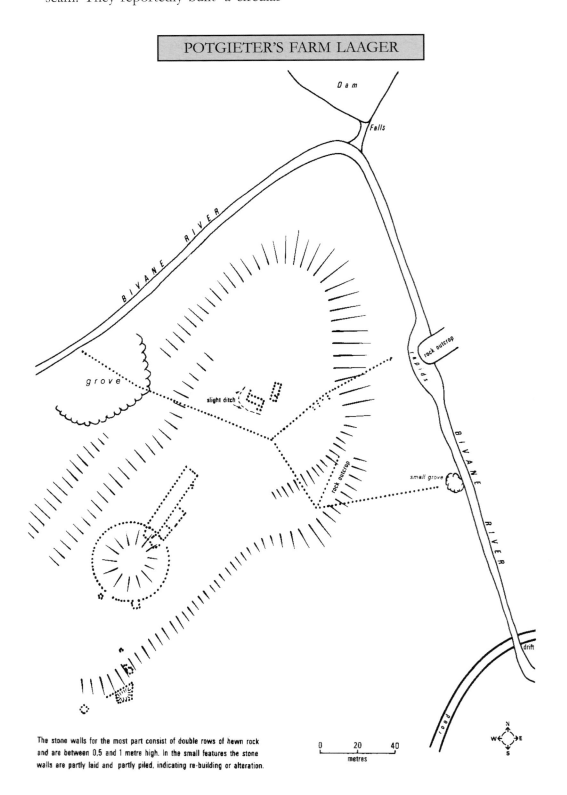

POTGIETER'S FARM LAAGER

The stone walls for the most part consist of double rows of hewn rock and are between 0.5 and 1 metre high. In the small features the stone walls are partly laid and partly piled, indicating re-building or alteration.

At **Utrecht** there was a stone settlers' laager. An adjoining military earthwork fort was built in December 1877 by men of the 80th. Nothing of them has survived.

The **Pivaan Laager** (sometimes referred to as 'Burgher's Laager' or 'Potgieter's Farm Laager') antedated the war. In late 1877, and at least once during early 1878, Boer families took shelter there. A small force of Dutch burghers, under Cmdt J.A. Rudolph, was at the laager in May 1879, though a month later they had left it and were camped close by Fort Lawrence.

In December 1877, preparatory to operations against Sekhukhune in the north-eastern Transvaal, men of the 80th Regiment built a military earthwork fort in Utrecht adjacent to the existing stonework settlers' laager. Throughout the war the fort protected the depot from which Wood's Column drew its supplies. Note the commissariat sheds within the perimeter.

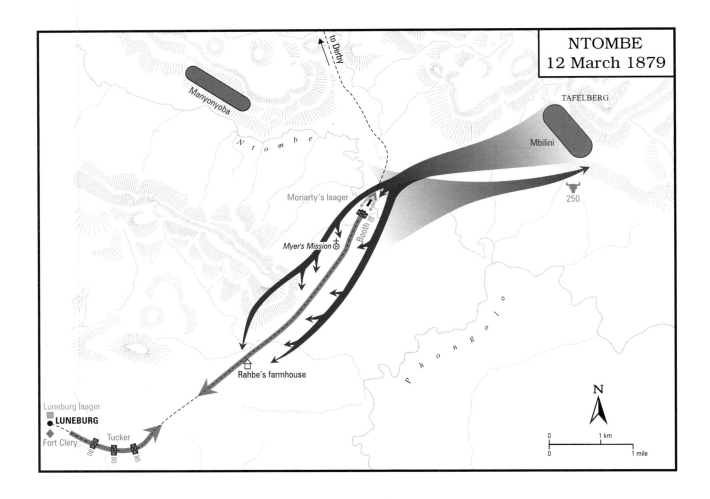

LUNEBURG SECTOR
Action at the Ntombe

A small but sharp action occurred at the drift across the Ntombe River on 12 March 1879 when Zulu irregulars overran a convoy and its escort of men from No. 5 Column.

The Zulu surprise the British camp
Supplies for the garrison of five companies of the 80th Regiment stationed at Luneburg were forwarded from Derby. On 7 March Maj Tucker, the officer in command at Luneburg, sent Capt Moriarty and a detachment of company strength to escort in a convoy of 18 wagons carrying ammunition and supplies. By 9 March the straggling convoy had closed up on the north bank of the Ntombe, but the rain-swollen river prevented all but two wagons crossing at Myer's Drift. While waiting for the river to subside, Moriarty and 71 of his men pitched camp on the north bank and formed a V-shaped laager with the wagons. This defensive arrangement was inadequate because the widely-spaced wagons were neither linked together nor otherwise fortified, and the flanks of the laager were not secured on the riverside in case its level rose and the camp became flooded. From 22 March 35 men commanded by Lt Harward remained on the south bank to guard the two wagons able to cross. Communication across the river was maintained by a raft of planks and empty barrels.

Presented with this soft target, Mbilini, the successful leader of Zulu irregulars in

the vicinity, concentrated his men on Tafelberg, the flat-topped mountain that was one of his fastnesses, 3 miles (about 5 km) north-east of Myer's Drift. On the evening of 11 March, Mbilini personally reconnoitred the British laager. Before dawn the next morning, and under cover of a thick river mist, he led some 800 of his men from Tafelberg against the sleeping camp. They approached unchallenged to within 70 yards (64 m) of the laager. At about 05h15 they fired a volley and rushed on Moriarty and his men with their spears. Taken by surprise, the British were overrun before they could form. On the opposite bank, Harward's detachment fired repeated volleys from the cover of the wagons and large anthills

British forces
No. 5 Column (detachment), Capt D. Moriarty commanding:
One company-strength detachment of the 80th Regiment (Staffordshire Volunteers).

Total: 106 officers and men.

Zulu forces
The irregulars commanded by Prince Mbilini waMswati are variously estimated at between 800 and 4 000 men, though the lower figure is the more likely.

British casualties
Killed: 1 officer and 60 men; a civil surgeon, 2 white wagon conductors and 15 black drivers.
Wounded: 1 man.

Zulu casualties
30 corpses were found on the banks of the Ntombe.
The Zulu were able to carry off their wounded, numbers unknown.

Capt David Barry Moriarty's tent was pitched outside the inadequate laager on the north bank of the Ntombe. When the Zulu attacked he rushed out of his tent and was immediately stabbed in his back with a spear. He nevertheless tried to reach the laager, but was shot in the chest as he clambered over a wagon. Falling onto his knees, he reportedly cried out, 'Fire away boys, death or glory; I am done.' He was later found lying on his face outside the laager. He was quite naked, but not disembowelled.

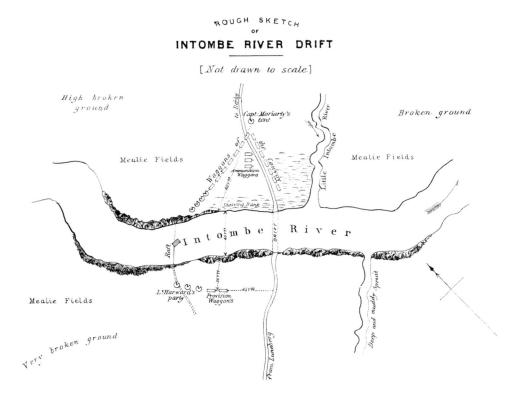

ROUGH SKETCH
OF
INTOMBE RIVER DRIFT

[*Not drawn to scale*]

'Just as I got to the river bank I was wounded in the head with an assegai . . . I waded up to my neck in the river, I then threw my rifle away . . . and being quite under water, and thinking I was drowning, I undid my belt . . . I managed to get hold of some grass and pulled myself up to the top of the bank . . . A Zulu came at me and attempted to stab me with an assegai, which I caught hold of, the blade cutting me between finger and thumb; we struggled, and the assegai broke, the blade being left in my hand, with it I stabbed the Zulu.'

(*Natal Witness*, 27 March 1879)

to cover the flight of a dozen fugitives across the river. Harward galloped away to Luneburg, ostensibly to get help.

The British fighting withdrawal

In his absence, and to avoid being surrounded by several hundred of Mbilini's men who were crossing the river to outflank his men, Sgt Booth rallied his small detachment and fell back in good order along the road towards Luneburg. At Myer's mission station, about half a mile (0.8 km) from the Ntombe, Booth's men made a brief stand. When Zulu skirmishers came up on either side, the British resumed their fighting withdrawal, foiling the Zulu attempt to rush them or cut them off with regular, well-directed volleys. The exhausted British halted once more at Rahbe's deserted farm-

house 3 miles (5 km) from the river. The Zulu came down in force from a hill to their left, but further volleys caused them to retire. Booth's men were able to continue their retreat to Luneburg almost unmolested, escorting the fugitives, all of whom were without arms, and some without clothes.

Harward reached Luneburg before 06h30, and Tucker immediately advanced to the Ntombe with most of the garrison. However, his lack of mounted men enabled Mbilini's force to withdraw unmolested in a dense column to Tafelberg. At the camp they had killed the dogs, shredded the tents and ritually disembowelled the dead. They drove off with them 250 cattle and took most of the ammunition and supplies that had been in the wagons.

Sgt A.C. Booth, 80th Regiment

The famous depiction by Lt B.W.R. Ussher, 80th Regiment, of Mbilini's dawn attack on Capt Moriarty's convoy and escort at the drift across the Ntombe River. Ussher's sketch was engraved and published by the Illustrated London News *on 12 March 1879. In the process, the shape of the low, flat-topped hills in the background were greatly exaggerated, as was the number of combatants.*

NEWCASTLE SECTOR

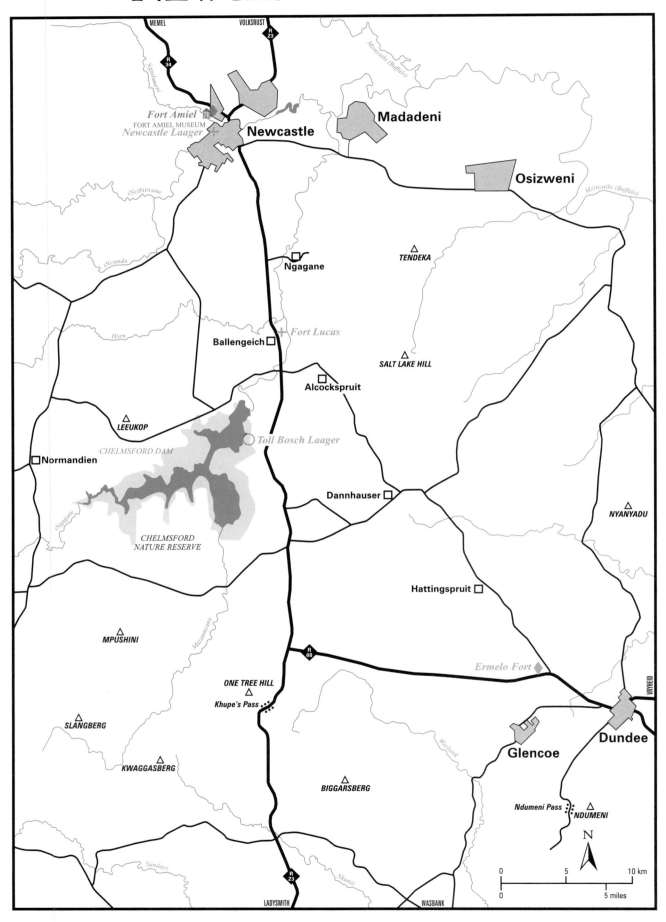

NEWCASTLE SECTOR
Fortifications

◆ The **Ermelo Fort** was begun in January 1878 on the initiative of the local settlers, and work on the stone laager was practically complete by mid-May. It seems that it was fleetingly used by a few settlers in the weeks of panic after Isandlwana.

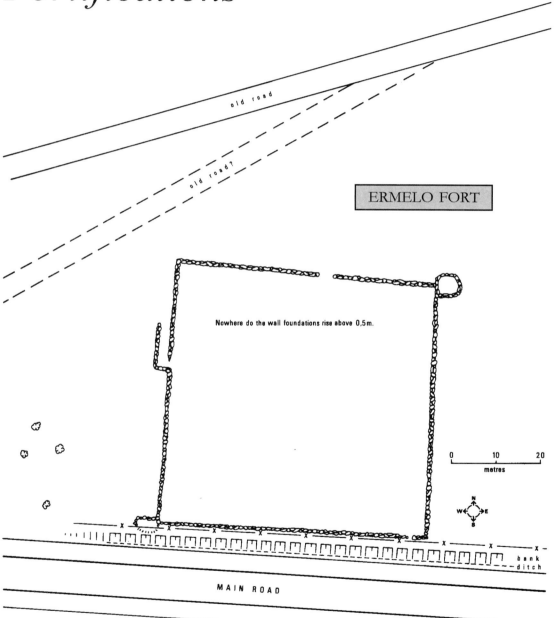

old road

old road?

ERMELO FORT

Nowhere do the wall foundations rise above 0,5m.

0   10   20
metres

N W E S

bank
ditch

MAIN ROAD

Fort Amiel, which commands Newcastle from the left bank of the Ncandu River, was built by the 80th Regiment (Staffordshire Volunteers), under Lt-Col C.F. Amiel, as a base for troops involved in the annexation of the Transvaal Colony in April 1877. During the war it was a rear depot and hospital for Wood's column. From mid-October 1878 until February 1879, when a company of the 2/4th (King's Own Royal) Regiment was posted there, a few invalids seem to have been the only defenders. The fort consisted then of some mud buildings enclosed by a rampart and stone wall surrounded by a ditch. During both the First and Second Anglo-Boer Wars the fort continued in use by the British, and was much altered and added to. Restored to the way it looked *circa* 1902, it now houses a museum.

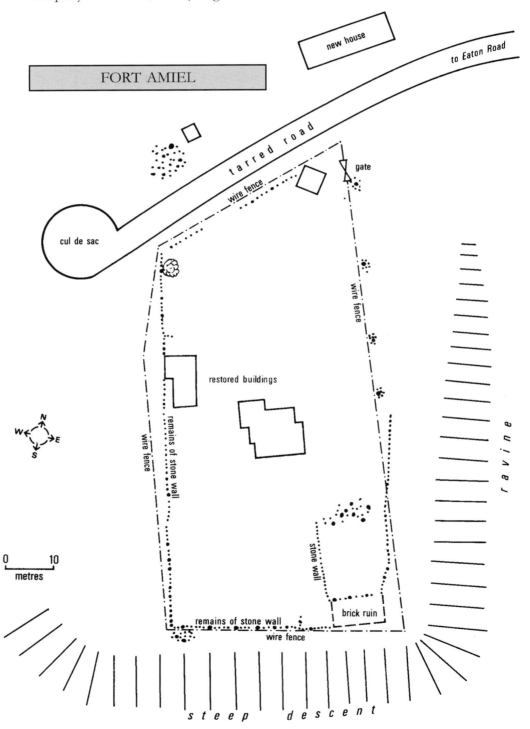

Mining operations at Ballengeich seem to have obliterated any remains of **Fort Lucas**, a pre-war fortification that was apparently not considered fit for use during 1879, although shown on certain wartime maps. Similarly, urban development has demolished the **Newcastle Laager**, which the Natal government built during 1877–8 in the centre of the town.

The **Toll Bosch Laager** (or 'Ingagane Laager') was started some time after January 1878 on Crown Land. However, the local settlers' building committee and the Natal government could not agree on the tenure and disposition of the site and surrounding land, so the settlers abandoned work on the laager, probably in July or August. The incomplete laager was never used during the war.

A view of Fort Amiel taken across the Ncandu River from the village of Newcastle in 1879. The fort and its environs were then being used as a transit camp, hospital and rear depot for Wood's Column. Note the military tents dotting the hillside in the distance, and the commissariat wagons and carts in the foreground.

ULUNDI SECTOR

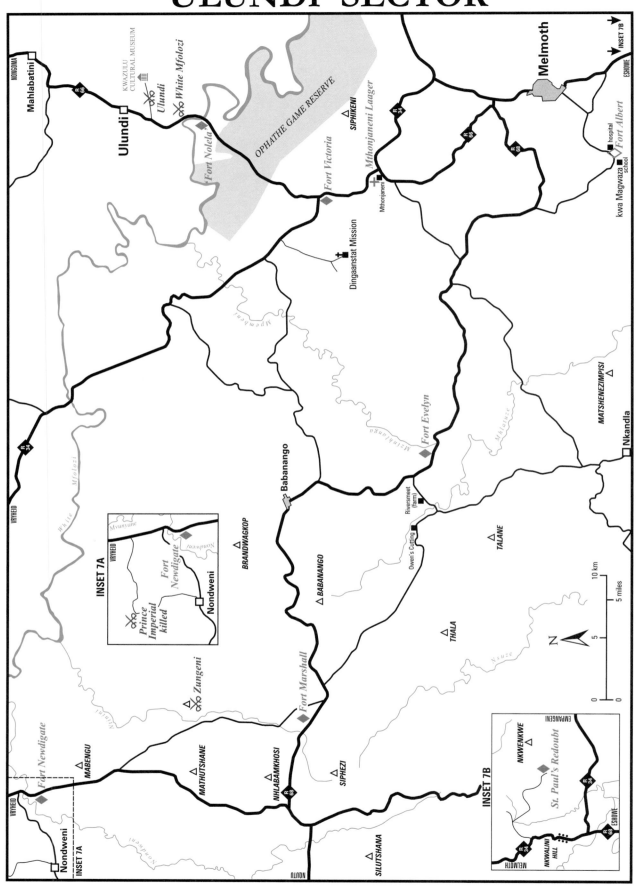

ULUNDI SECTOR

Fortifications

◆ The 2nd Division, South African Field Frce, built **Fort Newdigate** (named after Maj-Gen E. Newdigate, commander of the Division), on 6 June 1879 on its line of supply and communication in Zululand. It was garrisoned by two companies of the 2/21st Regiment (Royal Scots Fusiliers), a detachment of

No. 10 Battery, 7th Brigade, Royal Artillery, with two Gatling guns, and a company of the 2nd Battalion, Natal Native Contingent, with a squadron of the 1st (The King's) Dragoon Guards to maintain communications. The entire force was under the command of Maj J.C. Marter, KDG. Two companies of the 1/24th (2nd Warwickshire) Regiment replaced those of the 2/21st on or about 19 July. The Flying Column joined the 2nd Division on 18 June and they advanced together on oNdini, constructing several laagers and fort along their route.

FORT NEWDIGATE

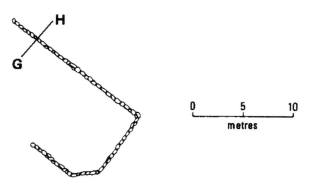

CROSS-SECTIONS

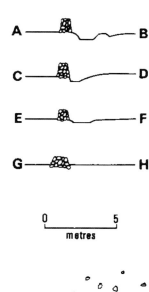

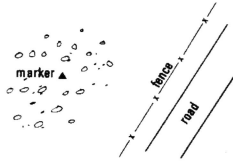

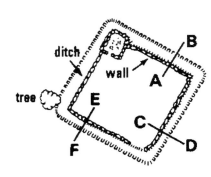

On 18 June the joint force built **Fort Marshall** (named after Maj-Gen F. Marshall, commander of the Cavalry Brigade attached to the 2nd Division). Two companies of the 2/21st garrisoned it, and two troops of the 17th (Duke of Cambridge's Own) Lancers were based there to protect the line forward. Col W.P. Collingwood, of the 21st, assumed command of Forts Marshall and Newdigate. From mid-August a company of the 58th (Rutlandshire) Regiment garrisoned Fort Marshall.

FORT MARSHALL

CROSS-SECTIONS

◆ **Fort Evelyn** (initially 'Fort Evelyn Wood') was built on 22–23 June by two companies of the 58th, who garrisoned it along with a division of N Battery, 6th Brigade, Royal Artillery, with two 7-pounders, a detachment of the 2nd Battalion, NNC, and a troop of the Natal Light Horse. Maj Foster of the 58th was in command.

FORT EVELYN

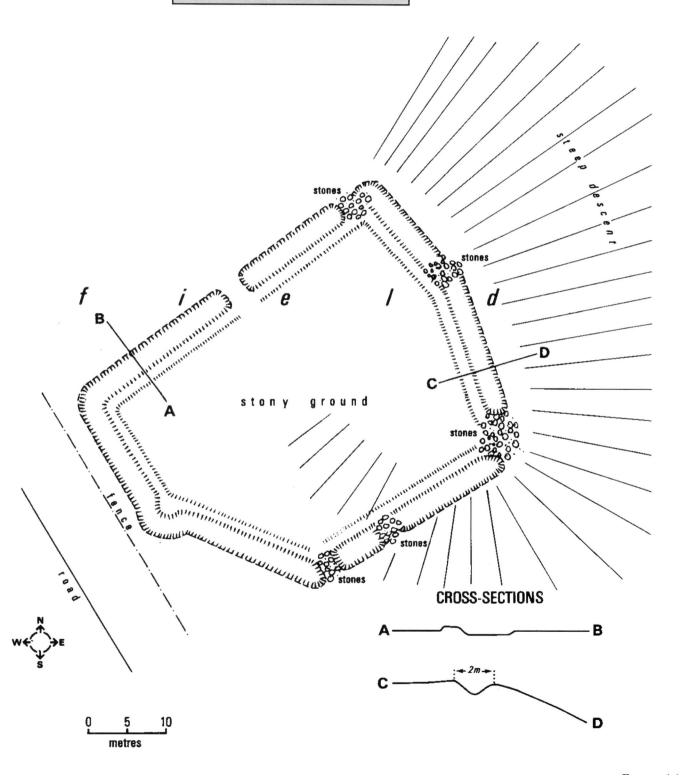

CROSS-SECTIONS

metres
0   5   10

PAGE 149

On 2 July men of the 2/21st built **'Fort Nolela'** (or 'Fort Ulundi', and sometimes erroneously called 'Fort Victoria') on the little hill commanding the double laager constructed by joint force on the banks of the White Mfolozi two days before the battle of Ulundi.

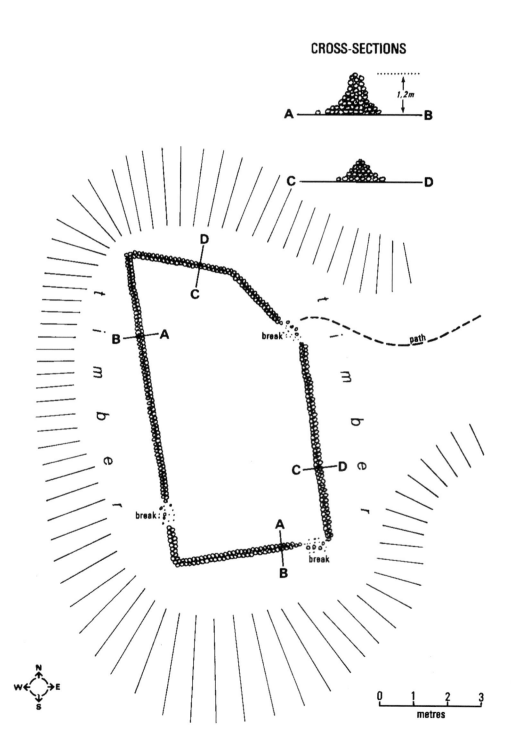

FORT NOLELA

CROSS-SECTIONS

Fort Victoria was built on 7 August by the 58th, whose headquarters and three companies remained there until 26 August, when the garrison was reduced to one company.

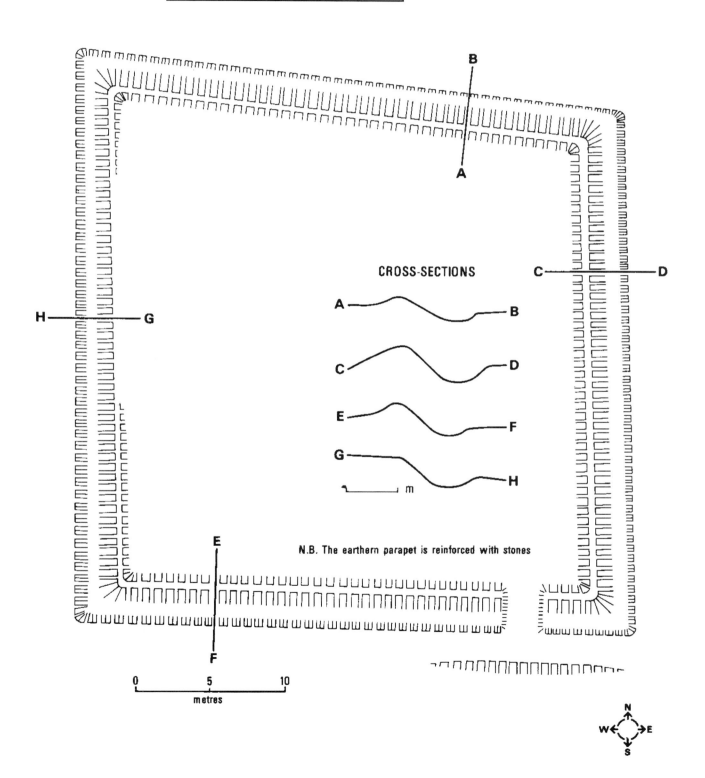

FORT VICTORIA

CROSS-SECTIONS

N.B. The earthern parapet is reinforced with stones

0   5   10
metres

◆ On the hill adjacent to **St Paul's** Anglican mission, the 5th Company, Royal Engineers, began a small redoubt on 28 July. It was garrisoned by men of the 90th Regiment (Perthshire Volunteers Light Infantry), stationed at the mission from 15 July until the end of September. After Zululand was annexed as a British colony in May 1887, a small detachment of the 1/1st Prince of Wales's (North Staffordshire) Regiment garrisoned the post from October 1887 to September 1888, and may have altered the redoubt.

ST PAUL'S REDOUBT

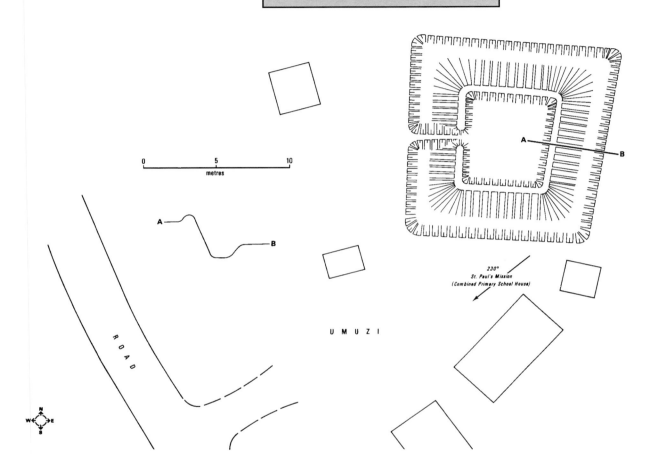

✚ On 29 June the 2nd Division and Flying Column built three laagers surrounded by a breastwork on the **Mthonjaneni heights**. When the joint force resumed its advance on oNdini on 30 June, Mthonjaneni was garrisoned by two companies of the 1/24th, one NCO and two privates from each company in the joint force, the 'weakly', a troop of Shepstone's Native Horse and a few of Baker's Horse. Major R. Upcher of the 24th was in command. The laager was broken up on 6 July, and no vestige remains. The extensive earthworks still to be seen on Mthonjaneni were begun in October 1887 when a British garrison was posted there following the annexation of Zululand. There are no remains of the various march laagers the joint force constructed along its line of advance into Zululand.

Fort Albert was built on 11–12 July by Clarke's Column and was initially named 'Fort Robertson' after the Revd R. Robertson of the KwaMagwaza Anglican mission nearby. The garrison consisted of two companies of the 94th Regiment and a division of N Battery, 6th Brigade, Royal Artillery, with two 9-pounders. Later, between June and September 1888, at the time of the uSuthu 'rebellion', a small detachment of the 1/1st North Staffordshires and the Eshowe Native Levy were posted there. The fort was a small enclosure, and there are remains of what may have been part of the wall and ditch at the site.

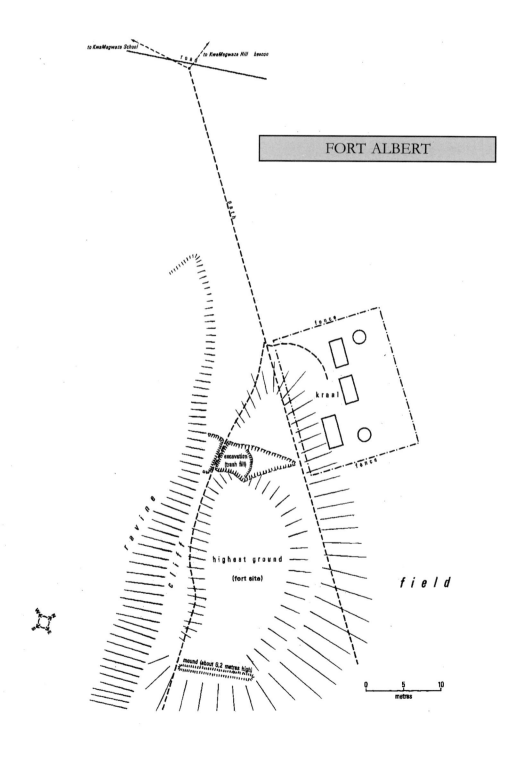

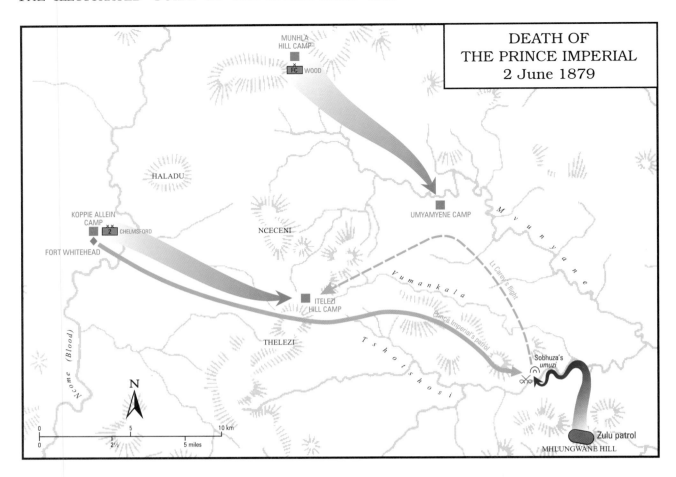

DEATH OF
THE PRINCE IMPERIAL
2 June 1879

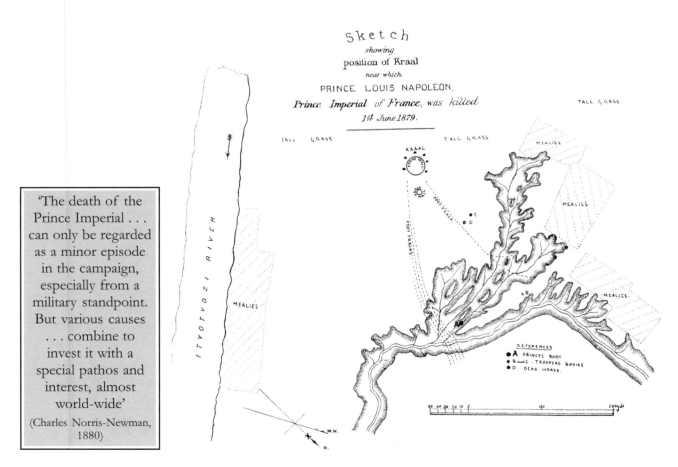

Sketch
showing
position of Kraal
near which
PRINCE LOUIS NAPOLEON,
Prince Imperial of France, was killed
1st June 1879.

'The death of the
Prince Imperial . . .
can only be regarded
as a minor episode
in the campaign,
especially from a
military standpoint.
But various causes
. . . combine to
invest it with a
special pathos and
interest, almost
world-wide'

(Charles Norris-Newman,
1880)

ULUNDI SECTOR

Death of the Prince Imperial

British forces
Louis Napoleon, Prince Imperial of France
No. 3 Troop, Natal Horse (Bettington's Horse) (detachment), Lt J.B. Carey.
Zulu guide.

Total: Prince Imperial, 1 officer, 6 men, 1 guide

Zulu forces
Small elements of the iNgobamakhosi, uMbonambi and uNokhenke *amabutho* numbering between 30 and 60 men.

British casualties
Killed: Prince Imperial, 2 troopers and 1 guide.

Zulu casualties
Nil.

The death on 1 June 1879 of the exiled Prince Imperial of France while on patrol near the Tshotshosi River caused more consternation in Britain than the battle of Isandlwana itself.

The Fatal Patrol

Louis Napoleon, the exiled Prince Imperial of France and Bonapartist pretender to the French throne, came to Natal as an observer in March 1879 with the British government's grudging permission. Lord Chelmsford attached him to his staff as an additional aide-de-camp. In May Chelmsford assigned the Prince to Lt-Col Harrison, Assistant Quartermaster-General in charge of supplying the 2nd Division, South African Field Force, and planning the route that it would take through Zululand. Twice during May 1879 the Prince was permitted to accompany patrols reconnoitring the country in advance of the 2nd Division.

On 1 June the Prince joined a patrol consisting of Lt Carey, 98th Foot, Sgt Willis, Cpl Grubb and Troopers Le Tocq, Abel, Cochrane and Rogers of Bettington's Horse, and a Zulu guide. Although Carey was the senior combatant officer present, he deferred to the Prince who effectively exercised command. Their orders were to select the future camping ground for the Division along the banks of the Tshotshosi River, and to examine the road ahead. From the reports of previous patrols, it was believed the area was free of Zulu combatants.

The patrol started from the camp at Koppie Alleen at 09h15 and soon after 10h00 reached Thelezi hill where the Division was to camp that night. The party then moved along the ridge between the Vumankala and Tshotshosi rivers, and at about 14h30 descended towards an

General view by Melton Prior, special artist for the Illustrated London News, of the scene of the Prince Imperial's death two days after the event. Sobhuza's umuzi, where the Prince's party off-saddled, is in the right centre ground (marked 3). The donga where the Prince died is in the centre (marked 1), and the place where the troopers fell is marked 2. The camp of the 2nd Division is to the left (marked 6). The Flying Column's camp is in the centre left distance (marked 4).

The Prince Imperial and the reconnoitring party at Sobhuza's umuzi *a few minutes before the Zulu attack. The Prince is seated on the ground, the Zulu guide is to the left, and Lt J.B. Carey stands in the centre in front of the troopers of Bettington's Horse. S. Durand drew the scene for the* Graphic *of 6 September 1879 based on information supplied by Lt Carey and on his inspection of the site.*

umuzi on the banks of the Tshotshosi. The *umuzi*, which belonged to Sobhuza and consisted of five huts, had been deserted by its occupants at the patrol's approach. When the Prince reached the *umuzi*, he ordered his men to off-saddle, make coffee and rest.

Meanwhile, a party of between 30 and 60 Zulu, who were also scouting in the area to monitor the advance of the British, spotted the Prince's patrol from their vantage point on Muhlungwane hill to the south-east. Realizing they had the numerical advantage, the Zulu decided to attack. They moved down a deep donga opening into the Tshotshosi and, under cover of the high river banks and mealie-fields, closed to within 15 yards (14 m) of the *umuzi*.

The Zulu ambush

At 15h35 Carey suggested saddling up but the Prince had decided to wait some minutes. Then at 15h50 the Zulu guide warned that he had detected enemy movements and the Prince ordered the patrol to prepare to move out. The stealthily approaching Zulu waited until the British were drawn up together ready to mount before firing a ragged volley. No one was hit but the British panicked and threw themselves as best they could into their saddles. The Zulu fired another volley as the British scattered, and charged forward, shouting their war-cry. Rogers, who had been unable to mount, was immediately speared. Abel was shot through the back as he galloped away. The Zulu then caught and killed the guide. One of their horses was also shot dead. Carey and the remaining four troopers who had galloped off safely, formed up on the other side of the donga, still under fire. One party of Zulu was following them and another was attempting to cut off their retreat across the ridge. Feeling under threat and presuming the Prince to be dead, Carey decided to make his way to the camp of the 2nd Division at Thelezi hill, where he reported to Chelmsford at 19h00.

The Prince Imperial brought to bay

Carey was correct in believing that the

Prince had failed to make his escape. His unmanageably excited grey had reared and broken away after the other horses before the Prince was in the saddle. He clung to the holster attached to the saddle for more than 100 yards (over 91 m) while he attempted to mount, before its leather strap broke. Kicked and winded as he fell, and having lost his sword, the Prince tried to run after his fleeing comrades. Several Zulu caught up with him in the donga 160 yards (146 m) from the *umuzi*. He gamely turned at bay and fired two to five shots (accounts differ) from his revolver, all of which missed. Zabanga threw a spear which struck the Prince in the thigh. The Prince pulled it out and brandished it at his foes. Langalibalele then threw a spear, followed once more by Zabanga and then Gwabakana. Mortally wounded, the Prince sank down and the Zulu rushed upon him, striking him with their spears. He suffered 18 wounds (any one of five would have proved fatal). As soon as the Prince was dead, Klabawathunga and Dabayane observed Zulu rites for the removal of the contagious ritual pollution that followed homicide (*umnyama*), and stripped the Prince in order to wear items of his apparel and slit his abdomen. The same was done to the two fallen troopers and guide.

The following day strong British parties located the Prince's body. It was taken to the camp at Koppie Alleen where it was embalmed and returned to England for burial. The two troopers were buried in the donga close to where the Prince had been found. In March 1880, a party commanded by Major H. Sparke Stabb, 32nd Regiment, erected a memorial stone cross paid for by Queen Victoria who 'desired' it to mark the spot where the Prince had fallen.

> 'The Prince ran to jump onto his horse and the horse reared up and he struck his belly and he fell back winded and holding himself. He made no further attempt to run for his horse which had gone. He stood and fired 3 quick shots with his revolver. I saw the look of surprise on his face that he hit nothing. He tried twice more slowly and still he hit nothing'.
> (M'Wunuzane, c. 1935)

Lt-Col Crealock's sketch of the Prince Imperial's left profile made on 3 June 1879, two days after his death. The other side of the Prince's face had been disfigured by a spear-wound through his right eye.

Melton Prior was present to sketch the body of the slain Prince Imperial being brought into the Itelezi Camp of the 2nd Division on 2 July 1879 by men of the 17th Lancers. In the background of the picture, which the London Illustrated News *published on 19 July 1879, Prior has shown the ambulance wagon in which the corpse had been transported.*

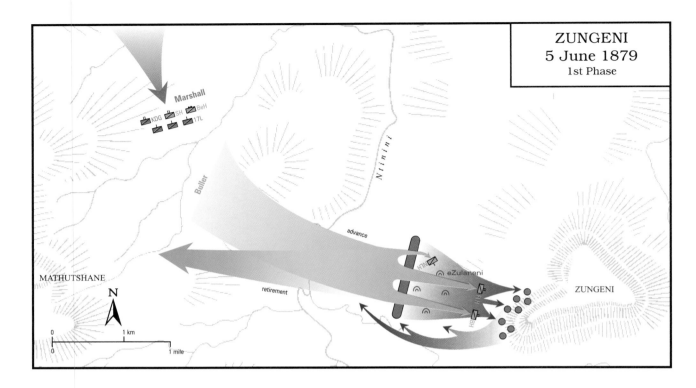

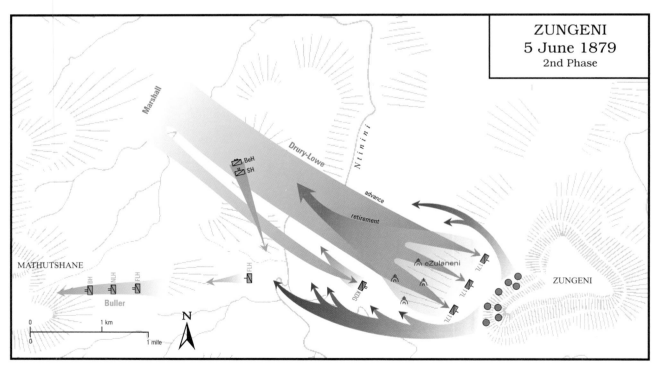

ULUNDI SECTOR
Skirmish at Zungeni

The skirmish at Zungeni Mountain on 4 June 1879 demonstrated the superiority of the tactical skills of colonial irregular horse over British regular cavalry, as well as Zulu effectiveness in skirmishing over broken terrain.

The irregular horse torch eZulaneni

On 4 June Baker's Horse, reconnoitring ahead of the Flying Column in the direction of Babanango Mountain, had a slight skirmish with a force of Zulu quartered in a cluster of four large *imizi* lying east across the Ntinini stream in a small, open plain, about 400 yards (366 m) from the steepish side of Zungeni Mountain. Known as eZulaneni, the cluster belonged to Sihayo kaXongo, the Qungebe chief. Three wagons and an ammunition cart, captured from the British at Isandlwana, were drawn up outside one of the *imizi*.

Lord Chelmsford feared that the Zulu at eZulaneni might be part of a large army concentrating ahead of him. To make certain, he ordered Lt-Col Buller and a force of irregular horse from the camp of the Flying Column on the southern bank of the Nondweni River to investigate further. At the same time, at dawn on 5 June, a section of the Cavalry Brigade under Maj-Gen Marshall set out in support from the camp of the 2nd Division, South African Field Force on the Tshotshosi River, 5 miles (8 km) to the Flying Column's rear.

Seeing Buller's force approaching, some 300 Zulu drew up in line in front of eZulaneni. With the Frontier Light Horse in the centre, Baker's Horse on the left and the Natal Light Horse on the right, Buller charged. The Zulu re-formed out of line into companies and scattered to take up position almost 300 yards (274 m) behind eZulaneni, on the lower slopes of Zungeni, which was seamed with dongas and covered in thorn trees and mimosa bush. From under cover of the bush they opened fire, many with Martini-Henry rifles. The Frontier Light Horse and Baker's Horse dismounted at between 200 and 275 yards (183 and 251 m) from the Zulu. While they exchanged fire, the Natal Light Horse put eZulaneni to the torch. After half an hour's shooting, Buller's men mounted their horses to retire. At that vulnerable moment the Zulu redoubled their fire, and some on their left rushed forward to outflank the British. At about 80 yards (73 m) they poured in volley, wounding two men of Baker's Horse and killing and injuring several horses. But Buller extricated his men and withdrew a mile (1.6 km) beyond the Ntinini.

> 'As we advanced, nearing the kraals, the enemy retired into the belt of thorn bush surrounding the base of the mountain . . . from which they poured a heavy fusilade on us as we advanced . . . Before we retired, a party of Zulus crept down the donga on the left . . . through the long grass, and poured in a volley.'
>
> (*Natal Mercury Supplement*, June 1879)

British forces
Cavalry Brigade, 2nd Division, South African Field Force (detachment), Maj-Gen F. Marshall commanding:
One squadron of the 1st (The King's) Dragoon Guards; three troops of the 17th (Duke of Cambridge's Own) Lancers.
One squadron of Shepstone's Native Horse and a detachment of No. 3 Troop, Natal Horse (Bettington's Horse).

Total: approx. 500 officers and men

Mounted Troops, Flying Column (detachment), Lt-Col R.H. Buller commanding:
One Squadron of the Frontier Light Horse; one squadron of Baker's Horse; and a troop of the Natal Light Horse.

Total: approx. 300 officers and men

Zulu forces
Some 300 Zulu quartered at eZulaneni

British casualties
Killed: 1 officer
Wounded: 2 men

Zulu casualties
On 8 June, a British mounted reconnaissance-in-force found 25 Zulu corpses

Between 7 and 17 June 1879 the 2nd Division remained encamped in the Ntinini (Phoko) valley across from Zungeni Mountain, the scene of the skirmish of 5 June 1879. In Lt-Col Crealock's water-colour drawing, the flat-topped Zungeni mountain with its bush-covered slopes can be seen on the right beyond the British camp, and Nhlazatshe Mountain with its rocky buttresses is in the distance to the left.

The cavalry repulsed

There Buller encountered Marshall and his force, who were eager for action. Although it was quite unnecessary, the 17th Lancers charged towards eZulaneni. At the burning *imizi* they came under Zulu fire and the adjutant, Lt Frith, was shot dead. The Lancers then advanced to within 145 yards (133 m) of the Zulu, where a troop dismounted and using their carbines exchanged fire with the Zulu. Marshall, seeing the Lancers engaged in unsuitable terrain, pushed the squadron of Dragoons across the Ntinini to support them on their flank and right rear as they fell back. The Zulu pursued the cavalry in skirmishing order, working around their flanks under cover, and keeping up a brisk, though inaccurate fire. Some crept down a donga and along the river bed to the right of the British and opened fire on a lingering troop of the Frontier Light Horse, which was saddling up preparatory to falling back. Shepstone's Horse advanced to give covering fire and drove off the Zulu. Buller then retired his men out of range over Mathutshane Mountain to the Flying Column's new camp. Marshall's men lingered in the plain to the west of the Ntinini in the hope of being able to charge the Zulu in the open, but the latter could not be drawn. Disappointed, the cavalry withdrew to the 2nd Division's camp, which had been advanced to the right side of the Nondweni.

ULUNDI SECTOR

Reconnaissance in force across the White Mfolozi

The mounted troops of the Flying Column only narrowly extricated themselves when, during their reconnaissance on 3 July across the White Mfolozi River preparatory to the battle of Ulundi the next day, they rode into a cunningly laid Zulu ambush.

The British camp at the White Mfolozi

On 2 July the 2nd Division moved forward to join the Flying Column already halted on the south bank of the White Mfolozi across from the Mahlabathini plain where nine *amakhanda*, including oNdini, were clustered, and where the Zulu army was concentrated.. The joint British force set about preparing a strong double laager anchored on a stone fort. Meanwhile, on his own initiative, Chief Zibhebhu ka-Maphitha (the most resourceful of the Zulu commanders) posted some thirty marksmen in the rocks of a high bluff overlooking the wagon drift across the river to fire on British watering and bathing parties. These snipers were still firing away the following day (3 July) when, at noon, Chelmsford finally broke off negotiations with King Cetshwayo who had been attempting to secure a last-minute cessation of hostilities.

With the parleying over, Chelmsford intended to advance into the Mahlabathini plain on the morning of 4 July to offer

battle. In preparation, he ordered Lt-Col Buller to make a reconnaissance in force across the river with all the mounted men of the Flying Column. Buller's objectives were to be, firstly, to drive off Zibhebhu's troublesome snipers; secondly, to approach as near as possible to oNdini to find the best position for Chelmsford's army to take up the following day; and, thirdly, to provoke the Zulu into responding to his sortie so as to give away their points of concentration and likely tactics.

Buller's sortie

Accordingly, at about 13h00 on 3 July Baker's Horse crossed the river by the wagon drift and made straight for the Zulu sharpshooters posted on the bluff. Supporting fire from two 9-pounder guns helped distract the enemy. Simultaneously, Buller led the larger part of the mounted men across a drift downstream of Baker's Horse and wheeled to take the Zulu in their flank. Disconcerted, the Zulu scattered, pursued for some way by Baker's Horse, who then halted and regrouped. Buller, meanwhile, continued across the plain having investigated the abandoned

> 'Zibebu went off to investigate what the enemy were doing at the Mfolozi. He observed some of them swimming in the river. He crept up on them through the bushes and fired on them. At once they set off in hot pursuit of him. They followed closely, firing at him. His pony galloped at top speed, ears drawn back, until near Ndabakawombe. There they left off the pursuit and went back. They said, "You'll see more of us tomorrow!"'
>
> (Mtshapi kaNoradu of the uMcijo *ibutho*, 6 April 1918)

British forces
Mounted Troops, Flying Column, Lt-Col R.H. Buller commanding:
One squadron of Mounted Infantry; two squadrons of Baker's Horse; two squadrons of the Frontier Light Horse; one squadron of the Natal Light Horse; two troops of the Natal Native Horse; one squadron of Raaf's Transvaal Rangers.

Total: approx. 500 officers and men

2nd Division, South African Field Force (detachment)
N Battery, 6th Brigade, Royal Artillery (two 9-pounder guns).
Three companies of the 1st Battalion, 24th (2nd Warwickshire) Regiment.

Total: approx. 300 officers and men

Zulu forces
Several thousand men from the *amabutho* stationed in the *amakhanda* in the Mahlabathini plain (perhaps as many as 10 000, though their precise number is entirely conjectural) played some part in the attempt to trap the British reconnaissance force. The uMxhapho *ibutho* took the lead in springing the ambush at the Mbilane stream. Zibhebhu kaMaphitha, the Mandlakazi chief and senior *induna* of the uDloko *ibutho*, devised the Zulu strategy and commanded the mounted scouts who lured the British forward.

British casualties
Killed: 3 troopers
Wounded: 4 troopers

Zulu casualties
Unknown

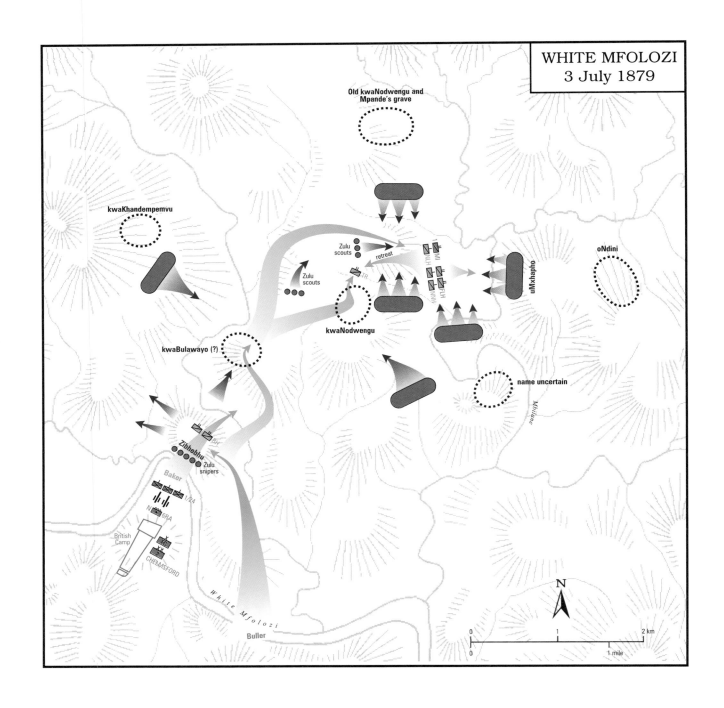

WHITE MFOLOZI
3 July 1879

Old kwaNodwengu and
Mpande's grave

kwaKhandempemvu

Zulu
scouts

retreat

oNdini

uMxhapho

Zulu
scouts

kwaNodwengu

kwaBulawayo (?)

name uncertain

Mbilane

Zibhebhu

Zulu
snipers

Baker

1/24

N   6RA

British
Camp

CHELMSFORD

White Mfolozi

Buller

N

0   1   2 km

0   1 mile

Capt Lord W.L. de la P. Beresford, 9th Lancers
Cmdt C.D. D'Arcy, Frontier Light Horse
Sgt E. O'Toole, Frontier Light Horse

Sgt-Maj S. Kambula, Natal Native
Horse

kwaBulawayo *ikhanda*. His horsemen encountered some twenty Zulu scouts who had been deliberately placed to entice them forward, and who ran on with great courage as far as the kwaNodwengu *ikhanda*. There they were relieved by another party of Zulu who, driving a large flock of goats, drew the pursuing British towards oNdini over the very ground where the next day's battle would be fought. Galloping Zulu horsemen, led by Zibhebhu, next took up the task, and lured Buller's men to the valley of the Mbilane stream.

The Zulu ambush

Buller, having met thus far with no serious Zulu opposition, was beginning to believe that the Zulu army might have withdrawn from the Mahlabithini plain, and that it would be possible to torch the lightly guarded oNdini, just across the Mbilane. But several thousand Zulu, among whom the uMxhapho *ibutho* was prominent, were concealed in two lines at right angles to the British front and right along the bed of the Mbilane and in a donga that ran into it. The long grass on the stream's banks had been carefully plaited to trip or impede the horses. Seeing this, Buller at last sensed a trap, and halted his men. At that, the Zulu rose up and poured a volley into the British at about 150 yds (137 m) range. Fortunately for the British, the Zulu fire was high and they suffered only four casualties. Buller instantly wheeled his men about, but they were still in grave danger. Two further Zulu forces of several thousand men each had been concealed on both flanks behind the British who had earlier passed unwittingly between them, and they now began to close together to cut off Buller's escape.

Buller extricates his men

Buller was saved partly by his foresight. During the advance, the Transvaal Rangers had reconnoitred the kwaNodwengu *ikhanda*, but found it empty, and Buller had ordered Cmdt Raaf to halt his men nearby as supports while he pushed forward. So when Buller pulled his horsemen back, firing by alternate ranks, Raaf was able to help cover his retreat. Baker's Horse, who were still stationed near the bluff, supplied

Chief Zibhebhu kaMaphitha of the Mandlakazi, photographed with one of his wives. A cousin of the king, he was one the most able and ambitious men in Zululand. He maintained close contacts with white traders and had acquired an informed appreciation of the value of firearms and horses in warfare. Nevertheless, though his personal courage and skills as a commander were widely acknowledged, and despite being the senior induna *of the uDloko ibutho, his relative youth at the age of 35 precluded him from a top command in the Zulu army.*

cover in their turn, and were supported by fire from over the river from the two 9-pounders and three hastily brought up companies of the 1/24th Regiment.

Nevertheless, Buller and his men were lucky to make their escape relatively unscathed. As they fell back, further

Cmdt Cecil D'Arcy (sitting) and Sgt Edmund O'Toole of the Frontier Light Horse, posing with the Victoria Crosses they were awarded for the gallantry they displayed during the reconnaissance of 3 July. D'Arcy turned back to rescue the unhorsed Tpr Raubenheim, but his horse then threw them both, injuring D'Arcy's back, and he was forced to leave Raubenheim to be stabbed to death by the Zulu. O'Toole rode back to provide covering fire for Capt Beresford who was rescuing Sgt Fitzmaurice. Beresford also received the Victoria Cross.

'Bill [Beresford] partly lifted, partly hustled the wounded man [Sgt John Fitzmaurice] into his saddle, then scrambled up somehow in front of him, and set the good little beast going after the other horsemen . . . There was a critical moment when their escape would have been impossible, but for the cool courage of Sergeant O'Toole, who rode back to the rescue, shot down Zulu after Zulu with his revolver as they tried to close in on the hapless pair, and then aided Beresford in keeping the wounded man in the saddle'.

(Archibald Forbes, 1891)

concentrations of Zulu moving to cut them off revealed themselves on the hills to the west and in the hollows of the plain. Some real acts of gallantry were elicited in this desperate situation, and three of the horsemen were subsequently awarded the Victoria Cross for risking death by turning back to rescue men who had been unhorsed. The Zulu exhibited equal dash and courage. They pursued the retiring British in excellent skirmishing order right down to the river's edge, valiantly disregarding the heavy rifle-fire from the infantry and the shrapnel and grape-shot from the guns on the opposite bank.

Later that day, some Zulu called out to the British outposts across the White Mfolozi, gloating with derisive laughs over their victory. But Buller had in fact achieved his objectives despite the perils he had run, and gathered the necessary intelligence for the next day's battle.

The striking representation in the Illustrated London News *of 6 September 1879 of Capt Lord William Beresford's 'encounter with a Zulu' during the reconnaissance of 3 July. 'Fighting Bill', as he was known, was Lt-Col Buller's Staff Officer and a notorious bruiser and all-round sportsman. When one of the running Zulu scouts turned at bay, Beresford parried his spear and, with the impetus of his galloping horse to aid him, stabbed him through the shield with his sabre straight in his heart. The Zulu's captured spear was destined to stand as a trophy in the corner of Beresford's mother's drawing-room.*

ULUNDI SECTOR

Battle of Ulundi

Drawn up in an infantry square in the Mahlabathini plain on 4 July 1879, the British finally crushed the Zulu army at what they called the battle of Ulundi. The Zulu normally referred to it as the battle of kwaNodwengu after the *ikhanda* nearest which it was fought, or as oCwecweni, the battle of the corrugated-iron sheets. The flashing of the bayonets, swords and gun barrels along the four sides of the impregnable British formation doubtless gave rise to this impression, though many Zulu (including King Cetshwayo) afterwards insisted that the British had fought from behind iron shields.

The British square

Lord Chelmsford's forces began their preparations at 03h45 on 4 July for their advance into the Mahlabathini plain from their fortified camp on the southern bank of the White Mfolozi. Buller's mounted irregulars of the Flying Column crossed by the lower drift at 06h00. They took up position commanding the upper drift across which the Flying Column and 2nd Division, South African Field Force moving in parallel columns, had both passed shortly after 07h00. The Zulu did not oppose the crossing. Col Bellairs remained behind in command of the garrison that was to hold the double wagon laager, anchored on a small, stone-built fort, should the Zulu attempt to seize it while the main force was committed in the plain.

Once it had moved out of bush onto open ground, the Flying Column halted at 07h30, about 1.5 miles (2.4 km) from the drift, and formed the front half of a hollow square, which was completed by the 2nd Division marching up behind it.

British forces
Lt-Gen Lord Chelmsford commanding.

2nd Division, South African Field Force, Maj-Gen E. Newdigate commanding:
1st (The King's) Dragoon Guards; 17th (Duke of Cambridge's Own) Lancers.
N Battery, 6th Brigade, Royal Artillery (six 9-pounder guns); N Battery, 5th Brigade, Royal Artillery (two 7-pounder guns).
2/21st Regiment (Royal Scots Fusiliers); 58th (Rutlandshire) Regiment; 94th Regiment.
Shepstone's Native Horse; No. 3 Troop, Natal Horse (Bettington's Horse).
2nd Battalion, Natal Native Contingent.
Army Medical Department.

Total: 132 officers, 1 752 white troops and 540 black troops, and 39 camp followers.

Flying Column, Brig-Gen H.E. Wood commanding:
No. 11 Battery, 7th Brigade, Royal Artillery (four 7-pounder guns); No. 10 Battery, 7th Brigade, Royal Artillery (two Gatling guns).
Detachment of Royal Engineers.
1/13th Regiment (1st Somersetshire) Prince Albert's Light Infantry; 80th Regiment (Staffordshire Volunteers); 90th Regiment (Perthshire Volunteers Light Infantry).
Mounted Infantry; Frontier Light Horse; Natal Light Horse; Natal Native Horse; Raaf's Transvaal Rangers;.
Wood's Irregulars; Natal Native Pioneer Corps.
Detachment of the Army Hospital Corps.

Total: 122 officers, 2 159 white troops and 465 black troops, and 108 camp followers.

Garrison holding the camp at the White Mfolozi, Col W. Bellairs commanding:
One company of Royal Engineers.
Five companies of the 1/24th (2nd Warwickshire) Regiment; other small detachments.

Total: 622 troops, of whom 93 were black.

Zulu forces
The Zulu forces, which had been concentrated in the *amakhanda* on the Mahlabathini plain, apparently consisted of elements of all the *amabutho*, save the iNdabakawombe and uDlambedlu guarding King Cetshwayo, who had departed the day before and was at the kwaMbonambi *ikhanda* during the battle. They numbered between 15 000 and 20 000, of whom some 5 000 were reserves, and were commanded by Prince Ziwedu kaMpande (Cetshwayo's brother). It is likely (though unconfirmed) that Chief Mnyamana kaNgqengelele, Chief Ntshingwayo kaMahole and other royal councillors and princes were present during the battle.

British casualties
Killed: 3 officers and 10 men.
Wounded: 69 men.

Zulu casualties
Zulu losses are estimated at up to about 1 500. Between 500 and 600 were killed within close range of the square, while the regular cavalry took credit for 150 and the irregular cavalry for at least another 450.

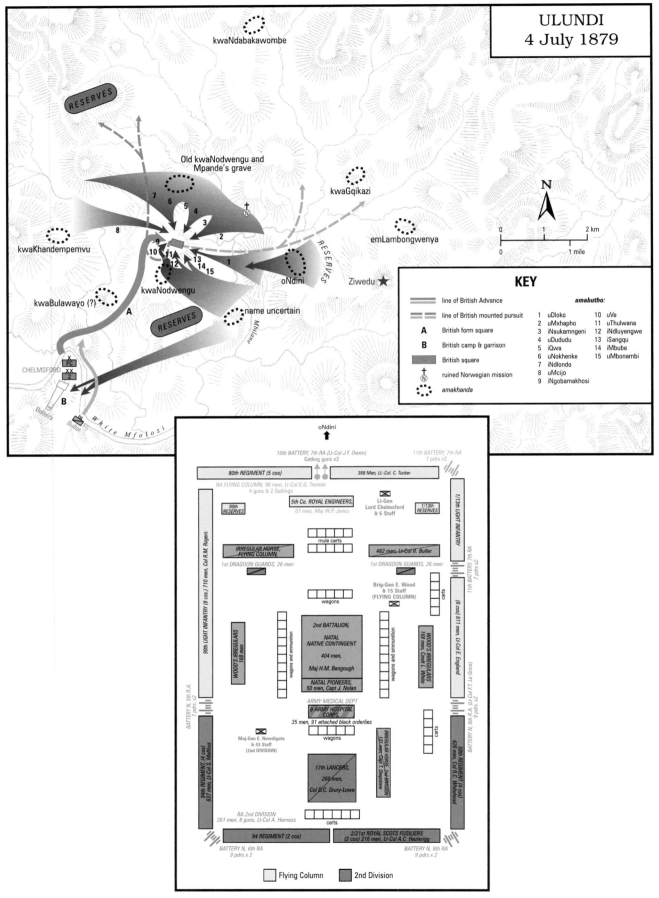

THE BRITISH SQUARE

During the battle of Ulundi Melton Prior was inside the British square, and worked up his picture from sketches made during the engagement, and from memory. It was published by the Illustrated London News on 23 August 1879. Lord Chelmsford and his staff are shown in the centre directing operations, dangerously exposed to fire on their horses, while members of the NNC crouch out of harm's way in the foreground, or help with the wounded.

Shortly before 08h00 the completed square resumed its march north-east across the plain in rather loose order. Buller's men fanned out in advance and about half a mile (0.8 km) off on the flanks to keep Zulu skirmishers away. The irregular horse of the Second Division made up the rearguard. Approaching the kwaNodwengu *ikhanda*, the square swung to its right, and at about 08h30 Chelmsford brought it to a halt facing oNdini about 1.5 miles (2.4 km) away. The position had been selected by Buller during a daring patrol the previous day, and was on the level top of a slight knoll with an excellent field of fire.

The Zulu attack
At about 08h00, the 15 000 to 20 000 Zulu concentrated in the plain began to manoeuvre with the aim of enveloping the British square, and by about 08h30 had completed their encirclement. The Zulu advanced in loose undulating lines with large masses in support behind, preceded by waves of skirmishers who opened a desultory and inaccurate fire at great range.

While the British square was advancing, about 5 000 Zulu moved on the fortified camp. The garrison went on to the alert at 08h10 as the Zulu approached the White Mfolozi drift. Some crossed the river to within 500 yards (457 m) of the camp. But this force never seriously threatened the garrison and soon melted away to join the battle developing in the plain.

Between 08h35 and 08h45 the irregular horse of the Flying Column and the 2nd Division engaged the advancing Zulu to draw them into effective range, retreating steadily before them until taking refuge in the square, where the regular cavalry had remained. At 08h45 the 9-pounder guns opened up, and the volley fire from the square became general at 08h50. Experience in previous battles had given the Zulu a better appreciation of the effectiveness of close-range and concentrated fire. They advanced at a run in crouching positions behind their shields, taking every advantage of natural cover, as well as the dense smoke from the British weapons and from kwaNodwengu, which the British had set alight. Despite great courage and determination, the Zulu were pinned down within 100 yards (91 m) of the square, unable to penetrate the zone of point-blank fire, and suffered particularly from the Gatling guns. The iNgobamakhosi and uVe came nearest to breaking through the cordon of fire at the right rear corner of the square, where they made good use of the shelter provided by kwaNodwengu and a depression in the land to the British rear. They charged to

'The Zulu continued to advance until they reached a spot not more than seventy yards from the face of the square . . . It was impossible for any force long to face the deadly storm of lead poured in among them at such short distance. A few now and then made an attempt to advance further . . . But it was no use.'

(*Natal Mercury Supplement*, July 1879: Phil Robinson)

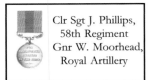

Clr Sgt J. Phillips,
58th Regiment
Gnr W. Moorhead,
Royal Artillery

Lt-Col Crealock's sketch of the mounted sortie out of the rear of the infantry square at Ulundi was made on the actual field of battle. The 17th Lancers are show in the centre of the picture charging the retiring Zulu who are rallying at the base of the hills to the right, while the colonial mounted men are moving up in support of the regular cavalry.

within 30 yards (27 m) of the corner, which Chelmsford had to reinforce before they were finally driven back.

With the Zulu assault pinned down at every quarter, the Zulu reserve moved out from oNdini in a dense column, but was driven from the field by fire from the 9-pounders. Further reserves, posted on the hills to the British north, and between them and the river, never came into action.

The Zulu rout

At about 09h15 the Zulu, unable to find a way around or through the British fire, began to falter. By 09h20 a disorderly withdrawal was under way. An air of demoralisation set in, and at 09h25 the regular cavalry charged out of the rear of the square and, wheeling right, pursued the Zulu to the lower slopes of the hills 2 miles (3 km) away. The Mounted Infantry moved out in the cavalry's support, taking the Zulu in the flank. The

irregular cavalry galloped out of the right front corner of the square a few minutes after the cavalry, and pursued the Zulu beyond oNdini and as far as the hills. At 09h40 the 9-pounders shelled the main body of the Zulu who were retreating in great masses over the hills to the north, and at 10h07 fired on oNdini and dispersed a large concentration of Zulu sheltering there. The NNC emerged from the square to assist the irregular horse in despatching the Zulu wounded and in burning all the *amakhanda* in the plain.

The square moved forward at 11h30 to the Mbilane stream. There the men rested, ate and tended the wounded. Meanwhile, mounted troops continued with their work of destruction, and oNdini was fired at 11h40. At about 14h00 the British returned to their camp at the White Mfolozi, reaching it in easy stages between 15h30 and 15h50. The defeated Zulu army rapidly dispersed.

dead men & wounded horses lying about

grass

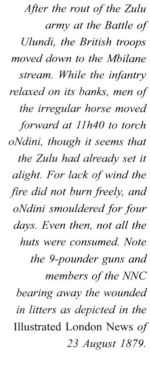

After the rout of the Zulu army at the Battle of Ulundi, the British troops moved down to the Mbilane stream. While the infantry relaxed on its banks, men of the irregular horse moved forward at 11h40 to torch oNdini, though it seems that the Zulu had already set it alight. For lack of wind the fire did not burn freely, and oNdini smouldered for four days. Even then, not all the huts were consumed. Note the 9-pounder guns and members of the NNC bearing away the wounded in litters as depicted in the Illustrated London News *of 23 August 1879.*

VRYHEID SECTOR

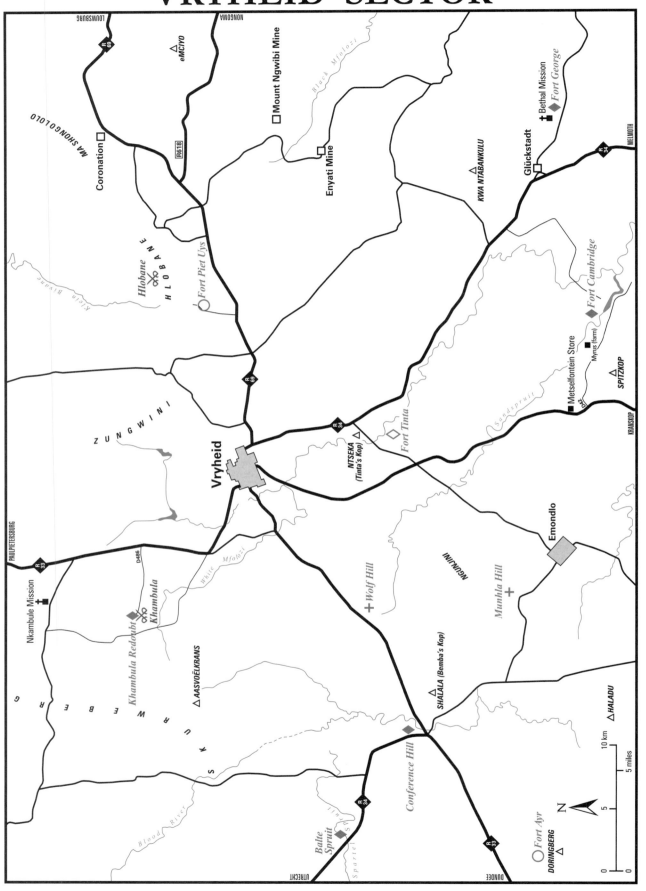

VRYHEID SECTOR

Fortifications

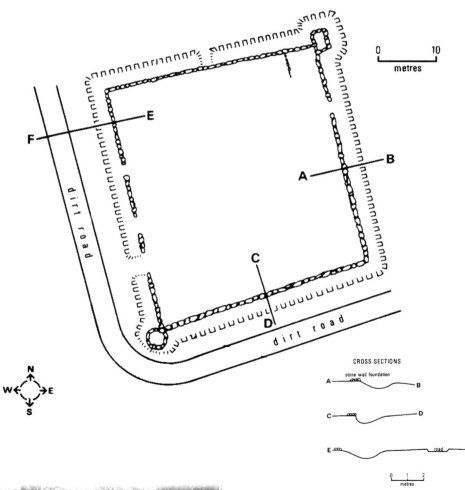

Balte Spruit Laager antedated the war. In the early part of 1877, and again at the end of that year, local Boers took refuge there. A meeting held at the laager on 20 May 1878 decided that it should not be abandoned in the face of the apparent Zulu menace. In late December Col Wood sent a detachment of 90 men who established a depot there for No. 4 Column, which came up from Utrecht in early January 1879. After the column moved forward into Zululand, Balte Spruit continued as an advanced depot. It was garrisoned by a division of No. 11 Battery, 7th Brigade, Royal Artillery, with two guns, and two companies of the 1/13th Regiment (1st Somersetshire) Prince Albert's Light Infantry, under Maj W.K. Leet, until relieved in February by a company of the 2/4th (King's Own Royal) Regiment. In August they were relieved in turn, apparently by troops of the 24th (2nd Warwickshire) Regiment. During January 1879, the Royal Engineers did some work at Balte Spruit, but the extent to which they altered the existing Boer fortifications is not clear. The small bastioned fort may well be the original Boer laager, subsequently modified by the British.

BALTE SPRUIT LAAGER

0 ... 10 metres

E

F

B

A

C

D

dirt road

dirt road

CROSS-SECTIONS

stone wall foundation

A ———— B

C ———— D

E ———— road ———— F

0 ... 1 ... 2 metres

N
W ← → E
S

◆ In early February 1879 two companies of the 2/4th, under Capt R.A. Knox, took up position at **Conference Hill**. Early in May the 94th Regiment, under Col S. Malthus, arrived and built a fort below the hill; while a company of the Royal Engineers built twin redoubts nearby to protect stores placed in-between them. It is not clear whether one or all of these were subsequently styled Fort Napoleon.

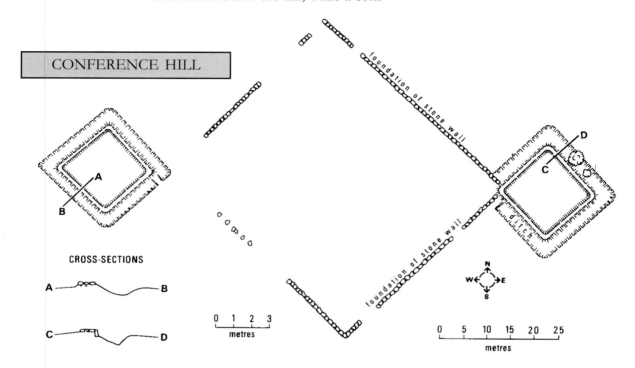

CONFERENCE HILL

CROSS-SECTIONS

◆ When No. 4 Column advanced into Zululand and encamped beyond the White Mfolozi, it built **Fort Khambula** between 11–13 February to command its entrenched camp, begun on 21 January and relocated 2 miles (3 km) higher up the spur on 11 February. This small redoubt played a significant part in the battle of Khambula on 29 March. After the Flying Column (as Wood's forces were re-designated on 13 April) moved camp 660 yards (603 m) to the west on 14 April, the redoubt continued to be occupied.

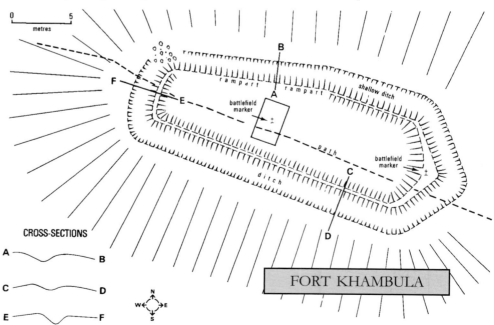

CROSS-SECTIONS

FORT KHAMBULA

It was finally abandoned on 5 May when the Flying Column began its advance on oNdini. On the break-up of the 2nd Division, South African Field Force, **Fort Cambridge** was thrown up on 26 July 1879 by the 2nd Company, Royal Engineers, and four companies of the 94th. Col Baker Russell's Flying Column encamped there from 5 to 9 August and left in garrison a company of the 94th, 200 men of the 2nd Battalion, Natal Native Contingent, and a dozen men of Lonsdale's Mounted Rifles.

FORT CAMBRIDGE

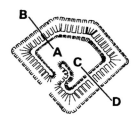

CROSS-SECTIONS

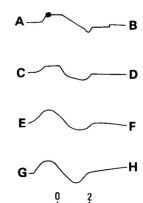

0   2
metres

0   10   20
metres

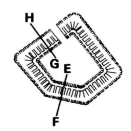

Fort George was built on 10 August as Baker Russell's forward base while he probed across the Black Mfolozi between 13 and 15 August. The column departed on 25 August, leaving in garrison two companies of the 94th and detachments of Raaf's Transvaal Rangers and the 2nd Battalion, NNC.

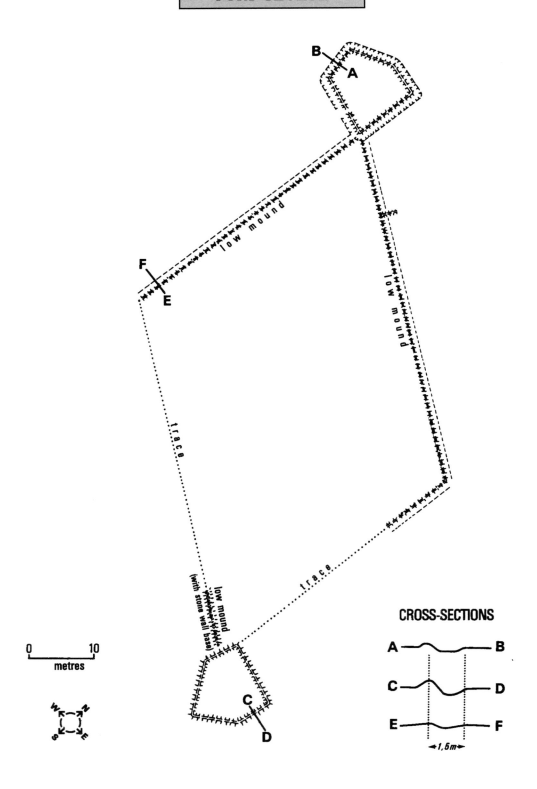

FORT GEORGE

CROSS-SECTIONS

◆ Overlooking the site of Tinta's Drift on the White Mfolozi are several stoneworks, one of which may be **Fort Tinta**, described contemporarily as a stone laager fort. It was built by Wood's column on 21 January 1879, and was garrisoned briefly (21–25 January) by a company apiece from the 1/13th and the 90th Regiment (Perthshire Volunteers Light Infantry).

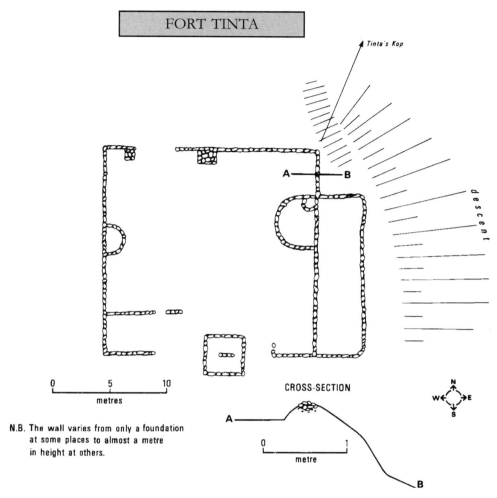

FORT TINTA

Tinta's Kop

descent

A — B

CROSS-SECTION

A

B

0   5   10
metres

N.B. The wall varies from only a foundation at some places to almost a metre in height at others.

0   1
metre

N
W ← → E
S

At **Wolf Hill** and **Munhla Hill** the advancing Flying Column threw up entrenchments (and at the latter place a redoubt and lunette as well) when they encamped there from 12 to 25 May and 25 May to 1 June, respectively. No remains of the works have been found. **Fort Piet Uys** was thrown up by Baker Russell's column on 29–30 August, and garrisoned by a company of the 94th. Ploughing has obliterated it.

○ On 26 April 1879 three companies of the 80th Regiment (Staffordshire Volunteers), under Maj C. Tucker, were sent to cut wood for fuel at the Doornberg (now called the Doringberg). At the 'northern extremity' they built an earthwork fort. On 8 May three companies of the 2/21st Regiment (Royal Scots Fusiliers), under Maj A.G. Hazlerigg, moved to the Doornberg from Landman's Drift and built **Fort Ayr**. The headquarters and another three companies of the 2/21st followed on 17 May. A newspaper report of mid-May refers to the detachments of both regiments – and a fort and a laager – under the command of Maj Tucker at the Doornberg. On 27 May the detachment of the 80th left, and two days later the 2/21st, to join their respective columns for the second invasion of Zululand. The exact sites of these works have not been located.

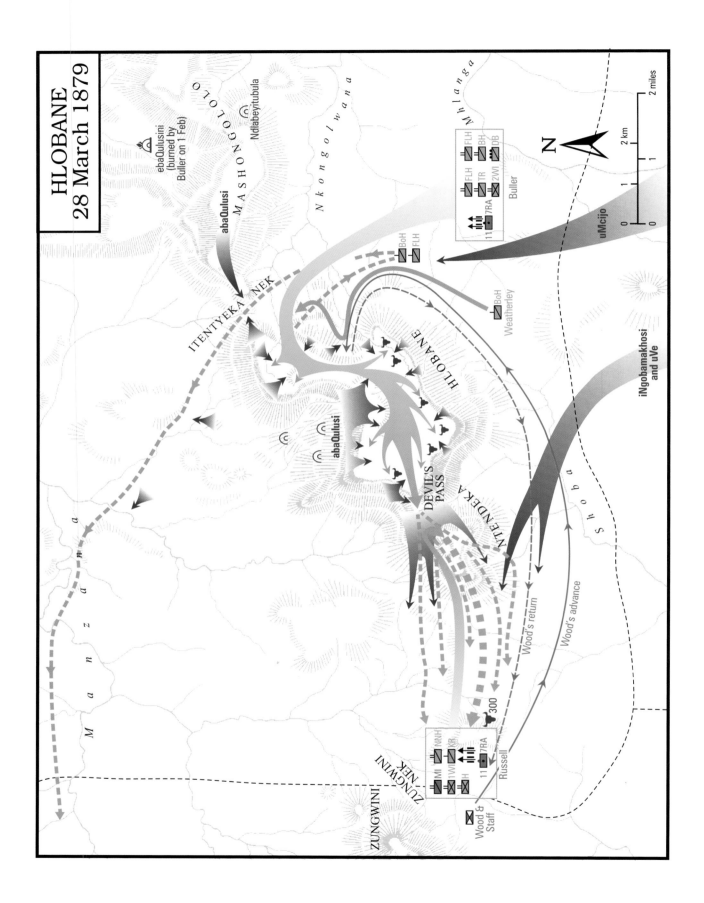

VRYHEID SECTOR
Battle of Hlobane

One of Wood's Irregulars (labour tenants on white farms in the Wakkerstroom and Utrecht Districts of the Transvaal Colony who had been pressed into service by their landdrosts), sketched by Lt-Col Crealock. They did their best to bring the captured Zulu cattle off Hlobane on 28 March 1879, though they believed they were left in the lurch by the rest of the rapidly retreating British troops.

During a running fight on Hlobane on 28 March 1879, Zulu irregulars and a detachment from the main Zulu army advancing on Khambula Camp cut off and routed the British raiding the mountain for cattle.

The British raid

Lord Chelmsford requested Col Wood to 'make any forward movement' from his camp at Khambula on or about 27 March to create a diversion in favour of the Eshowe Relief Column. Wood's decision to comply by raiding Hlobane Mountain neatly combined the required military objective with the tempting promise of considerable booty in the form of cattle. Hlobane was the central defensive position for the abaQulusi along a series of flat-topped mountains stretching from Ntendeka in the west to Mashongololo in the east. Mbilini, whose *umuzi*, Ndlabe-yitubula, was on the south-eastern slopes of Mashongololo, was their leader and the most effective commander of Zulu irregulars in north-western Zululand. He had concentrated most of the cattle herds of the region in temporary *imizi* the abaQulusi had built on the terraces around the precipitous sides of Hlobane, and grazed them in the plains below or on the flat summit.

For this raiding expedition (similar to raids very recently undertaken in the Ntombe valley and elsewhere), Wood decided to employ only his mounted units, supported by African auxiliaries.

British forces
No. 4 Column (detachment)
Col H.E. Wood commanding.

Lt-Col R.H. Buller's force:
No. 11 Battery, 7th Brigade, Royal Artillery (half a rocket battery).
Baker's Horse; Dutch Burghers; Frontier Light Horse; Raaf's Transvaal Rangers; Weatherley's Border Horse.
2nd Battalion of Wood's Irregulars.

Total: 675 officers and men.

Lt-Col J.C. Russell's force:
No. 11 Battery, 7th Brigade, Royal Artillery (half a rocket battery).
Mounted Infantry; Kaffrarian Rifles; Natal Native Horse.
1st Battalion of Wood's Irregulars; and the Ngenetsheni of Prince Hamu kaNzibe, Cetshwayo's brother, who had deserted the king and joined Wood earlier in March.

Total: 640 officers and men.

Zulu forces
Prince Mbilini waMswati was in command of the abaQulusi irregulars. Elements of the uMcijo, iNgobamakhosi and uVe *amabutho* were detached from army advancing on Khambula. Altogether, up to 2 000 Zulus might have been engaged.

British casualties
Killed: 15 officers and 79 men; probably over 100 Wood's Irregulars and Hamu's Ngenetsheni, the precise number of whose casualties is unknown.
Wounded: 1 officer and 7 men.

Zulu casualties
Unknown.

> 'When the Whitemen got to the top, seeing the mountain a nice level plain . . . but not the Qulusi who were hiding, they said "Hlobane is a fine place! it's like a man's headring". But the Qulusi heard all that, and sprang up on all sides and stabbed them.'
>
> (Magema M. Fuze, 1880)

The distance was too great for his British infantry who, in any case, were required to guard Khambula. Two forces would assault the mountain with its belt of nigh impenetrable cliffs in a pincer movement. Lt-Col Buller's force would go up one of the few points of access, which was on the eastern side where a stream had cut a notch in the cliffs, and would sweep west across Hlobane. Lt-Col Russell's men would ascend on the opposites side by way of Ntendeka, which was joined to Hlobane above by steep, rocky ridge, know as the Devil's Pass. Russell's role was to act in support of Buller, especially if he were attacked when retiring with the captured cattle. Wood planned to operate freely as an observer with his personal staff and a small escort. What he did not know was that the main Zulu army had left oNdini around 24 March and was marching towards Khambula.

On 27 March the units to be involved in the Hlobane raid rendezvoused in the vicinity of Zungwini Nek to the west of the mountain. Buller's men pushed on that afternoon at about 16h00 to a second bivouac south of the eastern extremity of Hlobane. At 03h30 on 28 March Buller's force set off to scale the eastern slopes of Hlobane. There was a jumble of great rocks at the foot of the cliffs and the abaQulusi had done their best to make ascent difficult by blocking the way up with lines of stones. They took up position in the natural caves and crevices and behind their improvised fortifications to ambush Buller's men as they struggled up the mountain in mist and rain. Neverthe-

less, Buller successfully led his men in skirmishing order through the heavy cross-fire to gain the summit. The Border Horse under Cmdt Weatherley, which had become separated from Buller in the dark and was still in the plain, was encountered by Wood and his escort as they moved east from Russell's bivouac around the base of the mountain. Wood took command and they followed Buller's track up Hlobane, skirmishing with the abaQulusi. Wood's party suffered several casualties, and Wood decided to retrace his steps to see how Russell was faring on Ntendeka. The Border Horse reached the summit, though they had been threatened in the flank by several hundred abaQulusi coming across Itentyeka Nek from their stronghold on Mashongololo to the east.

On the summit, Buller left a small rearguard to secure the way back down, and extended the rest of his force to drive west across the mountain top, brushing aside the sniping abaQulusi. His men rounded up about 2 000 cattle from the southern side of the plateau, and only halted when they reached the precipitous Devil's Pass at the western extremity. From there they exchanged fire with the abaQulusi who had built their *imizi* on the north-western side of Hlobane.

The British withdrawal and rout

It seems the abaQulusi on Hlobane were expecting the imminent arrival of the Zulu army, and had drawn Buller into a trap. Just before 09h00 Russell's column, which had scaled Ntendeka by 07h00 and was busy rounding up cattle, spotted the

Lt-Col Crealock's sketch of Hlobane and Ntendeka mountains from the top of Zungwini shows the precipitous Devil's Pass down which Buller retreated on 28 March 1879.

Zulu army on the range of hills to the south moving towards Khambula. Russell alerted Buller, who at 10h30 saw large numbers of Zulu advancing in battle formation across the flats from the south-east. An hour or so earlier he had begun to call in his scattered detachments preparatory to descending with the captured cattle. But the abaQulusi, reinforced from Mashongololo, mustered on the higher ground of the northern side of the plateau and emerged from their hiding-places all around the plateau, making Buller's withdrawal eastwards increasingly difficult. Harassed by the abaQulusi and alarmed by the presence of the Zulu army below, Buller realised that he must get off the opposite side of the mountain by way of Ntendeka, and herded the captured cattle in that direction. However, Russell was not there to support him. On seeing the Zulu army, he had moved Wood's Irregulars and the captured cattle to Zungwini Nek, and regrouped his mounted men at the foot of Ntendeka. Wood, who was moving back in his direction, ordered him to fall back on Zungwini Nek and evidently joined him there.

Harried with increasing boldness by the abaQulusi, and with no support on Ntendeka, Buller had nevertheless to scramble down the almost impassable Devil's Pass. The fleeing horsemen sustained many casualties in the descent (notably Piet Uys, the leader of the Dutch Burghers) and lost many horses. Once on Ntendeka they rallied, but were pursued for a considerable distance by the abaQulusi towards Zungwini. Once the abaQulusi gave up the pursuit, Russell withdrew to Khambula at about 11h15 with Buller's exhausted men, reaching the camp between 16h00 and 17h00. Most of the African auxiliaries had been cut off in the rout, but they had done their best to bring in the captured cattle. Indeed, the survivors succeeded in saving 300 head and were most indignant at the way in which the white troops had abandoned them.

Buller was fortunate that he had not been attacked by the main Zulu army. Evidently, the Zulu commanders did not wish to be diverted from their line of march towards Khambula, and were content to detach elements of the right horn to help intercept British fugitives in the plain. Buller had earlier ordered a troop of the Frontier Light Horse under Capt Barton and the Border Horse to return to Khambula via the south of Hlobane. When they rounded the shoulder of the mountain with the FLH in the lead, they ran straight into what was probably the uMcijo *ibutho*. They turned about and attempted to retreat over the precipitously steep Itentyeka Nek. Most were intercepted by the abaQulusi from both Hlobane and Mashongololo. The small number who broke through over the nek and escaped their pursuers eventually reached Khambula late that evening by way of Potter's store. Some way behind the uMcijo on the right flank of the Zulu army were the iNgobamakhosi and uVe. They crossed Nyembe hill and moved west along the base of the range of mountains, engaging stragglers who had come down the southern side of Ntendeka and harassing them as far as Zungwini. Later that afternoon the indefatigable Buller went out again on patrol to bring in the last few fugitives.

> 'The Zlobane retreat was a most aweful afair . . . I shall never forget the Zulus getting in amongst us and assegaying our fellows. Some of the cries for mercy from the poor fellows brought tears into our eyes.'
> (Lt Alfred Blaine, Frontier Light Horse, 31 March 1879)

Lt-Col R.H. Buller, 60th Rifles
Maj W.K. Leet, 1/13th Regiment
Lt E.S. Browne, 1/24th Regiment
Lt H. Lysons, 90th Light Infantry
Pte E. Fowler, 90th Light Infantry

Cpl W.D. Vinnicombe, Frontier Light Horse
Tpr R. Brown, Frontier Light Horse

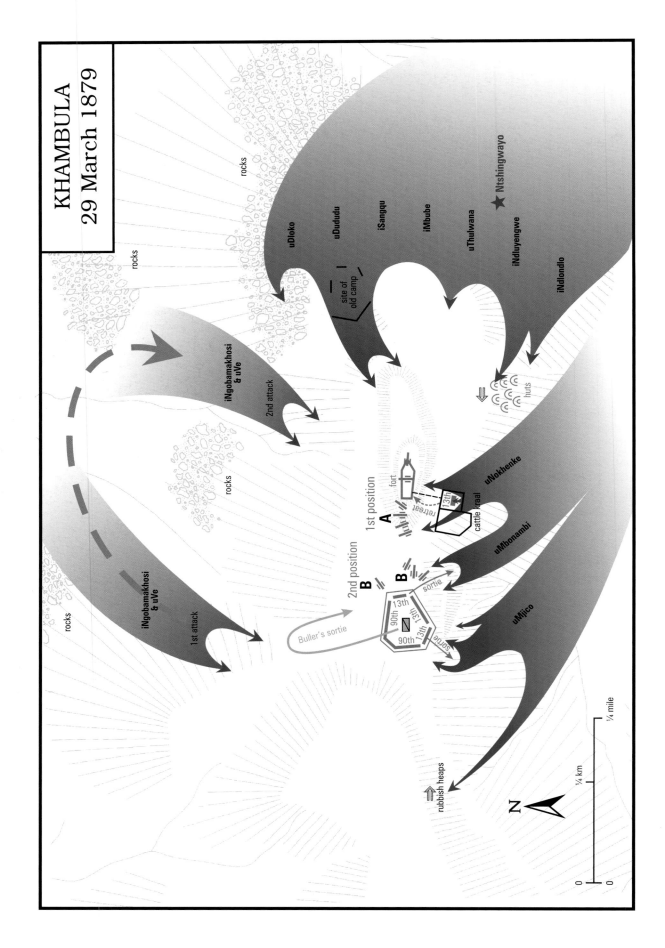

KHAMBULA
29 March 1879

rocks

rocks

rocks

uDloko

uDududu

iSangqu

iMbube

uThulwana

iNdluyengwe

iNdlondlo

★ Ntshingwayo

site of
old camp

huts

iNgobamakhosi
& uVe

2nd attack

rocks

iNgobamakhosi
& uVe

1st attack

fort

1st position

A

13th

retreat

cattle kraal

uNokhenke

uMbonambi

uMjico

2nd position

B

B

sortie

Buller's sortie

90th

13th

13th

90th 13th

sortie

rubbish heaps

N

¼ km

¼ mile

0

0

VRYHEID SECTOR
Battle of Khambula

Though not the best-known battle of the war, the action at Khambula on 29 March 1879 was the most decisive. The confident Zulu veterans of Isandlwana were repulsed and routed by the men of No. 4 Column, and Zulu morale never recovered from this defeat.

The Zulu advance

King Cetshwayo had carefully planned the Zulu attack on Khambula Camp in person. He had instructed his commanders not to assault the fortified camp, but to draw the British into the open by harassing them and threatening Utrecht and their line of supply. About 11h00 the Zulu army began its advance on Khambula in five columns from its bivouac on the banks of the White Mfolozi nearly 12 miles (19 km) away. The British were informed of its movements through spies and scouts and had time to complete their defensive arrangements. Their main force was stationed in a strongly fortified wagon laager, and smaller garrisons in a connected earthwork redoubt and a smaller cattle laager. Range-markers had been set up to aid the accuracy of the defenders' fire. At 12h45 the tents were struck and the men took up their battle stations.

The repulse of the Zulu right horn

Before midday, the Zulu halted for an hour on hills about 4 miles (6.4 km) southeast of the camp. There, on the insistence of the younger *amabutho*, the decision was taken not to bypass the camp and move

on Utrecht as their commanders urged, but to attack it. Accordingly, the Zulu began to deploy on a front extending over 10 miles (16 km) with the aim of surrounding the British position. The chest stayed where it was, while the uMcijo of the left horn wheeled to its right at about 13h00 and made a rapid advance on the camp, halting about 3 miles (5 km) away. The iNgobamakhosi and uVe of the right horn halted about 1.5 miles (2.4 km) north of the camp, just out of range of the guns. At 13h30 they began an unsup-

---

British Forces
No. 4 Column
Col H.E. Wood commanding.
No. 11 Battery, 7th Brigade Royal Artillery (six 7-pounder guns).
Eight companies of the 90th Regiment (Perthshire Volunteers Light Infantry); seven companies of the 1st Battalion, 13th Regiment (1st Somersetshire) Prince Albert's Light Infantry. One company of the 90th and one and a half of the 1/13th manned the cattle kraal. The remainder, including most of the mounted troops, were stationed in the laager.
Mounted troops: Lt-Col R.H. Buller:
One squadron of Mounted Infantry; four troops of the Frontier Light Horse; two troops of Raaf's Transvaal Rangers; and men of Baker's Horse, the Kaffrarian Rifles, Weatherley's Border Horse and Mounted Basutos. The Natal Native Horse remained outside the laager, harassing the Zulu.
There were also a few Royal Engineers present and members of the Dutch Burghers and Wood's Irregulars who had not decamped after the battle of Hlobane.

Total: 2 086 officers and men (of whom 132 were African), including 88 sick.

Zulu Forces
The Zulu army was under the supreme command of Chief Mnyamana kaNgqengelele of the Buthelezi and Cetshwayo's chief *induna*. Chief Ntshingwayo kaMahole, who had been one of the senior commanders at Isandlwana, led the army (which consisted mainly of veterans of that battle) into action. The iNgobamkhosi and uVe formed the right horn; the uDloko, uDududu, iSangqu, iMbube, uThulwana, iNdluyengwe and iNdlondlo the centre right; the uNokhenke and uMbonambi the centre left; and the uMcijo the left horn – a force of about 17 000. They were augmented by the abaQulusi *ibutho* and local irregulars, bringing the strength of their combined force up to 20 000 or more, and putting it on a par with the army sent against Isandlwana.

British Casualties
Killed: 3 officers and 25 men.
Wounded: 5 officers and 50 men.

Zulu Casualties
The Zulu lost well over 1 000 men; certainly no less than at Isandlwana and probably more. Within two days of the battle the British counted 785 Zulu dead within a 1-mile (1.6-km) radius of the camp, and another 157 along the line of the flight. For months afterwards Zulu corpses were found in the vicinity. Those *amabutho* that suffered the greatest casualties were, in order, the uMbonambi, uNokhenke, iNgobamakhosi and uVe. The abaQulusi irregulars lost most heavily in the rout. More men of high status were killed than in any other battle of the war.

Lt-Col Crealock sketched the Khambula battlefield from the west, showing the British wagon laager and the stone-built redoubt on its eminence beyond.

Kambula Fort attacked 29th March

> 'The attack on Khambula was premature, and not as was intended . . . but the success of the Zulus [at Hlobane] greatly elated them, and they thought if they attacked the camp next day they would obtain an easy victory.'
>
> (King Cetshwayo, February, 1880)

> 'We could not stand against the fire and had to retreat; the two regiments forming the horns were quite exhausted and useless, and we could not properly surround the position.'
>
> (Warrior of the uThulwana, 1882)

ported and rapid advance in column straight at the camp, probably to upstage their intense rivals, the uMcijo. Buller and two squadrons of mounted troops went forward when the iNgobamakhosi and uVe were just a little over half a mile (0.8 km) away, to provoke them into a fully committed but unsupported attack. The British artillery opened fire at 13h45 and the iNgobamakhosi and uVe were checked at 300 yards (274 m) by enfilading fire from the redoubt and laager, and forced to fall back to the cover of rocky outcrops north-east of the camp. The Zulu strategy was disrupted and their army was unable to complete its envelopment of the camp. The northern and western salients of the British position consequently remained unthreatened, freeing the garrison to concentrate on the Zulu attack from the opposite quarter.

The action becomes general
At about 14h15 the Zulu left and centre began to develop their belated attack, taking advantage of the dead ground to the south, and the cover afforded by the remains of the abandoned British camp to the east along the ridge. Undaunted by the heavy fire, they came in a series of great waves. The uNokhenke dislodged

the company of the 1/13th Light Infantry garrisoning the cattle kraal, while the uMbonambi's assault on the main laager was only repelled at about 15h00 by a sortie of two companies of the 90th Light Infantry. These in turn were caught in an enfilading fire by Zulu marksmen with Martini-Henry rifles posted in the huts of Wood's Irregulars and in the camp's refuse dump, and forced to retire. Also at about 15h00 a company of the 1/13th sortied to drive back at bayonet-point the uMcijo, who had reached the south-west corner of the laager.

The limit of Zulu success had been reached and the advantage now lay with the defenders. Nevertheless, for two further hours the Zulu continued to attack, at one point coming up to the trenches along the southern side of the redoubt. At 16h30 the Zulu centre switched the focus of their attack away from the south of the British position to the eastern face, while the iNgobamakhosi and uVe made a fresh advance from the north-east. But caught in a heavy cross-fire they were again held at about 300 yards (274 m) and forced to retire.

The Zulu rout and British pursuit
By about 17h00 the Zulu assault began to slacken. At 15h30 a company of the

Melton Prior's sketch of the battle of Khambula, engraved for the Illustrated London News *of 24 May 1879. It shows the entrenched laager of wagons to the left, the cattle laager to the right, and the palisade connecting it to the redoubt on the hill, the height of which has been exaggerated. The guns are being fought in the open between the fortified points. The struck tents are lying on the ground behind the firing line of two companies of the 90th Light Infantry who are making a sortie. The ground to the right of the cattle laager does not fall away nearly so precipitously as depicted, and in reality provided the Zulu with cover without impeding their assault.*

1/13th cleared the cattle kraal, and Wood advanced a company of the 90th to fire on the Zulu sheltering in the dead ground. The Zulu then began to retire in an orderly fashion under heavy fire. Three columns of British mounted troops under Buller charged out and transformed the withdrawal into a rout. Attempts by the Zulu commanders to rally their completely exhausted men failed, and until night fell the British harried them mercilessly as far as Zungwini Mountain, 10 miles (16 km) away. British infantry and their African auxiliaries scoured the immediate neighbourhood of the camp and killed all those lying wounded or hidden.

'We were then pursued by the horsemen from the camp, who rode after our retreating army and turned them about like cattle. We were completely beaten.'

(Sihlala, 3 June 1879)

'The flying Zulus . . . became exhausted, and shooting them down would have taken too much time; so we took the assegais from the dead men, and rushed among the living ones, stabbing them right and left'

(*Natal Mercury Supplement*, April 1879 : Cmdt Schermburcker)

Sgt-Maj Learda, Natal Native Horse
Sgt E. Quigley, 1/13th Regiment
Pte A. Page, 1/13th Regiment

PIETERMARITZBURG SECTOR

BARRICADING AND LOOPHOLING THE WINDOWS OF THE COURT HOUSE IN ANTICIPATION OF AN ATTACK, JAN. 26

The Pietermaritzburg Court House, one of the substantial buildings upon which the improvised laager of barricades was anchored, being prepared for defence during the last week of January 1879. (The Graphic, *8 March 1879).*

The Colonial Buildings in Church Street, where the officials of the Natal administration had their offices, with the shutters loopholed against anticipated Zulu attack. The latest bulletins from the front and instructions for the defence of the city were posted on the notice-board near the right-hand end of the building.

PIETERMARITZBURG SECTOR
Fortifications

◆ The City of Pietermaritzburg was a special Colonial Sub-District under direct command of the Colonial Secretary, Lt-Col C.B.H. Mitchell. When news of Isandlwana reached the city on 24 January, the white citizens hastily improvised the **Pietermaritzburg Laager** for their protection. It was to be defended chiefly by the City Guard, and when completed in mid-February consisted of a number of substantial buildings prepared for defence through the loopholing

of walls and the fitting of reinforced and loopholed doors and shutters. These buildings were connected by barricades of sandbags and boxes filled with earth. The openings left for the passage of normal traffic down the streets could readily be closed with similar material kept at hand for the purpose. The laager never had to be used since no Zulu incursion ever occurred, and it was dismantled in July 1879. Two buildings on which the defensive system was anchored still survive: the government building of 1871 in Commercial Road, which housed the Supreme Court and Legislative Council, and is now the home of the Tatham Art Gallery; and the Presbyterian church of 1852 in Church Street, which is today the Phemba Kahle Cultural Centre. The substantially unaltered **Gaol** of 1861 on Burger Street (now the premises of the Gateway Project) was also prepared for defence. Officials from nearby Government House were to have repaired there in an emergency.

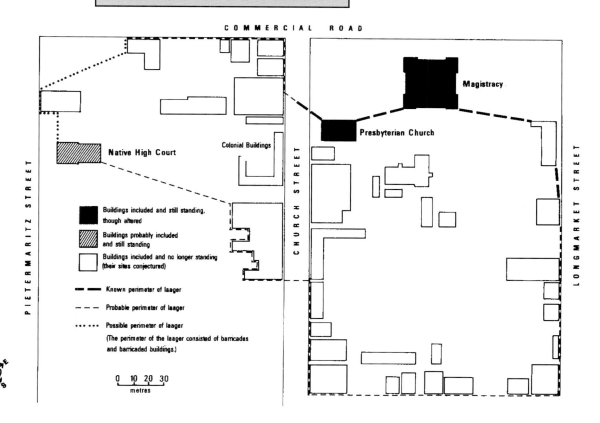

The rectangle of brick barracks at Fort Napier is shown in this photograph of 1879 enclosed by the earthworks built in 1876, which were strengthened by stone redoubts and gun emplacements.

The **Fort Napier** military station was the headquarters of the permanent British garrison in Natal until 1914. The fort itself was begun in 1843, and by 1845 consisted of a rectangle of brick barracks, whose outer walls were loopholed for defence, flanked by two stone bastions at opposite corners. The design of the fort seems to have been continually modified over the next thirty years, and in August 1876 a 10-foot (3.05-m) deep trench with corresponding earthwork walls was made to enclose the fort buildings. To increase the defensibility of the post, stone walls and gun emplacements were built at various angles of the new earthworks, while the main roadways to the fort were protected by drawbridges. During the Anglo-Zulu War the fort was garrisoned successively by detachments of the 88th Regiment (Connaught Rangers), the 2/21st Regiment (Royal Scots Fusiliers), and the 99th (Duke of Edinburgh's Lanarkshire) Regiment. Nothing of the earthworks remains, but the basic trace of the fort is still discernible in the surviving though altered buildings.

View of Pietermaritzburg in 1879 from a gun emplacement at Fort Napier. The house and stables of the Anglican Bishop of Maritzburg, William Macrorie, are visible just above the earthwork parapet to the right. The wooded grounds of Government House are to the left at the intersection of West and Longmarket streets. At the far end of Longmarket Street, the steeply pitched skylight of the Court House stands out above the other buildings.

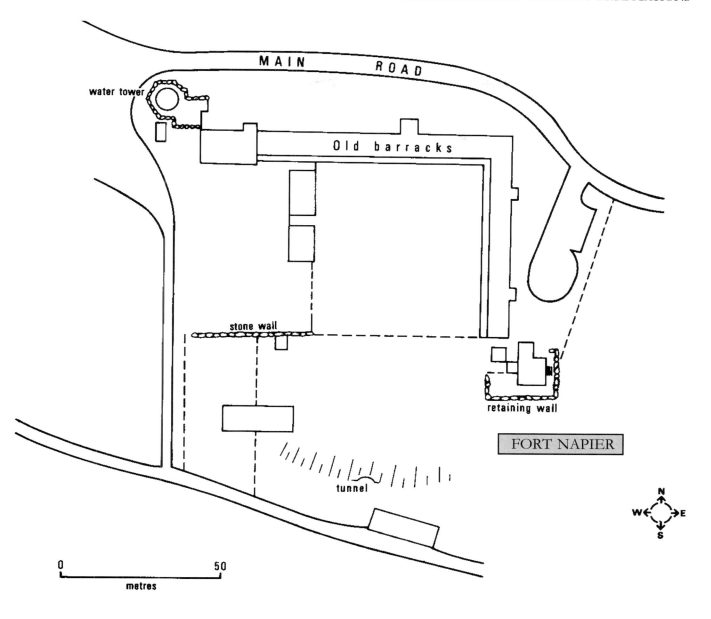

'On Sunday morning the preparations for defence commenced . . . Wagons with ammunition and stores rattled through the streets; carpenters were noisily at work barricading the windows and open spaces; wells were being sunk in the grounds . . . A few people were afraid, a good many were anxious, while the remainder looked upon these precautions with amusement, as being unnecessary altogether or ill-timed.'

(*Natal Witness*, 28 January 1879)

DURBAN SECTOR

After Isandlwana the Court House in Durban (now the Local History Museum) was prepared for defence as part of the Town Laager. The photograph was taken in September 1880 during the elections for the Legislative Council of Natal.

DURBAN SECTOR
Fortifications

◆ The **Durban Redoubt**, or 'Old Fort' as it is now known, was begun in 1842 for the defence of the permanent British garrison stationed in the town. During the Anglo-Zulu War it was garrisoned successively by single companies of the 99th (Duke of Edinburgh's Lanarkshire) Regiment, the 88th Regiment (Connaught Rangers), the 58th (Rutlandshire) Regiment and again of the 99th. The remains of the fort indicate that the trace of the earthworks was approximately rectangular with two bastions at opposite corners. The scale model of the fort, just inside the Molyneux Gate, represents the fortified camp of 1842, and bears no relation to the existing earthwork. Along with Fort Napier in Pietermaritzburg, it was probably the prototype for many earthworks and stone laagers built in Natal before and during the war. After Isandlwana, the **Court House** was prepared for defence by storing ammunition inside, loopholing its walls and doors, and sandbagging its parapets. In the event of a Zulu attack, it was to be defended by an ensign and 50 men of the 88th. The Old Court House building today houses the Local History Museum.

DURBAN REDOUBT (OLD FORT)

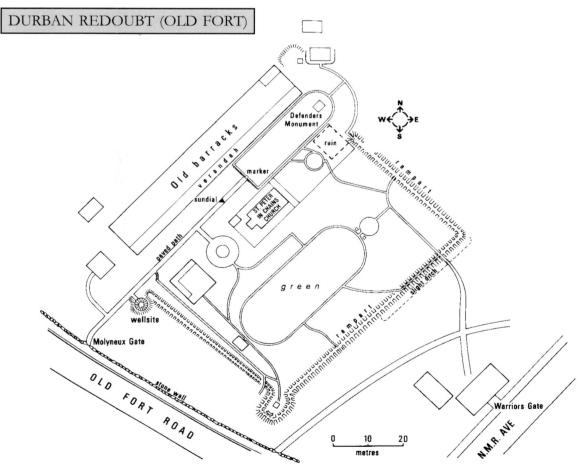

✚ The Colonial Commandant of Durban Sub-District, Maj J.W. Huskisson, 56th Foot, refused as impracticable and unnecessary the townspeople's clamour after Isandlwana for Durban to be entirely encircled by fortifications. Instead, in accordance with the principles for the defence of an open town, he assigned local volunteer units to a number of key buildings in Durban (in addition to the Court House), some of which were fortified. This network of buildings, which made up the **Town Laager**, were not linked by any barricades. Apart from the Court House, and perhaps the old portions of the gaol, nothing appears to remain of them. After Isandlwana, a stockade was erected across the **Point**, behind which the white women and children and Indian and African refugees were to retire should Durban be attacked. A redoubt was also built towards Red Hill, overlooking the **Western Vlei**. Both these works have disappeared.

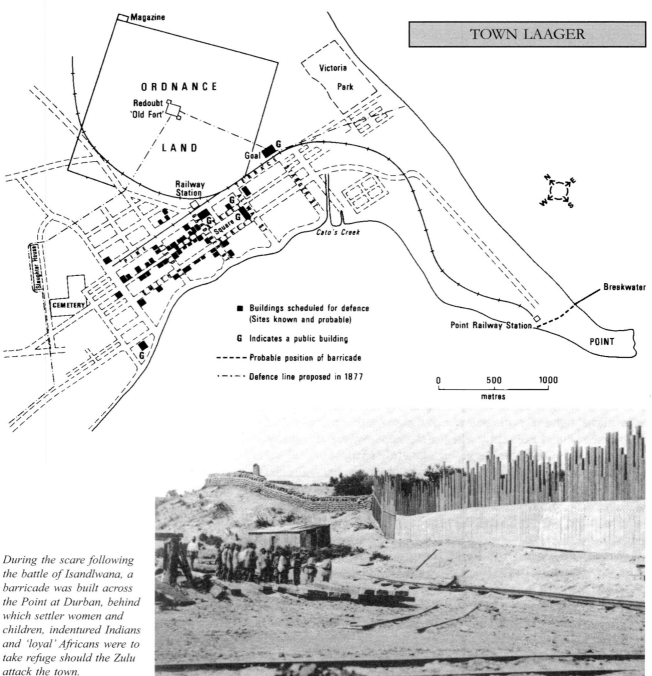

TOWN LAAGER

■ Buildings scheduled for defence (Sites known and probable)

G Indicates a public building

- - - - - Probable position of barricade

·—·—· Defence line proposed in 1877

0   500   1000
metres

During the scare following the battle of Isandlwana, a barricade was built across the Point at Durban, behind which settler women and children, indentured Indians and 'loyal' Africans were to take refuge should the Zulu attack the town.

References

The Anglo-Zulu War generated a considerable number of published works, both during its course and in its immediate aftermath. Reminiscences by participants continued to be published for decades after. Interest in the war revived in the late 1960s, and has continued to grow. Consequently, there are not only numerous books and articles available which have been brought out in recent years, but many annotated collections and editions of contemporary manuscript and published sources, as well as reprints of some of the standard contemporary works. In this select bibliography we have listed only those published works which we believe the reader will find of most value.

Naturally, any serious researcher into the Anglo-Zulu War would also need to work with the numerous manuscript sources held in repositories in South Africa and the United Kingdom. The Chelmsford Papers in the National Army Museum, Chelsea; the War Office Papers relating to the war of 1879 in the Public Record Office, Kew; the Wood Papers divided between the Killie Campbell Africana Library, Durban, and the Pietermaritzburg Archives Repository; and the papers of the Colonial Secretary and Secretary for Native Affairs, Natal, both in the Pietermaritburg Archives Repository, are among the most important. The published series of *British Parliamentary Papers* and *African Confidential Print* are also essential sources. So too are the newspapers and periodicals of the time, both British and colonial. The bibliographies in the more scholarly modern secondary works listed below will provide the necessary guidance.

Official Printed Sources

Callwell, Col C.E. *Small Wars: Their Principles and Practice*, London, 3rd edition, 1906.

Fynney, F. *The Zulu Army and Zulu Headmen. Published by Direction of the Lieut.-General Commanding*, Pietermaritzburg, April 1879.

Chelmsford, Lt-Gen Lord. *Regulations: Field Forces, South Africa, 1878*, Pietermaritzburg, November 1878.

His Excellency the Lieutenant-General Commanding (Chelmsford, Lt-Gen Lord). *Special Instructions regarding the Management of Ox Transport on the Line of March, and for the Conducting of the Line of March when Troops March with Ox Wagon Transport, and for Forming Wagon Laagers*, Durban, 1879.

Infantry, Field Exercises and Evolutions of, pocket edition, London, 1877.

Intelligence Branch of the War Office. *Narrative of the Field Operations Connected with the Zulu War of 1879*, London, 1881.

Intelligence Division of the War Office. *Précis of Information Concerning Zululand*, London, 1895.

Unofficial Contemporary Printed Sources

Articles

Brown, Surgeon D. Blair. 'Surgical notes on the Zulu War', *Lancet*, II, 5, July 1879.

Colley, Col Sir G. Pomeroy. 'Army', *Encyclopaedia Britannica*, Edinburgh, 9th edition, 1875, vol. II.

Forbes, A. 'Lord Chelmsford and the Zulu War', *Nineteenth Century*, February 1880.

Fripp, C.E. 'Reminiscences of the Zulu War, 1879', *Pall Mall Magazine*, XX, 1900.

Harness, Lt-Col A. 'The Zulu campaign from a military point of view', *Fraser's Magazine*, CI, April 1880.

Hutton, Lt-Gen Sir E. 'Some recollections of the Zulu War', *Army Quarterly*, XVI, April 1921.

Montgomery, A.N. 'Isandhlwana: A visit six months after the disaster', *Leisure Hours Magazine*, 1892.

Nugent, Col Sir C. 'Fortification', *Encyclopaedia Britannica*, Edinburgh, 9th edition, 1875, vol. IX.

Ross, Capt. J. 'Through the Zulu War with General Wood's Flying Column, *Canadian Military Institute: Selected Papers*, 5, 1893–4.

Schermbrucker, F. 'Zhlobane and Kambula', *South African Catholic Magazine*, 111, 30 and 31, 1893.

'The Zulu War: With Colonal Pearson at Eshowe: By one who was there', *Blackwood's Edinburgh Magazine*, DCCLX, CXXVI, July 1879.

Books and pamphlets

Colenso, F.E., assisted by Durnford, Lt-Col E. *History of the Zulu War and its Origin*, London, 1880.

Colenso, F.E. *The Ruin of Zululand*, London, 1884–5.

Colenso, Bishop J.W. and Colenso, H.E. *Digest of Zulu Affairs Compiled by Bishop Colenso and Continued after his Death by his Daughter Harriette Emily*

Colenso, Bishopstowe, 1878–8, series no.1, parts I and II, December 1878 – April 1881.

Dawnay, G.C. *Private Journal of Guy C. Dawnay. Campaigns: Zulu 1879; Egypt 1887; Suakim 1885*, printed for private circulation, n.d.

Deleage, P. *Trois Mois chez les Zoulous et les Deniers Jours du Prince Imperial,* Paris, 1879.

Durnford, Lt-Col E. *Isandhlwana, 22nd January, 1879: A Narrative, Compiled from Official and Reliable Sources*, London, 1879.

— (ed.) *A Soldier's Life and Work in South Africa, 1872–1879: A Memory of the Late Colonel A.W. Durnford, Royal Engineers*, London, 1882.

Gibson, J.Y. *The Story of the Zulus*, London, 1911.

'H' (Heron-Maxwell, W.) *Reminiscences of a Red Coat*, London, 1895.

Haggard, H. Rider. *Cetywayo and his White Neighbours; or, Remarks on Recent Events in Zululand, Natal and the Transvaal*, London, 1888.

Hamilton-Browne, Col G. *A Lost Legionary in South Africa*, London, 19[?].

Harrison, Gen Sir R. *Recollections of a Life in the British Army*, London, 1908.

Historical Records of the 2nd Battalion, 24th Regiment, for the Campaign in South Africa, 1877–78–79; Embracing the Kaffir and Zulu Wars, confidential, Secunderabad, January 1882.

Holden, W.C. *British Rule in South Africa: Illustrated in the Rule of Kama and his Tribe, and of the War in Zululand*, London, 1879.

Holt, H.P. *The Mounted Police of Natal*, London, 1913.

Lucas, T.J. *The Zulus and the British Frontiers*, London, 1879.

Ludlow, Capt W.R. *Zululand and Cetywayo*, London and Birmingham, 1882.

Mackinnon, J.P. and Shadbolt, S. (comps) *The South African Campaign, 1879*, London, 1882.

Malet, T.St.L. *Extracts from a Diary in Zululand*, Upper Norwood, 1880.

Marter, Lt-Col R.J.C. *The Capture of Cetywayo, King of the Zulus*, private, 1880.

McToy, E.D. *A Brief History of the 13th Regiment (P.A.L.I.) in South Africa during the Transvaal and Zulu Difficulties*, Devonport, 1880.

Mitford, B. *Through the Zulu Country: Its Battlefields and its People*, London, 1883.

Molyneux, Maj W.C.F. *Notes on Hasty Defences as Practised in South Africa*, private circulation of notes made in 1879.

Molyneux, Maj-Gen W.C.F. *Campaigning in South Africa and Egypt*, London, 1896.

Montague, Capt W.E. *Campaigning in South Africa: Reminiscences of an Officer in 1879*, Edinburgh and London, 1880.

Moodie, D.C.F. (ed.) *John Dunn, Cetywayo and the Three Generals*, Pietermaritzburg, 1886.

Mossop, G. *Running the Gauntlet*, London, 1937.

Mynors, A.C.B. *Letters and Diary of the Late Arthur C.B. Mynors, Lieut 3rd. Batt., 60th Rifles, Who Died at Fort Pearson, Natal, the 25th of April, 1879*, Margate, 1879.

Norbury, Fleet-Surgeon H.F. *The Naval Brigade in South Africa during the Years 1877–78–79*, London, 1880.

Norris-Newman, C.L. *In Zululand with the British throughout the War of 1879*, London, 1880.

Parr, Capt H. Hallam. *A Sketch of the Kafir and Zulu Wars*, London, 1880.

Paton, Col G., Glennie, Col F. and Penn Symons, W. (eds) *Historical Records of the 24th Regiment from its Formation, in 1689*, London, 1892.

Plé, J. *Les Laagers dans la Guerre des Zoulous*, Paris, 1882.

Richards, W. *Her Majesty's Army: A Descriptive Account of the Various Regiments now Comprising the Queen's Forces, from their First Establishment*, London, 188[?].

Samuelson, R.C.A. *Long, Long Ago*, Durban, 1929.

Smith-Dorrien, Gen Sir H. *Memories of Forty-eight Years' Service*, London, 1925.

Special Reporter of the *Cape Times* (Murray, R.W.). *Cetywayo, from the Battle of Ulundi to the Cape of Good Hope*, Cape Town, 16 September 1879.

Tomasson, W.H. *With the Irregulars in the Transvaal and Zululand*, London, 1881.

Vijn, C. (tr. from the Dutch and edited with preface and notes by the Rt. Rev. J.W. Colenso, Bishop of Natal). *Cetshwayo's Dutchman: Being the Private Journal of a White Trader in Zululand during the British Invasion*, London, 1880.

Wood, Field Marshal Sir E. *From Midshipman to Field Marshal*, London, 1906, vol. II.

Later Edited, Annotated and Printed Contemporary Sources

Ashe, Maj W. and Wyatt Edgell, Capt the Hon. E.V. *The Story of the Zulu Campaign*, London, 1880 (reprinted with introduction by J.P.C. Laband, Constantia, 1989).

Bennett, Lt-Col I.H.W. *Eyewitness in Zululand: The Campaign Reminiscences of Colonel W.A. Dunne, CB: South Africa, 1877–1881*, London, 1989.

Butterfield, P.H. (ed.) *War and Peace in South Africa 1879–1881: The Writings of Philip Anstruther and Edward Essex*, Melville, 1987.

Child, D. (ed.) *The Zulu War Journal of Colonel Henry Harford, C.B.*, Pietermaritzburg, 1978.

Clarke, S. (ed.) *Invasion of Zululand 1879: Anglo-Zulu War Experiences of Arthur Harness; John Jervis, 4th Viscount St Vincent; and Sir Henry Bulwer*, Houghton, 1979.

— *Zululand at War 1879: The Conduct of the Anglo-Zulu War*, Houghton, 1984.

Emery, F. *The Red Soldier: Letters from the Zulu War, 1879*, London, 1977.

— *Marching over Africa: Letters from Victorian Soldiers*, London, 1986.

Fannin, N. (ed.) *The Fannin Papers: Pioneer Days in South Africa*, Durban, 1932.

Filter, H. (comp.), Bourquin, S. (tr. and ed.) *Paulina Dlamini: Servant of Two Kings*, Durban and Pietermaritzburg, 1986; reprinted 1998.

Fuze, M.M. (Lugg, H.C. (tr.) and Cope, A.T. (ed.)) *The Black People and Whence They Came: A Zulu View*, Pietermaritzburg and Durban, 1979; reprinted 1998.

Greaves, A. (ed.) 'What happened to the guns after Isandlwana? A compilation of letters by Lt H.T. Curling, RA', *The Journal of the Anglo-Zulu War Historical Society*, 3, June 1998.

Hall, H.L. 'With assegai and rifle: reminiscences of a transport conductor in the Zulu War', *Military History Journal*, IV, 5, June 1979, Appendix VIII.

Hart-Synnot, B.M. (ed.) *Letters of Major-General Fitzroy Hart-Synnot CB, CMG*, London, 1912.

Hattersley, A.F. *Later Annals of Natal*, London, 1938.

Holme, N. (comp.) *The Silver Wreath: Being the 24th Regiment at Isandlwana and Rorke's Drift*, London, 1979.

Jones, L.T. (ed.) *Reminiscences of the Zulu War by John Maxwell*, Cape Town, 1979.

Knight, I. (ed.) *'By the Orders of the Great White Queen': Campaigning in Zululand through the Eyes of the British Soldier, 1879*, London, 1992.

— (ed.) '"Kill me in the shadows": The Bowden Collection of Anglo-Zulu War oral history', *Soldiers of the Queen*, 74, September 1993.

Laband, J. *Fight us in the Open: The Anglo-Zulu War through Zulu Eyes*, Pietermaritzburg and Ulundi, 1985.

— (ed.) *Lord Chelmsford's Zululand Campaign 1878–1879*, Stroud and Dover NH, 1994.

— and Knight, I. *The War Correspondents: The Anglo-Zulu War*, Stroud 1996.

Lloyd, Lt W.N. 'The defence of Ekowe', *Natalia*, V, December 1975.

Moodie, D.C.F. *Moodie's Zulu War*, Constantia, 1988 (selection from Moodie's *The History of the Battles and Adventures of the British, the Boers and the Zulus in Southern Africa, from 1495 to 1879, Including Every Particular of the Zulu War of 1879, with a Chronology*, Sidney, Melbourne and Adelaide, 1879, with an introduction by J.P.C. Laband).

Preston, A. (ed.) *Sir Garnet Wolseley's South African Journal, 1879–1880*, Cape Town, 1973.

Webb, C.deB. and Wright, J.B. (eds) *A Zulu King Speaks: Statements Made by Cetshwayo kaMpande on the History and Customs of his People*, Pietermaritzburg and Durban, 1978.

— *The James Stuart Archive of Recorded Oral Evidence Relating to the History of the Zulu and Neighbouring Peoples*, Pietermaritzburg and Durban, 1976, 1979, 1982, 1986, vols. 1–4.

Webb, C.deB. (ed.) 'A Zulu boy's recollections of the Zulu War', *Natalia*, VIII, December 1978.

Whitehouse, H. (ed.) *'A Widow-Making War': The Life and Death of a British Officer in Zululand, 1879*, Nuneaton, 1995 (reprint with introduction of Wynne, W.R.C. *Memoir of Capt W.R.C. Wynne, RE*, for private circulation, Southampton, n.d.).

Later Printed Sources

Articles

Bailes, H. 'Technology and imperialism: a case study of the Victorian army in Africa', *Victorian Studies*, XXIV, 1, autumn 1980.

Benyon, J.A. 'Isandhlwana and the passing of a proconsul', *Natalia*, VIII, December 1978.

Bourquin, S. 'The Zulu military organization and challenge of 1879', *Military History Journal*, IV, 4, January 1979.

Burroughs, P. 'Imperial defence and the Victorian army', *Journal of Imperial and Commonwealth History*, XV, 1, October 1986.

Edgecombe, R. 'Appendix: the battle of Hlobane' in *The Constancy of Change: A History of Hlobane Colliery 1898–1998*, Vryheid, 1998.

Emery, F. 'Geography and imperialism: The role of Sir Bartle Frere (1815–84)', *Geographical Journal*, L, 3, November 1984.

Guy, J. 'A note on firearms in the Zulu kingdom with special reference to the Anglo-Zulu War, 1879', *Journal of African History*, XII, 4, 1971.

Hall, Maj. D.D. 'Artillery in the Zulu War, 1879', *Military History Journal*, IV, 4, January 1979.

Jackson, F.W.D. 'Isandhlwana, 1879: The sources re-examined', *Journal of the Society for Army Historical Research*, XLIX, 173, 175, 176, 1965.

— 'Isandhlwana revisited: A letter to the editor', *Soldiers of the Queen*, XXXIII, July 1983.

Jones, H.M. 'Why Khambula?' *Soldiers of the Queen*, 74, September 1993.

— 'Blood on the Painted Mountain: A review article', *Soldiers of the Queen*, 84, March 1996.

— 'Hlobane: A new perspective', *Natalia*, 27, 1997.

The Journal of the Anglo Zulu War Historical Society, 1–5, 1997–1999, passim.

Knight, I. 'Ammunition at Isandlwana: A reply', *Journal of the Society for Army Historical Research*, LXXIII, 296, winter 1995.

Laband, J.P.C. 'Introduction', *Companion to Narrative of Field Operations Connected with the Zulu War of 1879*, Constantia, 1989.

— '"Chopping wood with a razor": The skirmish at Zungeni Mountain and the unnecessary death of Lieutenant Frith, 5 June 1879', *Soldiers of the Queen*, 74, September 1993.

— '"He fought like a lion": An assessment of Zulu accounts of the death of the Prince Imperial of France during the Anglo-Zulu War of 1879', *Journal of the Society for Army Historical Research*, LXXXVI, 307, autumn 1998.

Morris, D. 'Isandhlwana', *Soldiers of the Queen*, XXIX/XXX, summer 1982.

Tylden, Maj G. 'The Waggon Laager', *Journal of the Society for Army Historical Research*, XLI, 168, 1963.

Verbeek, J.A. and Bresler, V. 'The role of the ammunition boxes in the disaster at Isandhlwana, 22nd January, 1879', *The Journal of the Historical Firearms Society of South Africa*, 7, 6, December 1977.

Webb, C.deB. 'Lines of power: The High Commissioner, the telegraph and the war of 1879', *Natalia*, VIII, December 1978.

Whybra, J. 'Contemporary sources and the composition of the main Zulu impi, January 1879', *Soldiers of the Queen*, LIII, June 1988.

Books

Ballard, C. *John Dunn: The White Chief of Zululand*, Craighall, 1985.

Benyon, J.A. *Proconsul and Paramountcy in South Africa. The High Commission, British Supremacy and the Sub-Continent, 1806–1910*, Pietermaritzburg, 1980.

Binns, C.T. *The Last Zulu King: The Life and Death of Cetshwayo*, London, 1963.

Brown, R.A. *The Road to Ulundi: The Water-Colour Drawings of John North Crealock (the Zulu War of 1879)*, Pietermaritzburg, 1969.

Castle, I. and Knight, J. *Fearful Hard Times: The Siege and Relief of Eshowe, 1879*, London, 1994.

Chadwick, G.A. and Hobson, E.G. (eds) *The Zulu War and the Colony of Natal*, Mandini, 1979.

Cope, R. *Ploughshare of War: The Origins of the Anglo-Zulu War, 1879*, Pietermaritzburg, 1999.

Coupland, Sir R. *Zulu battlepiece: Isandhlwana*, London, 1948.

Drooglever, R.W.F. *The Road to Isandhlwana: Colonel Anthony Durnford in Natal and Zululand*, London and Novato, California, 1992.

Duminy, A. and Ballard, C. (eds) *The Anglo-Zulu War: New Perspectives*, Pietermaritzburg, 1981.

— and Guest, B. (eds) *Natal and Zululand from Earliest Times to 1910: A New History*, Pietermaritzburg, 1989.

Edgerton, R.B. *Like Lions They Fought: The Zulu War and the Last Black Empire in South Africa*, Bergvlei, 1988.

Featherstone, D. *Weapons and Equipment of the Victorian Soldier*, Poole, 1978.

French, Maj the Hon. G. *Lord Chelmsford and the Zulu War*, London, 1939.

Goetzsche, E. *'Rough but Ready': An Official History of the Natal Mounted Rifles and its Antecedent and Associated Units*, Durban, 1973.

Gon, P. *The Road to Isandlwana: The Years of an Imperial Battalion*, Johannesburg, 1979.

Guy, J. *The Destruction of the Zulu Kingdom: The Civil War in Zululand,1879–1884*, 3rd edition, Pietermaritzburg, 1998.

Hurst, G.T. *Short History of the Volunteer Regiments of Natal and East Griqualand: Past and Present*, Durban, 1945.

Knight, I.J. (ed.) *There Will Be an Awful Row at Home about This*, Shoreham-by-Sea, 1987.

— *Brave Men's Blood: The Epic of the Zulu War, 1879*, London, 1990.

— *Zulu: Isandlwana and Rorke's Drift 22nd–23rd January 1879*, London, 1992.

— *Nothing Left but to Fight: The Defence of Rorke's Drift, 1879*, London, 1993.

— and Castle, I. *The Zulu War: Then and Now*, London, 1993.

— *The Anatomy of the Zulu Army from Shaka to Cetshway 1818–1879*, London, 1995.

— *Go to Your God like a Soldier: The British Soldier Fighting for Empire, 1837–1902*, London, 1996.

Krige, E. *The Social System of the Zulus*, Pietermaritzburg, 1974.

Laband, J.P.C. and Thompson, P.S. *War Comes to Umvoti: The Natal-Zululand Border, 1878–9*, Durban, 1980.

— and Thompson, P.S. with Henderson, S. *The Buffalo Border 1879: The Anglo-Zulu War in Northern Natal*, Durban, 1983.

— and Wright, J. *King Cetshwayo kaMpande (c. 1832–1884)*, Pietermaritzburg and Ulundi, 1983.

— and Thompson, P.S. *Field Guide to the War in Zululand and the Defence of Natal 1879*, Pietermaritzburg, 2nd revised edition, 1983; reprinted with minor revisions, 1987.

— *The Battle of Ulundi*, Pietermaritzburg and Ulundi, 1988.

— and Thompson, P.S. *Kingdom and Colony at War: Sixteen Studies on the Anglo-Zulu War of 1879*, Pietermaritzburg and Constantia, 1990.

— and Mathews, J. *Isandlwana*, Pietermaritzburg and Ulundi, 1992.

— *Kingdom in Crisis: The Zulu Response to the British Invasion of 1879*, Manchester and New York, 1992.

— *Rope of Sand: The Rise and Fall of the Zulu Kingdom in the Nineteenth Century*, Johannesburg, 1995 (issued in the UK and USA as *The Rise and Fall of the Zulu Nation*, London and New York, 1997).

Lock, R. *Blood on the Painted Mountain: Zulu Victory and Defeat, Hlobane and Kambula, 1879*, London, 1995.

Lugg, H.C. *Historic Natal and Zululand*, Pietermaritzburg, 1949.

Morris, D.R. *The Washing of the Spears: A History of the Rise of the Zulu Nation under Shaka and its Fall in the Zulu War of 1879*, London, 1966.

Peires, J.B. (ed.) *Before and after Shaka: Papers in Nguni History*, Grahamstown, 1981.

Rogers, Col H.C.B. *Weapons of the British Soldier*, Great Britain, 1972.

Smail, J.L. *From the Land of the Zulu Kings: An Historical Guide for Those Restless Years in Natal and Zululand 1497 to 1879*, Durban, 1979.

Strachan, H. *European Armies and the Conduct of War*, London, 1983.

Thompson, P.S. *The Natal Native Contingent in the Anglo-Zulu War 1879*, Pietermaritzburg, 1997.

Van Lingen, G. et al. *Battlefields of South Africa*, Johannesburg, 1991.

Whitehouse, H. *Battle in Africa, 1879–1914*, Mansfield, 1987.

Wilkinson-Latham, C. *Uniforms and Weapons of the Zulu War*, London, 1978.

Unpublished Theses

Dominy, G.A. 'Routine of empire: The use of force to maintain authority and impose peace as a principle of imperial administration; the cases of Waikato 1863 and Zululand 1879 compared', MA thesis, University College of Cork, 1983.

Kennedy, P.A. 'Fatal diplomacy: Sir Theophilus Shepstone and the Zulu kings, 1839–1879', PhD thesis, University of California, 1976.

Machin, I.M. 'The levying of forced African labour and military service by the colonial state of Natal', PhD thesis, University of Natal, 1996.

Mathews, J. 'Lord Chelmsford and the problems of transport and supply during the Anglo-Zulu War of 1879', MA thesis, University of Natal, 1979.

— 'Lord Chelmsford: British general in southern Africa, 1878–1879', D Litt et Phil thesis, University of South Africa, 1986.

Quotation Box Acknowledgements

Laband, J. *Fight Us in the Open: The Anglo-Zulu War through Zulu Eyes,* Pietermaritzburg and Ulundi, 1985: pp. 49 (bottom), 50, 52, 54 (bottom), 62, 84 (bottom), 102, 106 (top), 112, 182 (bottom), 183 (top).

— (ed.) *Lord Chelmsford's Zululand Campaign 1878–1879,* Stroud, 1994: pp. 22, 30, 31, 35, 38, 44 (top), 51, 61.

— and Knight, I. *The War Correspondents: The Anglo-Zulu War,* Stroud, 1996: pp. 7, 21, 23, 24, 36, 44 (bottom), 49 (top), 54 (top), 60, 84 (top), 88 (top and bottom), 91, 100 (top and bottom), 108 (bottom), 131, 140, 159, 164, 167, 183 (bottom), 187.

Knight, I. (ed.) ' "Kill me in the shadows": The Bowden Collection of Anglo-Zulu War oral history', *Soldiers of the Queen,* 74 (September 1993), pp. 9–18: pp. 15 (top), 46, 104 (bottom), 106 (bottom), 108 (top), 157.

Moodie, D.C.F (edited and introduced by Laband, J.) *Moodie's Zulu War,* Cape Town, 1988: p. 179.

Webb, C. de B. and Wright, J.B. (eds) *A Zulu King Speaks: Statements Made by Cetshwayo kaMpande on the History and Customs of His People,* Pietermaritzburg and Durban, 1998: pp. 5, 182 (top).

— *The James Stuart Archive of Recorded Oral Evidence Relating to the History of the Zulu and Neighbouring Peoples,* Pietermaritzburg and Durban, 1982, vol. III: pp. 15 (bottom), 16, 17, 18, 19, 129, 161.

Picture Acknowledgements

Angas, G.F. *The Kafirs Illustrated,* London, J. Hogarth, 1849: p. 9.

Courtesy of S.B. Bourquin: pp. 7, 8 (top), 12 (bottom), 22, 29 (top), 31, 36, 39, 50, 78 (top), 110.

British Parliamentary Papers LIII of 1878–9 (C. 2367): p. 79 (top left).

British Parliamentary Papers L of 1880 (C. 2505): pp. 11, 75 (bottom), 77 (top), 78 (bottom left), 80 (top left), 81.

Brown, R.A. (ed.), *The Road to Ulundi: The Water-Colour Drawings of John North Crealock (The Zulu War of 1879),* Pietermaritzburg, University of Natal Press, 1969: pp. 6, 33 (top), 51 (top and bottom), 52, 59 (bottom), 69 (bottom), 70, 88, 102–3 (top), 130 (top), 157 (top), 160, 168–9 (bottom), 177, 178, 182.

Campbell Collections, University of Natal, Durban: pp. 41, 75 (top), 80 (bottom), 96, 100, 190.

Courtesy of the Cecil Renaud Library, University of Natal, Pietermaritzburg: pp. 4, 8 (bottom), 13, 112, 137, 145, 186 (top and bottom).

Drawings by Christine Grant, pp. 14, 25.

Graphic, 1879 (courtesy of the Natal Society Library, Pietermaritzburg): pp. 10, 17, 24, 25, 26, 28, 32, 37, 43, 61, 64, 79 (bottom), 89, 96 (top left), 108, 126, 127, 131, 156, 184 (top).

Illustrated London News, 1879 (courtesy of the Natal Society Library, Pietermaritzburg): pp. 20, 27, 29 (bottom), 33 (bottom), 40 (bottom), 42, 45, 47, 56, 58 (top), 60, 62, 66, 97, 98, 124, 130, 141, 155, 157 (bottom), 164, 167, 169, 183.

Intelligence Branch of the War Office, *Narrative of the Field Operations Connected with the Zulu War of 1879,* London, War Office, 1881: pp. 71, 140, 154 (bottom).

Courtesy of Ian Knight: p. 69 (top), 93.

Local History Museum, Durban: p. 188.

Mackinnon, J.P. and Shadbolt, S.H. *The South African Campaign of 1879,* London, Sampson Low, Marston, Searle and Rivington, 1880: p. 103 (middle and bottom), 139.

Natal Museum Library, Pietermaritzburg: p. 117.

Courtesy of the *Natal Witness* Collection, Pietermaritzburg: p. 58 (bottom).

Pietermaritzburg Archives Repository: pp. 3, 5, 40 (top), 65, 163 (top and bottom), 184 (bottom).

Punch, 1879: pp. 59 (top), 113.

The Queen's Empire: A Pictorial and Descriptive Record, London, Cassell, 1897: pp. 12 (top), 35.

Vanity Fair, 15 March 1879: p. 56 (top).

Index

Helpmekaar heights   36, 49, 50, 109, 112
Henderson, Lt A.F.   99
Hicks Beach, Sir M.   4, 6
Hlobane, battle of   vii, 51, 52, 54, 65, 176–9, 181
Houshold, W.F.   129, 130, 131
Huskisson, Maj J.W.   190

I

Imperial units (raised locally)
  Irregular Horse   41, 51, 167, 168, 182
    Baker's Horse   152, 159, 161, 163, 177, 181
    Dutch Burghers   177, 179, 181
    Frontier Light Horse   24, 159, 160, 161, 163, 165, 177, 179, 181
    Jantzi's Native Horse   87
    Kaffrarian Rifles   133, 134, 177, 181
    Lonsdale's Mounted Rifles   173
    Mafunzi's Mounted Natives   87
    Mounted Basutos   181
    Natal Horse
      No. 1 Troop   87
      No. 3 Troop (Bettington's Horse)   155, 156, 159, 165
    Natal Light Horse   149, 159, 161, 163, 165
    Natal Native Horse   23, 24, 88, 99, 103, 161, 163, 165, 177, 181
      Edendale Troop   23, 99, 103
      Hlubi's Troop   99, 103, 109
      Sikali's Horse   99, 103, 109
    Raaf's Transvaal Rangers   161, 163, 165, 174, 177, 181
    Shepstone's Native Horse   23, 152, 159, 160, 165
    Weatherley's Border Horse   177, 178, 179, 181
  Infantry
    Native Foot Scouts (Dunn's Scouts)   87
    Natal Native Contingent   22, 23, 24, 26, 28, 37, 38, 39, 41, 59
      1st Battalion   38, 124, 125, 131
      2nd Battalion   22, 38, 59, 92, 93, 147, 149, 165, 167, 168, 169, 173, 174
      3rd Battalion   38, 124, 131
      4th Battalion   87, 88
      5th Battalion   80, 87, 88
      1st Regiment   38, 99, 103, 104
      2nd Regiment   38, 50, 83
      3rd Regiment   38, 49, 99, 100, 102, 104, 107, 109
    Natal Native Pioneer Corps   23, 37, 83, 84, 99, 100, 165
    Weenen Contingent   38
    Wood's Irregulars   23, 165, 177, 179, 181, 182
    Carrier Corps   62
Isandlwana
  Hill   49, 50, 59, 99, 102
  battle of   vii, 12, 16, 17, 18, 22, 26, 27, 30, 31, 32, 37, 38, 50, 51, 52, 60, 66, 69, 83, 91, 92, 93, 96, 99–108, 109, 113, 124, 127, 143, 159, 181, 193

J

Jones, Capt W. Parke   96
KwaJimu, *see* Rorke's Drift

K

Khambula, battle of   51, 52, 54, 56, 58, 172, 180–3

Knox, Capt R.A.   172
Koppie Alleen   60, 95
Kranskop   38, 49, 61, 129, 130
Krohn, Capt R.   99, 104, 106
Kubheka people   51, 52, 54, 64, 65

L

Ladysmith   36, 38, 49, 59
Landman's Drift   60
Law, Lt-Col F.T.A.   87
Lawrence, Capt H.B.   135, 136
Leet, Maj W.K.   171, 179
Lloyd, J.   7
Lonsdale, Capt J.F.   99, 102, 104, 106
Lonsdale, Cmdt R. de la T.   50, 100
Louis Napoleon, Prince Imperial of France   60, 154–7
Lower Thukela Drift   36, 38, 42, 49, 56, 69, 75, 81
Lucas, Capt. G.A.   54, 59, 80
Luneburg   5, 52, 54, 60, 62, 65, 139, 140
Lysons, Lt H.   58, 179

M

MacKenzie, F.R.   31
KwaMagwaza mission station   62, 153
Mahlabathini plain   10, 11, 15, 58, 61, 62, 70, 161–5
Mahubulwana kaDumisela, Qulusi *induna*   65
Malthus, Col S.   172
Manyonyoba kaMaqondo, Kubheka chief   51, 52, 65
Marshall, Maj-Gen F.   59, 66, 148, 159, 160
Marter, Maj R.J.C.   64, 147
Masegwane kaSopigwasi, Cetshwayo's *inceku*   83, 87
Matshana kaMondisa, Sithole chief   50, 99, 103
Matshiya kaMshandu, Nzuzu chief   83
Mavumengwana kaNdlela, Ntuli chief   49, 52, 87, 99, 100, 129
Mbambo, Mbilini's *induna*   50
Mbilane stream   163, 168
Mbilini waMswati, exiled Swazi prince   50, 51, 52, 54, 138–41, 177
Mbilwane kaMhlanganiso, *induna* of kwaGingi-ndlovu   83, 87
McPhail, Quartermaster D.   99
Melvill, Lt T.   93, 108
Mfunzi, Zulu royal messenger   65, 124
Mhlathuze River   11, 49, 56, 58, 62
Middle Drift   43, 46, 54, 61, 65, 125, 126,
  raid at   128–31
Milne, Lt A.B.   41, 100
Mitchell, Lt-Col C.B.H.   181
Mlalazi River   56
Mnyamana kaNgqengele, Buthelezi chief and Cetshwayo chief *induna*   54, 64, 165, 181
Montgomery, Cmdt A.N.   125
Moriarty, Capt D.   52, 138–9, 141
Mostyn Capt W.E.   99, 104
Mpande kaSenzangakhona, Zulu king   9
Msebe kaMadaka, Qulusi *induna*   50
Mthonjaneni heights   61, 62, 152
Myer's mission station   140
Mzinyathi River   6, 36, 38, 39, 42, 49, 50, 54, 59, 69, 93, 100, 107, 108, 109, 112